THE PHILOSOPHICAL STRUCTURE OF
HISTORICAL EXPLANATION

THE PHILOSOPHICAL STRUCTURE OF HISTORICAL EXPLANATION

Paul A. Roth

Northwestern University Press
Evanston, Illinois

Northwestern University Press
www.nupress.northwestern.edu

Copyright © 2020 by Northwestern University Press. Published 2020. All rights reserved.

Printed in the United States of America

10 9 8 7 6 5 4 3 2 1

Library of Congress Cataloging-in-Publication Data

Names: Roth, Paul Andrew, 1948– author.
Title: The philosophical structure of historical explanation / Paul A. Roth.
Description: Evanston, Illinois : Northwestern University Press, 2020. | Includes bibliographical references and index.
Identifiers: LCCN 2019017365 | ISBN 9780810140875 (paper text : alk. paper) | ISBN 9780810140882 (cloth text : alk. paper) | ISBN 9780810140899 (e-book)
Subjects: LCSH: History—Philosophy. | Historiography—Philosophy.
Classification: LCC D16.8 .R849 2019 | DDC 901—dc23
LC record available at https://lccn.loc.gov/2019017365

Except where otherwise noted, this book is licensed under a Creative Commons Attribution-NonCommercial-NoDerivatives 4.0 International License. To view a copy of this license, visit http://creativecommons.org/licenses/by-nc-nd/4.0/.

In all cases attribution should include the following information:
Roth, Paul A. *The Philosophical Structure of Historical Explanation.* Evanston, Ill.: Northwestern University Press, 2020.

The following material is excluded from the license:
Previously published material.

For permissions beyond the scope of this license, visit http://www.nupress.northwestern.edu/.

Knowledge Unlatched

An electronic version of this book is freely available, thanks to the support of libraries working with Knowledge Unlatched. KU is a collaborative initiative designed to make high-quality books open access for the public good. More information about the initiative and links to the open-access version can be found at www.knowledgeunlatched.org.

Contents

	Acknowledgments	vii
	Preface	xi
1	Reviving Analytical Philosophy of History	3
2	Problems for Narrative Explanations: The Case of History	22
3	The Pasts	35
4	Essentially Narrative Explanations	65
5	The Silence of the Norms	82
6	Kuhn's Narrative Construction of Normal Science	97
7	Methodological Naturalism and Its Consequences	113
	Conclusion	139
	Notes	149
	Works Cited	173
	Index	185

Acknowledgments

> Light dawns gradually over the whole.
> —Ludwig Wittgenstein, *On Certainty*, #141

Numerous people over many, many years have shaped, influenced, and aided me in this project. Louis Mink, who taught me at Wesleyan University and in a program there he helped create—the College of Social Studies—impacted my thinking in ways that proved determinative. Alan Donagan made a place for me in the Philosophy Department at the University of Chicago and provided an additional opportunity to study further issues such as philosophy of history that first fired my interest in philosophy. Hayden White's work I have always found to be a source of inspiration and provocation. Hayden White became, after I moved to Santa Cruz, a friend and an invaluable conversational partner. It was Hayden who first insisted to me that I needed to present my thoughts as a book, and who none too patiently prodded me along that path. Hayden passed away after my manuscript had been accepted but before it had been published.

Three thinkers decisively influenced my views as developed in this book: Arthur Danto, Louis Mink, and Hayden White. Danto's notion of a narrative sentence I have come to appreciate as a foundational insight into what makes an event historical in some philosophically interesting and relevant sense of that term. Anything that I attempt to say regarding what I learned from Mink would be inadequate to the task. Instead I will simply register that Mink's writings provided me not only with the critical insights but also with the inspiration to develop and extend Danto's device of narrative sentences. But beyond anything found on the written page, his influence and example as a teacher and a thinker have remained living and vivid for me.

Although Hayden White will be the person least directly discussed in the ensuing pages, his work also has been determinative of my own thinking on this topic. As I told him, for many years I had taped to my computer screen a quote from him that also ultimately served as an epigraph for my paper "The Pasts": "We choose our past in the same way that we choose our future." What I often imagine myself to be doing is offering an account of why I take this to be correct by reformulating his insights as a conclusion of a type of philosophical argument.

Regarding then Danto, Mink, and White, much of this book consists in efforts to knit together insights gleaned from each within an epistemological perspective forged by my readings of W. V. O. Quine and T. S. Kuhn. This allows me to answer questions regarding historical explanation debated since the nineteenth century (see Patton 2015; Dewulf 2017b).

A key portion of this book originated from an invitation to develop my views by Mary Morgan and Norton Wise. I received helpful challenges and intellectual impetus as well from conversations with and questions by John Beatty and Ken Waters. As a consequence of their questions I briefly venture to discuss in chapter 4 narratives in science. However, it remained a primary goal for me to address how narrative explanation, and so histories as a form of empirical inquiry, relate to disciplines unproblematically taken to be sciences.

At the very beginning of my efforts to weld some three decades of writings into a unified line of thought, Lisa Clark provided invaluable assistance, and to her I owe an immense debt. She diligently worked through a very rough early version of my manuscript with patience, intelligence, and insight. Without her editorial help and extensive suggestions, I doubt that I would have found the project doable. I can list names of only some of the many people whose feedback on one part or another of this project over the years has been of importance to me: Mark Bevir, Adrian Currie, Larry Davis, Ewa Domanska, Barry Gottfried, Michael Hicks, David Hoy, Jouni-Matti Kuukkanen, Chris Lorenz, Jon McGinnis, Allan Megill, Mary Morgan, Martin Paleček, Mariana Imaz Sheinbaum, Preston Stovall, Karsten Stueber, Eleanor Stump, Stephen Turner, Thomas Uebel, John Vandenbrink, Norton Wise, John Zammito, and Eugen Zeleňák. Students in my graduate seminar in spring 2018 also provided invaluable feedback on the manuscript.

My writing has been enabled by sabbaticals from the University of California–Santa Cruz. Work on this book was also supported in part by a visiting professorship at the University of Hradec Králové in fall 2017.

My wife, Renee C. Winter, read numerous drafts of many of my papers, including precursors to chapters of this book. She improved them all. But I also often hear her wistfully remark, "Another beautiful

ACKNOWLEDGMENTS

day," as I sit in sunny Santa Cruz hunched over my computer, unwilling to venture out. She tolerates this, and much more. To her and to my daughter, Emma, I owe that special debt one incurs to those whom you love, and who love and accept you, even while taking countless hours away to pursue those idiosyncratic obsessions that form the substance of much academic work.

This book emerged to my surprise as an outcome of multiple forays over many years into the topic of historical explanation. Indeed, material central to the positive account took shape only relatively recently. Until that happened, I never thought that I had a book to offer. Doubtless like many who have struggled long to articulate and unravel philosophical puzzles that one finds important yet elusive, I resonate to the somber concluding remark of Wittgenstein's preface to the *Philosophical Investigations*: "I should have liked to produce a good book. This has not come about, but the time is past in which I could improve it." In my case, bringing some form of closure to this project reflects less a matter of time than of ability. For better or for worse I have said what I have to say. I no longer know how to improve it. My hope would be that what I have written in some way merits the time and effort others gave on my behalf.

Santa Cruz, California
June 2017

Preface

> The aim of philosophy, abstractly formulated, is to understand how things in the broadest possible sense of the term hang together in the broadest possible sense of the term.
> —Wilfrid Sellars, "Philosophy and the Scientific Image of Man"

What counts as explaining how things hang together? An analytical philosopher typically answers questions such as this by providing an underlying *logical* structure, for logic makes inferential moves explicit and so aids in evaluating rational rectitude. For reasons that I attempt to make convincing and compelling, the focus in the first four chapters is on how this evaluative process unfolds in the case of historical explanation. As will be noted in chapter 1, an important reason for this approach is that history has lived in the methodological shadows since its emergence as an academic discipline. On the one hand, histories are a form of empirical inquiry, and as such claim to provide a type of knowledge. On the other hand, the form that histories typically take—narratives, stories—has always appeared at odds for one reason or another with explanatory formats found in other recognized sciences.

This seeming incongruity in explanatory approaches has created a standing philosophical puzzle regarding how to rationally evaluate historical explanations with regard to their epistemic legitimacy. For the type of inference structures used in other sciences could not be squared with what narrative form seemed to provide. This tension between a logic of science and the study of narrative form can be heard in a remark once made by the philosopher of science Clark Glymour (1980, ix): "If it is true that there are but two kinds of people in the world—the logical positivists and the god-damned English professors—then I suppose I am a logical positivist." The philosophically minded, as I understand Glymour's complaint, look for demonstrably logical evaluative criteria. The rest, including presumably narrative theorists, make do with something less. For many decades, this bleak dichotomy seemed both depressingly apt and yet also a nearly insurmountable challenge for those who, like myself, wished to see narrative as a legitimate form of explanation (see also, e.g., Kuukkanen 2015).

Indeed, for the entire existence of analytical philosophy of history as a subfield debates within it on the topic of historical explanation have been configured by theoretical discourses drawn from either logical positivism or narrative theorizing. A few philosophical voices attempted to alter this conversation (e.g., Louis Mink and Leon Goldstein). For reasons yet unknown, these efforts to keep the philosophical conversation afloat were swamped by a tsunami of narrative theorizing initiated by the work of Hayden White (see especially chapter 5). This wave swept aside all discussions of explanatory or epistemic norms (see Roth 1992). And in any case analytical philosophical discussion regarding the epistemic status of narrative history never managed to fully free itself from the grip of positivism. For even with the fall of positivism from philosophical ascendency, no alternative analyses of logical form or of explanation arose that took narrative per se as legitimate.

From a purely analytical perspective, no evaluative significance attaches to White's "content of the form"—the narrative structures that must be imposed to provide meaning to a morass of data.[1] Narrative theorists for their part pursue analyses of narrative which quite pointedly do *not* include concerns for the verification of causal or factual claims or in general any matter related to issues of epistemic evaluation. Nor is there any obvious reason why they should. What makes for the structural coherence of a narrative need not intersect with a philosopher's interest in a logical link between explanans and explanandum. Thus, narrative theory neither exhibits an interest in nor offers any resources for addressing philosophical concerns. But historians at least both write narratives *and* claim to be offering nonfiction, viz., knowledge of what happened and why. So histories as narratives fully square neither with the focus of philosophical analysis nor with that of narrative theorists. In consequence, the epistemic and evaluative questions raised by narratives qua explanations remain unanswered.

This lacuna effectively precluded making explanations in narrative form candidates for rational evaluation. As a result, what has come to mark philosophy or theory of history is that issues and concerns primary for philosophers have no bearing on the interests of the dominant narrativist discourse. Even worse, positions polarized and became increasingly

PREFACE

antagonistic insofar as individuals in each of Glymour's groupings came to view those not in their theoretical cadre as offering only irrelevancies.

In order to move past this long-standing impasse in debate within philosophy and theory of history, this book demonstrates that there exists an unrecognized alternative to the grim dichotomy explicitly stated by Glymour and implicitly accepted by many in this field. In developing this, it aims to be a successor project to a tradition in analytical philosophy of history that links back to work by Arthur C. Danto and Louis Mink. For in their work can be found a basis for making narrative explanation once again a theoretically viable and practically relevant issue. However, this book also endorses the primacy of narrative form in the case of historical explanation, and thus the constructivist position long advocated by Hayden White and the narrativist theorizing that follows from his work.

But the narrativist and constructivist orientation of the latter have implicitly been taken to be orthogonal to the normative and evaluative concerns of analytical philosophy. This is a false dichotomy. The arc of discussion this book transcribes begins in chapter 1 by identifying those problems of historical explanation that concern me both in terms of debates within analytical philosophy and in terms of characteristics specific to narratives qua explanations. Chapter 1 also addresses what work the term 'narrative' does throughout the book and why narrative form typifies and is essential to historical explanations.

Part of the puzzle here, as I note in several places, is why the topic fell off the philosophical map in the 1970s. (For various thoughts about why this happens, see D'Oro 2008; Kuukkanen 2015; the essays by Herman Paul and Piotr Kowalewski in Brzechczyn 2018.) As Thomas Uebel first suggested to me, it is an interesting question as to why Hempel, then a recently resettled émigré to the United States, chooses in 1942 to publish on historical explanation as one of his very first works in English. (Fons Dewulf illuminatingly and suggestively addresses this topic in his 2018 dissertation, "A Genealogy of Scientific Explanation.") For reasons given in detail by Dewulf and sketched in this book, for all intents and purposes the debate takes contemporary shape with this article by Hempel. But it also remains worth noting that dating the debate in this way results (yet again!) from *retrospective* reflection on how discussion took shape. Hempel's article did not achieve canonical stature, as nearly as I can tell, until at least a dozen years after initial publication. I find little evidence of any great impact (e.g., by study of citations) that Hempel's article had around the time of its initial publication (e.g., Cohen 1952; Dray 1967; see esp. Dewulf 2017a, 2017c, 2018).

Having thus set the historical and intellectual stage in chapter 1, I begin chapter 2 by identifying two types of objections to considering narrative explanations as legitimate. The first I term the metaphysical and the second the methodological. The methodological objection I divide into problems of logical formlessness and evaluative intractability. I answer the metaphysical objections in chapters 2 and 3 and the methodological objections in chapter 4. The metaphysical objections addressed in chapters 2 and 3 have a common root in a type of historical realism, a view that Mink labels "Universal History." Chapter 2 examines the problems by detailing some alleged obstacles to considering narrative as a form of explanation and offers an argument for the incoherence of this sort of metaphysical realism about history (the view that the past exists as a fixed object or an "untold story").

Chapters 3 and 4 detail why these alleged metaphysical and methodological problems prove to be only apparent and how to surmount them. Chapter 3 in particular attempts a more ambitious, positive argument as to why there is no determinate, fixed history but rather that there must be multiple pasts. This view I term "historical irrealism," borrowing from both Nelson Goodman and Ian Hacking. This account of irrealism in chapter 3 serves to motivate the explanatory strategy developed in chapter 4, which then formulates the specifics of what I call "essentially narrative explanations." Here I address the methodological objections identified as problems of logical formlessness and evaluative intractability. This reveals a structure that shows how irrealism and those features that define narrative explanations as I understand them—nonaggregativity, nonstandardization, nondetachability, and an explanandum expressed (or expressible) as a Dantoian narrative sentence—tell against the methodological objections.

Chapters 5, 6, and 7 elaborate the response incipient in chapter 4 to the more general epistemic and methodological question of how historical inquiry fits with other modes of scientific investigation. Chapters 5 and 6 in particular extend the reach of my positive account of narrative explanation to encompass an understanding of whatever comes to be called a science.

As I complain, especially in chapter 5, it remains an unsolved philosophical mystery just why the topic of historical explanation suffers in academic silence for so long. Chapters 5 and 6 together make a case for a deep interdependence between natural science and history, arguing that a narrative history of natural science ironically proves critical to providing a basis for characterizing what now passes as a science. Chapter 6 in this regard is the linchpin of my more general argument. This chapter also makes plain how my case proves contingent on defending a Kuhnian history of science, at least as I read Kuhn. As I construe naturalism, this strikes me as exactly the right result.

PREFACE

Inasmuch as narrative explanation turns out to be required for explaining what theories come to have status as scientific, this book maintains that the issue of how to tie narrative historical explanation back into the general catalog of accounts of what happens cannot be avoided. As illustrated throughout, narrative explanations work to shape philosophical practice even with regard to philosophers who self-identify with the analytical tradition. And in light of the enduring influence of Thomas Kuhn's work in the history of science on the philosophy of science, the continued slighting by philosophers of this topic represents professional bad faith. What licenses deliberately trafficking in an explanatory form whose norms go unexplicated?

Related to obstacles posed to any effort to articulate logical form is an implicit question whether or not narrative has a specifically cognitive role. Does narrative constitute a fundamental way rational beings make sense of the world? Formulating a positive answer to the question of how narrative form functions as a "cognitive instrument" (as Mink terms it) provides a further rationale for including narrative within any list of scientifically acceptable explanatory methods. So while chapter 4 offers an account of the logical form of narrative explanations, chapters 5 and 6 explicitly argue that narrative explanation cannot be considered an outlier to forms of scientific explanation inasmuch as narrative proves ineliminable for purposes of accounting for what passes as science. Narrative form is among the basic cognitive instruments that serve to fashion explanations of the theoretical outlooks that sciences have.

Chapter 7 then elaborates how narrative explanation fits within a fully naturalized account of empirical knowledge. The chapter completes my case for how various disciplines, each with distinctive explanatory approaches, fit comfortably and intelligibly within a certain understanding of philosophical naturalism. But as I suggest at the end of the chapter, an epistemological consequence of irrealism and naturalism will be that evaluating many histories will turn less on questions of fact than on framing.

Nothing in this book represents a proposal to reform historical practice. Ironically, at least relative to where this debate begins, it is philosophical attitudes and standards that need to change regarding what to count as an explanation. What this book offers to historians is a heightened methodological self-consciousness about existing habits of constructing histories. Hayden White demonstrated the ways in which moral implications attach to a choice of narrative form, and that historians bear responsibility for these choices. In short, choices of form impact content. They are not normatively neutral. But in saying that historians make choices of forms, this in and of itself does not imply that their accounts remain unconstrained by evidence. Exploring alternative accounts of what happens in history, like studies in the history and philosophy of science more generally, offers fascinating examples of how evidence (however what counts as such gets settled) proves compatible with competing explanations.[2]

The final three chapters thus offer a very specifically philosophical argument regarding the status of narrative explanation within the context of naturalism, at least as I develop that position. What the book has to offer historians lies in the examples used and the logic they make explicit, especially as developed in chapters 1–4. If successful, the extended argument of this book should lay to rest those long-standing questions regarding the supposed problematic relation of history to other forms of empirical inquiry.

But as the epigraph to this preface suggests, the case made for the acceptability of narrative explanation reaches beyond the bounds of the particular subfield initially addressed and the specific disciplinary vocabulary employed. For by extending narrative explanations to include a Kuhnian history of science, the book's ambition ranges beyond historical explanation as a merely disciplinary concern and contributes to a general account of empirical knowledge.

THE PHILOSOPHICAL STRUCTURE OF
HISTORICAL EXPLANATION

1

Reviving Analytical Philosophy of History

A call to revive philosophy of history will, I expect, quickly prompt at least the following two questions: What exactly would this revival revive? and Why bother? Those skeptically inclined might counsel indefinite postponement, inasmuch as this subfield has remained mostly deserted since the 1970s. My primary concern will be to outline where certain key issues now stand with regard to the first question, i.e., with an aim to identifying those aspects within philosophy of history that both merit and demand renewed philosophical consideration. Specifically, I focus on those features that make historical explanation distinctive and yet belong in any satisfactory catalog of explanatory strategies. I conclude with some examples meant to illustrate how an answer to the first question answers as well the second. In this case, it does so by suggesting how our professional lives exist enmeshed in agendas set by historical narratives.

Philosophy of history in the sense that primarily interests me connects to issues that concern the nature of historical explanation. These arose in discussions originating in the philosophical literature in the nineteenth century and in terms that still dominate. Varieties of positivism, whether of Comtean or Vienna Circle style, advocated for forms of explanation modeled on their idealization of the natural sciences. Historians protested that all such models ill fit their actual practices. In reaction, theoretically minded historians and sympathetic philosophers sought to specify why history as practiced counts as a science, even if not of a form scouted by assorted positivists. (See Patton 2015 for an excellent historical overview.)

A terminology specific to that debate invokes a distinction between nomothetic and idiographic modes of explanation. The former explains by regimenting statements of fact into explanatory patterns so as to reveal how such patterns instantiate laws or law-like connections. The latter mode explains by elaborating those contexts in which things happen; on this account, the specifics of a situation provide what is needed by way of explanation. Later discussions that feature a contrast between thin and thick descriptions, where the former invoke highly schematic accounts of what rationality consists in, and the latter study rationality as construed in situ, evoke and invoke this contrast. Economists gone modeling and ethnographers gone native provide contemporary instances of these different explanatory strategies in action.

A distinction between explanation and understanding evolves in tandem with these differing notions of explanation, the suggestion being that nomothetic explanations provide causes, and idiographic accounts engender understanding. That is, causal explanatory accounts imply underlying scientific laws or at least their simulacra, and so do not depend on time and context (see Habermas 1988, esp. 1–42; Apel 1984, esp. 1–68). As Hegel remarks, nature has no history (Kolb 2008, 6). Understanding ties to context typically by seeking to comprehend what counts in a particular situation as good or sufficient reasons for action. No claim is made that the goodness of the reasons generalizes; such matters will be specific to time and place.

Toward this end, it helps to recall how analytical philosophy of history comes to exist as a subfield. If one were to construct a type of genealogical chart, it would show analytical philosophy of history as the runt of a litter of topics that sprang from philosophy of science in its youth. Birth could plausibly be dated to coincide with the publication of Hempel's (1942) classic article, "The Function of General Laws in History" (see also Nagel [1961], esp. the chapter "Problems in the Logic of Historical Inquiry"). Hempel's explication effectively mandates the de facto exile of academic history from the realm of the legitimate sciences.[1] Analytical philosophy of history, for the twenty-five years following Hempel's article, by and large consists in critiques or defenses of the applicability of this model to historical explanation.[2]

Indeed, Hempel's essay became a near exclusive focus of discussion both in and out of philosophy by (in)famously insisting that historical explanations in their usual guise constitute at best "explanation sketches." Such sketches then have to be completed by citing some law or law-like connection between the explanandum statement and those putatively serving as explanantia. The problem notoriously was not that historians had carelessly neglected to insert the relevant laws, like rushed students who omit lines in a proof, and so simply needed to tidy their presentations a bit. Rather, historians have no laws to insert, and so it seems no genuine explanations on offer.

In any case, in the subsequent three decades of debate triggered by Hempel's essay,[3] one of the most notable responses can be found in Danto's (1965) important work, *Analytical Philosophy of History*. It is in Danto's work that I first find the phrase "narrative explanation" (237).[4] What makes this point noteworthy is that it has come to name that form of explanation specific to history and connotes for our purposes those differences already in play prior to Hempel's article. Danto's specific ways of motivating consideration of this term and Mink's (1987) subsequent crucial modifications and elaborations of Danto's insights remain central to any serious consideration of this topic.[5]

Note, however, that the term 'narrative explanation' as now used has been evacuated of the substantive content it has in Danto and in Mink. Evidence for this loss can be found in one of the very few recent articles in the analytical literature to seemingly bear on the subject of concern here, viz., David Velleman's (2003) "Narrative Explanation." Velleman begins by unproblematically assuming a working contrast between scientific and narrative explanations: "Can we account for the explanatory force of narrative with the models of explanation available in the philosophy of science? Or does narrative convey a different kind of understanding, which requires a different model and perhaps even a term other than 'explanation'?" (1). Although Velleman displays some passing awareness of earlier work in philosophy of history by, e.g., Mink, as well as some contemporary work by Noël Carroll (2001),[6] he nonetheless misses entirely Carroll's deliberate use of a classic example of Danto's, and in at least this important respect fails to understand a chief target of Carroll's own work on narrative explanation.[7] Velleman's (2003, 22) lack of awareness of the history of the topic helps account for, I suspect, his expressed frustration—"I began reading the vast literature on narrative, and by the end of the first semester I was utterly lost. I decided to work on a different project, so as to have something to show for the year"—with the entire topic as well as his ultimate rejection of the notion of narrative explanation.

In a similar vein, a recent article in the Blackwell Companions series dedicated to philosophy of history unfortunately only repeats the nineteenth-century distinction between idiographic and nomothetic explanation without advancing it: "Narrative explanation can be distinctively particular; it can pay due attention to a particular context in all its complexity, and provide satisfactory explanation of actions arising from those contexts without resorting to fanciful or trumped-up laws. It can do this while remaining faithful to the spirit of the generalist [Hempelian] position: all explanations must reduce to the sheer contingency of what is explained. It does this because the factors cited in narrative explanations are causally related (in various ways) to the events they explain" (MacDonald and MacDonald 2009, 139–40). But the parenthetical remark in this quote only serves to reiterate the standing problem: How does providing context explain? It provides no hint of an answer. One may almost sympathize here with Velleman.

Mutatis mutandis, these points apply as well to Daniel Little's interesting and thoughtful recent survey of issues in philosophy of history. Little and I agree on any number of very basic issues, including the wrongful neglect of philosophy of history. On the one hand, Little (2010, 28) freely acknowledges that "representing history often takes the form of creating a *narrative* of events." He offers the following helpful gloss of what he takes 'narrative' to mean: "It is an account of the unfolding of a series of events, along with an effort to explain how and why these processes and events came to be. A narrative is intended to provide an account of how a complex historical event unfolded and why.... So a narrative seeks to provide hermeneutic understanding of the outcome ... and causal explanation" (29). This, of course, echoes Weber.[8] In any case, I take Little to say as much as needs to be said for philosophical purposes about what a *narrative* is.

In this regard, I concur with Little in questioning the value of pursuing further literary analyses of narrative. To use jargon currently popular, *philosophical* discussions focus on normative issues, i.e., "the cognitive and semantic content of historical knowledge. The key issues are to be able to provide good interpretations of the causal analysis of social processes and empirically supportable interpretations of historical actors that play central roles in historical explanations" (Little 2010, 29n6). The thought is that a primary philosophical concern is to evaluate the putative "goodness" of explanations offered in narrative form. In addition and quite importantly, Little writes, "It has to be acknowledged that there are often multiple truthful, unbiased narratives that can be told for a complex event.... Each of these may be truthful, objective, unbiased—and inconsistent in important ways with the others.... And there is no such thing as an exhaustive and comprehensive telling of the story—only various tellings that emphasize one set of themes or another" (30). The need, in short, is to identify those structural features critical to evaluating narrative explanations. Philosophically, as I argue, focus should fall on how narrative functions qua explanation.[9]

On the other hand, Little does not attempt to justify this critical claim there can be multiple narrative explanations, all (as he puts it) truthful, objective, unbiased, and yet inconsistent with each other. He mentions underdetermination in passing, but underdetermination alone does not license an inference to a metaphysical multiplicity of possibilities. Rather, underdetermination reminds us that evidence alone cannot force which epistemic choice to make.

In addition and because he commits himself to a particular notion of mechanism, Little (2010, 213) postulates that "there are social mechanism through which ... bundles of knowledge are transmitted across generations and across space time." These "bundles of knowledge" mean to answer questions such as "What are the social processes through which this body of knowledge is transmitted relatively intact from one generation to the next? What are the social mechanisms of transmission through which these clusters of human knowledge and their variations are conveyed across space and across social groups (from village to village)?" (213). One important concern here is whether this search for a transmission mechanism for "bundles of knowledge" already sends social inquiry down a road leading nowhere (see esp. Turner 1994). In addition, without such a transmission story, narratives specify no mechanism and so by Little's own account offer no explanation. But this dismal conclusion proves contrary to what Little himself maintains.

This brief survey serves to emphasize that even with the waning of overt philosophical enthusiasm for some unitary model of scientific explanation, the problems attending historical explanation remain unchanged from their origins well over a century ago. In this respect, i.e., by virtue of implicitly or explicitly placing a demand on historical practice that emanates from philosophical preconceptions regarding the logical form of scientific explanation, I have termed the putative problem of historical explanation as one of our (i.e., philosophers') own making (Roth 2008b, 226).

Part of the problem with appreciating narrative as a form of explanation results, I suggest, from a misplaced obsession regarding how to unpack the notion of a narrative. (See Martin 1986 for a helpful overview.) Literary theorists typically have concerns with narrative in terms of stylistic devices, e.g., what structural elements stories of certain types require, and narrative theorists often then offer a catalog of these and how these forms influence the type of narrative that results. These considerations are certainly not irrelevant to what historians do insofar as they construct narratives. And as Hayden White famously and rightly emphasizes, a choice of narrative form comes politically and morally freighted. But narrative qua narrative seemingly has no discernible bearing on evaluating *epistemic* goodness or *inferential* connections, and so any talk of narrative explanation remains problematic, at least for these reasons, among philosophers.

Showing how narratives address and impact epistemic concerns—i.e., indicating how narratives becomes part of a *justification* of a claim to know, in some relevant sense of that term—constitutes my primary reason for bringing discussion back to Danto. For in that moment of the debate there exists not only a sharp focus on epistemic issues but also at least the beginnings of an answer. This promise dies aborning for a number of reasons. For one, while Danto does develop his own account of narrative as a form of explanation, it ultimately overlooks a number of his own best insights regarding what makes narrative peculiar to how to evaluate historical claims. Mink, in crucial respects, sees better than does Danto himself what Danto's account achieves for purposes of elucidating and clarifying the justificatory role of a historical narrative.

Danto's notion of a narrative sentence and his attendant account of the Ideal Chronicle and Ideal Chronicler rank as crucially important insights that he develops in *Analytical Philosophy of History* (Danto 1965, ch. 8; this reprints Danto 1962). This thought experiment establishes that statements true of a particular time t cannot be comprehensively known at t, not even by someone capable of recording all that happens when it happens (the Ideal Chronicler). Danto's now canonical example is this: "The Thirty Years War began in 1618." This statement is true of what happens in 1618 but is not knowable in 1618, not even by an Ideal Chronicler. Danto calls these "narrative sentences," and they demonstrate that there will be truths about any time t not knowable at t; truths about time t continue to accumulate after t. Narrative sentences also create a relation between the two events, and in a minimalist sense imply a narrative, a relating of the passage of time that conceptually links a later event and an earlier one. In this regard, Mink observes, even histories with an apparent nonnarrative structure—he mentions as an example Huizinga's *The Waning of the Middle Ages*—betray in their title a narrative perspective.

Historical events exist only as events under a description, and descriptions typically continue to emerge retrospectively. Mink (1987, 138–39) in short acutely grasps the nub of a key insight caught by Danto's reasons for taking narrative sentences to demonstrate the impossibility of an Ideal Chronicle:

> The general pattern of argument is to show that we already believe that there are true descriptions of past events such that *no one could have experienced those events under these descriptions*. . . . And such 'narrative sentences' belong to stories which historians alone can tell. . . . A present event may belong to indefinitely many stories, none of which can be told until it is completed. The description of the past does not come closer and closer to an Ideal Chronicle but departs further and further from it as more descriptions become available which were not earlier available even in principle.

Certain descriptions could not be known at the time because what will be historically significant about some events will emerge only later. As Danto (1965, 142) puts matters, "Completely to describe an event is to locate it in all the right stories, and this we cannot do. We cannot because we are temporally provincial with regard to the future.... The complete description then presupposes a narrative organization, and narrative organization is something that we do. Not merely that, but the imposition of a narrative organization logically involves us with an inexpungible subjective factor. There is an element of sheer arbitrariness in it." This hints of a philosophical rationale for the metaphysical plurality and epistemic legitimacy of competing narratives that Little acknowledges yet leaves unaccounted. In short, historians look to justify an explanation of an event under a particular description, a description tied to a retrospective and so narrative perspective. Danto's notion of a narrative sentence receives further development in chapter 2 and figures crucially in my discussion throughout, but especially in chapter 4.

This brings out the first of three key characteristics that critically distinguish between historical events and those that scientific theories target for purposes of explanation, what I shall term going forward the *nonstandardization* thesis. It concerns the fact that historical events do not begin as constructs of some articulated theory of which they are a part. Indeed, on rough analogy with Donald Davidson's discussion of anomalous monism, there exists at present no reason to believe that the sort of events that interest humans for purposes of historical elucidation will be captured by any theory that utilizes anything like laws. Mink (1987, 139) puts the point this way:

> A scientific account of an event determines a standard description of the event, by counting, say, statements of the mass and velocity of a moving body as relevant descriptions, and statements about its color . . . as irrelevant. History, on the other hand, reports how descriptions change over time, that is, how "The author of *Rameau's Nephew* was born in 1713" came to be true. . . . There can be a history of science, that is, of changes in the kinds of descriptions accepted as standard at different times, but no science of history, that is, a complete description of events which includes or subsumes all possible descriptions.

As Mink (1987, 139) also notes, "Danto's argument depends on bringing out with maximum forcefulness the point that there are many descriptions of an event, and no standard or complete description."[10] As a result, "the description of the past does not come closer and closer to an ideal chronicle but departs further and further from it as more descriptions become available which were not earlier available even in principle" (139). In short, we understand what it means to do normal science in Kuhn's sense because of theoretical standardization. But there exists no analog in the writing of human histories to what permits of this type of normal

CHAPTER 1

science. Nothing answers to "normal history" because there exists no theory that normalizes historical events in this respect.

Of course, some social sciences attempt to normalize the social and historical in just the Kuhnian sense. Economists construct for purposes of measurement various theoretical entities, e.g., the gross domestic product, and likewise talk of certain events, e.g., inflation, as happenings in the world based on certain ways of theoretically conceiving the world that humans make and inhabit. And while it might seem to be an open question whether all historical events could be so characterized, further considerations attending to narrative sentences argue otherwise.

In this regard, while Danto emphasizes the *temporal* asymmetries that narrative sentences produce and reveal and how this frustrates any hypothesized Ideal Chronicle, Mink elucidates a point related to non-standardization left undeveloped by Danto. Mink identifies what he terms a *conceptual asymmetry* that narrative sentences may reveal. By "conceptual asymmetry" Mink (1987, 140) means "descriptions possible only after the event because they depend on later conceptual modes of interpretation and analysis, e.g., 'the unpropertied citizens of Rome constituted the first urban proletariat.'" This importantly complicates any understanding of the process just noted by which historical events become constituted for purposes of inquiry. Conceptual asymmetries represent a further principled barrier to any hope of normalizing descriptions of historical events inasmuch as "concepts belong to narratives of human action in two ways, there are the concepts which inform our understanding of past events, and there are the concepts which at least in part were constitutive of past actions, in the sense that they were necessarily involved in the agents' understanding of what they were doing. We could not understand Greek civilization without the concept of *moira*, which is not part of our conceptual systems, nor without a concept of culture, which was not part of theirs" (141). Danto neglects to spell out the consequences of conceptual asymmetries, Mink complains. As a result, Danto overlooks a related critical limitation on historical knowledge: "For just as we cannot tell a story whose descriptions refer to future events which we cannot predict, so we cannot tell a story whose descriptions depend on concepts which we do not yet possess" (142). Critical race theory and feminist perspectives serve as examples here. Put another way, historians employ retrospective understanding in ways that involve truths not knowable at earlier times using concepts not then available. Later concepts do not standardize events, but redescribe them to make plain relations previously unobservable.[11]

Yet Danto's use of the term 'narrative' invites confusion between, on the one hand, conceptually relating an earlier time to some later one and, on the other hand, offering an actual narrative that develops that relation. Only the latter counts as what theorists in this area think of as a narrative. Narrative sentences, that is, do not constitute a narrative in any theoretically relevant sense of that term, but typically they imply one. Even more, Danto's still important analysis of temporal language and his coinage of the term 'narrative explanation' does not signal any interest or basis in his own work for a defense of narrative as itself a legitimate form of historical explanation. Rather, his notion of a narrative sentence makes vivid and compelling a reason why our human relationship to history will always be dynamic and not static. Danto takes such "antecedents revealed in retrospect" as a defining mark of the historical. For reasons developed in later chapters, I take this to be correct. For the passage of time inevitably reveals truths about the significance of past times not knowable at those moments.

What I take my account to bring to the fore involves the fact that histories, and so those who author them, constitute the events they explain under nonstandardized descriptions. Further, these descriptions resist any assimilation to standardization, at least as would seem to be required for their theoretical normalization. This does not make the history unscientific. Rather, it implicates narrative structure in the very constitution of the explanandum. It marks in this respect a critical difference between how historians constitute what they study and how such events importantly differ from those that, e.g., chemists or physicists examine and explain.

Acknowledging nonstandardization of explananda allows us to better comprehend just how Velleman fails to join issue with what Mink has to say about what makes narrative importantly different for purposes of explanation. Velleman (2003, 8) begins his assessment of Mink with an unfortunate and incorrect characterization of Mink's motivation as arising from a dissatisfaction "with the suggestion that historical narrative render events intelligible by revealing their causes." This sets up a pernicious contrast between the causal and the narrational, a contrast not part of Mink's thought. Mink never claims that historians lack a concern with causes or argues against offering causal explanations.[12]

Velleman cites in this connection Mink's discussion of Morton White's moderated defense of the applicability of Hempel's covering law model to historical explanation. Apropos that discussion, Mink (1987, 129–30) does say, "White's insistence that 'cause' is used univocally throughout ordinary and historical discourse comes very near to legislating the meanings of 'cause,' as the covering-law model in other versions does to legislating the meaning of 'explain.'" Mink goes on to complain about White, "White's mode of analysis, despite its gestures towards narrative, depends essentially on redescribing the sequences of a story so that they can be regarded as the states of a system, isolated from each other for purposes of description and connected only by causal relations specified by general theories" (131). In short, only by redescribing what historians seek to explain does White effect a rapprochement of what historians do and what Hempel's model would require them to do.

Against this general view, Mink (1987, 131) makes the following telling observation:

> Even though histories may be reconstructed as a series of causal statements about sequences and connections of events, such an interpretation and reconstruction conceptually inhibit insight into other important features of histories. In a similar way, it has been argued . . . [e.g., by Kuhn and Toulmin] that the rational reconstruction of natural science as a set of hypothetico-deductive theories inhibits insight into the process and conditions of scientific discovery. What White's account rules out are the concepts of *novelty, development,* and *growth.* Historical interest to a very great extent is in the irruption of new ideas and institutions. . . . 'Singular explanatory statements' are thin instruments indeed for dealing with such phenomena.

In short, White's reconstruction eliminates all narrative sentences, and so turns an event as constituted for purposes of historical explanation into something else, something that *lacks* the very feature that historians seek to explain. White's demand that 'causal' be legislated so as to fit a deductive-nomological model elides those events that historians seek to explain.

I take something like this point to be the main thrust of Karsten Stueber's (2015, 404) objection as well. However, Stueber's own thoughts do not strike me as fully consistent on this key point. On the one hand, he asserts, "The need for narrative arises because there is no overarching theory and generalization about the relations between types of events in light of which the feature of event . . . can be accounted for" (404). However, barely a page later he writes as if using multiple theories can then solve the problem: "It [a narrative] only excludes appeal to generalities that would subsume all the events of the narrative under *one* theory" (405; emphasis mine; see also 408). First, either these "multiple theories" as Stueber imagines them are consistent or they are not. If they are, then narratives simply can be rewritten using the relevant generalizations, contrary to what Stueber otherwise suggests (e.g., 401). If they are not, then appeal to multiple theories comes at the cost of embedding inconsistency into the narrative, and surely that satisfies no one's notion of explanation.

So far as I can tell, Stueber offers at best a sophisticated updating of the position found in Morton White, which, for reasons already rehearsed, cannot satisfy the defining criteria of events understood in historical perspective, a perspective that, as noted, Stueber professes to share (403–4).

Oddly, given Mink's own relentless proclivity for actual historical examples, Velleman's chosen counterexample to Mink rests on Velleman's discussion of Robert Louis Stevenson's novel *Treasure Island*. Velleman's (2003, 9–10) criticism is this: understanding does not "rest on an explanation of the events understood.... In short, how comprehensible the story is, in Mink's sense of the term, does not depend on how well it explains why the treasure was found." But so described, even Mink would agree. However, Mink never sets out to equate comprehensibility and explanation. Why would one? Rather, as Mink (1987, 135) notes, "the logic of explanation should have something to do with the phenomenology of understanding; the former, one hopes, should serve to correct the latter and the latter to enrich the former." In order to bring out the relationship between comprehension and explanation, he underlines the centrality of retrospection for determining the explanandum:

> And when we tell the story, we retrace forward what we already traced backward. Thus what may be contingent in the occurrence of events is not in their narration.... The judge of an historical narrative is not the naïve reader ... but the sophisticated one who has been through this garden before.... Yet of course he too "follows" with interest. Why? Not, of course, to learn the outcome, nor ... to see that the outcome could have been predicted by anyone knowing what we know now, but precisely to see as intelligible a pattern of relationships.... And its peculiar characteristic is that the intelligibility it affords is possible only in historical reconstruction; it is retrospective intelligibility which no contemporary witness could have achieved simply because he could not trace backwards from outcomes not yet known. (Mink 1987, 136–37)

The point in sum is that a historian constitutes events that could not have been known prospectively; this much one learns from Danto on narrative sentences. Prediction cannot then be the point of historical explanation. Events do not come prepackaged, like elements on some periodic table, and so determinately conjoinable.

But even more to the explanatory point, since what calls for explanation emerges only in retrospect, and while the narrative charts a developmental path from earlier to later, the path it carves exists in a landscape of its—the narrative's—own making. Mink's holistic characterization of narrative implies the second distinctive feature of narrative explanation, what I shall call the *nondetachability thesis*: "But despite the fact that an historian may 'summarize' conclusions in his final chapter, it seems clear that these are seldom or never detachable conclusions.... The significant conclusions ... are ingredient[s] in the argument itself ... in the sense that they are represented by the narrative order itself. As ingredient conclusions they are exhibited rather than demonstrated" (Mink 1987, 79; see also 172, 11). In a sense elaborated below, events explained by histories exist qua events only as constructions of those histories. Primarily as a consequence of this feature narratives explain only by virtue of the narrative order itself. Not, of course, because the world it depicts does not exist; rather, the narrative selectively orders materials. That results, I have maintained, from the fact that the events to be explained, and the events used to explain it, turn out to be part and parcel of the narrative to which they belong. A narrative constructs both the explanans and the explanandum.

Indeed, nonstandardization underwrites nondetachability at least in the following way. Because there exists no standardized way of demarcating either event types (e.g., revolutions) or specific historical events (e.g., the American Civil War) these become nondetachable from histories that discuss them (see, e.g., Towers 2011). No prior theories function to "standardize" such events, and neither do they constitute natural kinds. Thus, historical events "exist" only as part of some narrative or other.

Mink's reflections also tell against any assumption that human history has a natural or intrinsic structure and so against any idea that there exists just one human past. More specifically, in addition to the aforementioned nonstandardization thesis and nondetachability thesis, I now add as a third defining characteristic of narrative as a form of explanation: the *nonaggregativity thesis*. This builds on observations that Mink makes regarding the very intelligibility of Danto's thought experiment. Mink (1987, 194) notes that Danto's setup for the Ideal Chronicle seems plausible because one finds nothing obviously unimaginable in the initial suggestion of an Ideal Chronicle as a totality of the historical record: "To say that we still presuppose ... a concept of universal history, means: we assume that everything that has happened belongs to a single and determinate realm of unchanging actuality." So while Danto offers a *reductio* of the possibility of any such chronicle, Mink discerns an additional important epistemological consequence. This involves an assumption that histories can or should aggregate. Aggregation presupposes that all the events could belong to some one narrative, an implied unifying perspective. But there can no more be a single story than there can be an Ideal Chronicle, for new and different events and new and different stories constantly come into being (Mink 1987, 197). Moreover, in order to aggregate, events would have to be detachable and standardized, but narratives allow for neither.

"The Past" cannot as a result exist as a static object about which one may hope to know more and more, as in Kuhn's image of normal science. For nothing now licenses an assumption of The Past conceived as an untold or partially told story, but always nonetheless the same story, a human past narratable *sub specie aeternitatis*. Rather, one confronts the fact that what these various histories "have in common is the impossibility of being gathered together under any rubric of 'universal history.' . . . Instead of the belief that there is a single story embracing the ensemble of human events, we believe that there are many stories, not only different stories about different events, but even different stories about the same event" (Mink 1987, 193–94). Absent a "master narrative," no One True History lies waiting to be discovered in what evidence provides. (I develop this point in chapter 3.) As the nonstandardization thesis implies, histories rather create pasts by the way particular events come to be fashioned and accounted for. Nonaggregativity adds that these histories cannot therefore be expected to cohere, to theoretically aggregate into one seamless account of The Past.

Mink (1987, 184) powerfully puts this point in terms of the lingering but unacknowledged appeal of the notion of a Universal History: "The determinateness of the past is part of common-sense ontology; it is not a theory but a presupposition of unreflective common experience." Referring to Danto's conception of an Ideal Chronicle, Mink observes, "We could not conceive or imagine an Ideal Chronicle at all *unless* we already had the concept of a totality of 'what really happened.' We reject the possibility of a historiographical representation of this totality, but the very rejection presupposes the concept of the totality itself. It is in that presupposition that the idea of Universal History lives on" (195). Put another way, Mink makes his claim as follows: "If we accept that the description of events is a function of particular narrative structure, we cannot at the same time suppose that the actuality of the past is an untold story. There can in fact be no untold stories. . . . There can only be past facts not yet described in a context of narrative form" (201). Either there exists a Universal History, a single past, all of whose events can be expressed as part of a single account, or there exists no events, and so nothing for historians to explain, until given a narrative form. "The many stories have their own beginnings, middles, and ends, and are at least in principle fully intelligible without ensconcing them within a more comprehensive narrative, whose form is not fully visible in the segment that they represent" (194). I find no middle ground between these alternatives.

Consider some examples now that exemplify how nonstandardization, nondetachability, and nonaggregativity function to define narrative explanations. My first case focuses on the evolution of discussion of the Holocaust—the pursuit by the Nazis of a deliberate policy of extermination against the Jews and selected others. As those who track debates surrounding historical explanation realize, this example is not randomly or casually chosen (see, e.g., Friedländer 1992). For any view that smacks of a type of relativism, as mine certainly does, quickly comes to be charged with denying, e.g., the "reality" of the Holocaust as a consequence of claiming that explananda exist only as products of a narrative process.

And, indeed, my view does understand the Holocaust as a social construction, at least in the following sense. Were it not, I would claim, for the publication of Raul Hilberg's (1985) *The Destruction of the European Jews*, it would be highly unlikely that discussion of Nazi policy with respect to the Jews would have received the scholarly attention it does. Hilberg does not in that work use that term, but his work arguably proves central to the creation of a historiographical focus that does. As Hilberg's own account notes, he was strongly advised against even attempting to publish his work. (His dissertation advisor at Columbia was himself someone who had fled Nazi Germany.) (For details, see Browning 2004; Bush 2010; Trevor-Roper 1962.)

Put another way, one could have histories of the Second World War or the rise and fall of the Third Reich that did not feature this aspect of that period. All could agree that people died, that the Nazis had racial laws, etc., and yet none of this might be marked out for any special attention or study. Just one more unfortunate set of facts associated with that time. Further, anyone familiar with Hannah Arendt's influential *Eichmann in Jerusalem* quickly realizes how her own narrative framing of Eichmann's significance draws upon and requires Hilberg's account. In short, discussion of the Holocaust as an event in its own right, as one that grimly foreshadows what happens repetitively going forward in the twentieth century, as a basis for rethinking the limits of nation-states for the purpose of judging war crimes, etc., depends in many key respects on how Hilberg bequeaths to us a way of thinking about that time.

The structuring of Hilberg's narrative surely aims to be causal, but not in terms of events linked by laws. (Hilberg himself claims that the signing of the Nuremberg laws makes Auschwitz inevitable, but I leave that to others to debate.) Characterizing what at least Hilberg intends to specify by speaking of the destruction of the European Jews cannot, I maintain, be separated from his narrative that links together in grim and overwhelming detail all the various elements that were orchestrated to constitute the Final Solution. As Hilberg (1985, 993–94; emphasis mine) puts it, "The Germans killed five million Jews. The onslaught did not come from the void; it was brought into being because it had meaning to its perpetrators. . . . *In retrospect it may be possible to view the entire design as a mosaic of small pieces, each commonplace and lusterless by itself.* Yet this progression of everyday activities, these file notes, memoranda and telegrams, embedded in habit, routine, and tradition, were fashioned into a massive destruction process. Ordinary men were to perform extraordinary tasks. A phalanx of functionaries in public offices and private enterprises was reaching for the ultimate." Here Hilberg interestingly erases himself as author, as creator of this genuinely great and incredible history. Yet he crafted this mosaic; to him goes the credit of providing the world a new way of seeing familiar pieces. His "mosaic" depicts that destruction as a deliberate, careful policy. Hardly less interesting has been the postwar, and even the post-Wall reaction of German historians, betraying an anxiety to somehow "seal off" this period from any grander narrative of German history. Thus, Hilberg's explanation cannot be detached from the narrative he provides; what he explains does not exist as a standardized event; and as even a casual survey of Holocaust historiography makes evident, the various histories do not aggregate.

Does this mean that every history has only some such narrative to offer? Certainly not. To take another example from this genre, consider Christopher Browning's (1998) compelling book, *Ordinary Men*. Browning asks the question of how a group of "ordinary men"—his title deliberately echoes Hilberg here—in this case older German males who served as a police force behind the lines in conquered territories in the East, were transformed into ruthless death squads who executed large numbers of civilians: the elderly, women, children, etc. Browning employs now well-known results from social psychology, primarily work by Milgram and Zimbardo, to argue that the transformation can be viewed as a type of natural experiment of their sort (see Roth 2004). The results, down to the percentage of participants in the mass killings (all of this documented on the basis of archival evidence and postwar interviews), chillingly conforms to results obtained many years later in storefronts in New Haven and a classroom basement in Palo Alto. In short, Hilberg provides a narrative while Browning mixes narrative and more familiar modes that employ explanatory generalizations. But in each case the narratives create the events discussed, and in each case the narratives not only mean to but also plausibly do explain events so constituted. Indeed, no other way exists, so far as I know, to exhibit and so explain these events. The narrative and the explanation are of a piece.

Still, it remains to be asked: What makes questions of historical explanation relevant to analytical philosophy of science, of social science, of scientific practices? A case for taking narrative as a form of explanation thus builds on the fact—and it is a fact—that philosophers pervasively use narratives to explain and that these exhibit the three previously noted defining features of historical narratives: the nondetachability of conclusions, the nonstandardization of events explained, and the nonaggregativity of narrative explanations. Absent then some demarcation criterion, it would be more plausible to simply admit narrative histories to any list of legitimate forms of explanation rather than to continue to exclude them in theory while honoring them in practice. Examining some well-known "histories of reason," Alan Richardson (2002) provides further test cases illustrating how narratives function as a sui generis type explanation. In this regard, I briefly consider some well-known works by Thomas Kuhn and Michael Friedman, including writing by Friedman on the history of analytical philosophy.

Kuhn's work generates disputes persisting to this day regarding the relation of the history of science and the philosophy of science. A great if unintended irony regarding philosophical reception of *The Structure of Scientific Revolutions* can be glimpsed in the following remark by Danto (1995, 72): "Kuhn advanced a view of history so powerful that, rather than being an applied science as Hempel holds history to be, history came to be the matrix for viewing all the sciences." *Danto's remark gives voice to the important, albeit still unacknowledged fact that Kuhn's great work effectively reverses the received order of epistemic authority*. In particular, Kuhn can be read as upending philosophical views that true science moves by an inexorable logic that transcends time and place. He replaces this with a history of reason, where what counts as good reasoning even within science will vary with the theory in disciplinary ascendance.

Kuhn worries about how history relates to science but never satisfactorily resolves his concerns on this score. (Chapters 5 and 6 develop this point.) The title of Kuhn's famous book adumbrates a narrative sentence, inasmuch as what counts as a revolution (scientific or otherwise) appears only in retrospect. One can attempt to date its beginning after the fact, but that becomes a fact true of the earlier time only when seen in retrospect. The title is of course also ironic, since Kuhn's argument shows that changes in theoretical fashion have a "structure" only in a somewhat hand-waving sense of the term. This follows from his challenges to both Hempelian and Popperian orthodoxies regarding the rationality of scientific change insofar as neither verification nor falsification can explain historically significant theoretical transitions in what passes as a science.

What persistently escapes notice, however, involves just how Kuhn's book itself embodies a form of explanation that neither Hempel nor Popper could accommodate. Note in this regard that even what to count as a science appears known retrospectively. That a discipline has successive paradigms related in certain ways—has a particular history—creates a lineage for physics and chemistry as sciences but not, e.g., for astrology and alchemy. Kuhn's narrative also exhibits that what passes as scientific rationality has a history. The "argument" for his history of reason consists in showing how different cases of theoretical transition also alter what makes for proper procedures within a science. Kuhn's emplotment of these successive transitions shows them resistant to any overarching analysis of scientific rationality.

Indeed, *Structure* manifests exactly those characteristics of a narrative explanation sketched above. For the argument regarding the general significance of paradigm shifts cannot be detached from how Kuhn narrates key episodes within his history of science. The events discussed do not exist in any standardized form, and so the endless complaints regarding how Kuhn uses the term 'paradigm.' And one of the most notorious consequences he draws from his argument—the inability to make clear sense of any notion of scientific progress—instantiates the inability of histories to aggregate, at least with respect to some story of progress. (Kuhn endorses Mink's work here. See chapter 5 for details.) In addition, his narrative does not aggregate either as a history of a stable something known as "science" or with traditional histories of science.

In important work over the past fifteen years, Michael Friedman challenges Kuhn's history of science but has done so using specifically narrative means. Commenting on Friedman's (2001) *The Dynamics of Reason*, Richard Creath (2010, 504) remarks, "Friedman's historical narrative is, in effect, an explication of the role of reason within the particular historical context in which these [mathematical and scientific] revolutions take place. . . . So the historical narrative does real work for Friedman's account. The history is not an illustration of his argument. . . . It is the argument itself—a powerful one." Friedman (2010, 792n317; see also 712ff.) emphatically endorses this characterization of his "argument." "Whatever the fate of this new philosophy of science may be, it is clear beyond the shadow of a doubt, I think, that careful and sensitive attention to the history of science must remain absolutely central in any serious philosophical consideration of science" (Friedman 1993, 37). Friedman also did early and well-known work on explanation. Like Kuhn, he cannot be charged in this regard with a lack of familiarity with philosophical debates about explanation or an ignorance of scientific theories and mathematics or an inability to work in those terms. Yet, also like Kuhn, although Friedman self-consciously uses historical narrative to reshape thinking about what science is, he never considers how narratives explain.

Further, it is worth reflecting in this regard on Friedman's (2000) *A Parting of the Ways*. Here too Friedman offers a very interesting explanation, indeed a specifically historical narrative explanation in the sense rehearsed above. Additionally, I suggest that his explanation has important implications for contemporary debate regarding the state and nature of what has come to be called analytical philosophy (itself, of course, now the topic of multiple conflicting histories). Indeed, Friedman provides a narrative explanation that shapes and influences not only how one conceives of what philosophers did but also of what they *ought* to do.

Friedman's title does display exactly the sort of narrative structure that Danto teaches us to attend to. The debate between Cassirer and Heidegger at Davos comes to mark, on Friedman's telling, a parting of the ways. But, of course, this appears only retrospectively; those at Davos could not have used some model of explanation available then or now (or, I would venture to speculate, ever) to predict what later became marked as the "continental divide" (to echo the title of Peter Gordon's [2010] fine book). Friedman roots his tale of that encounter in two very different and influential ways in which the Kantian project has been appropriated in Germany at that time. Having situated his narrative in that way, he can then locate the confrontation at Davos between Cassirer and Heidegger as a critical moment in a much broader intellectual story, one fraught with great significance with respect to understanding the purposes of those who gave our discipline key elements critical to its current shape, and so determinative of current professional self-understanding.

As Friedman (2000, xi) puts it, he proposes to "show" (his term, having in context the connotation of 'prove' or 'explain') "that the Davos encounter between Carnap, Cassirer, and Heidegger has particular importance for our understanding of the ensuing split between what we now call the analytical and continental philosophical traditions. Before this encounter there was no such split. . . . I further hope to show that carefully attending to the very different ways in which the thought of all three philosophers evolved in sharply diverging directions from a common neo-Kantian core can greatly illuminate the nature and sources of the analytical/continental divide." Just as Peter Novick's (1988) recounting of the history of the American Historical Association turns an uncomfortable light on the founding but contested and elusive intellectual assumptions present at the creation of history as a profession, Friedman means to demonstrate how a present unanticipatable in the past nonetheless came to be the intellectual and professional space that we inhabit. This conforms, I take it, with exactly the points on which Danto and Mink insist.

Historical explanation qua narrative explanation concerns itself with a *developmental* process that emerges only in retrospect. A narrative traces a path of development, a path not defined or marked by any known laws or the like. The event emerges as an event only because our interests call it into being; events so constituted do not embody some natural kind. Following that path might well change our perception of how to proceed on the basis of an altered understanding of that past.[13] As Friedman (2000, 147) writes, "We have now arrived at the beginning of our own particular story, and also at a fundamental intellectual crossroads." One need not agree with Friedman in all the particulars to share his sense that philosophy does stand at a crossroads, one rooted in divergent and deeply contested ways of understanding the legacies of Frege, Russell, Carnap, Wittgenstein, Quine, Sellars.[14]

I have no doubt that a deeply instilled craving for generality will prompt dismissal out of hand of the very particularist and pluralist view of narrative explanation such as I have begun to outline. As explanations, narratives will only whet and cannot slake a thirst for a general theory. But histories, like ethnographies and literature more generally, thrive on displaying the peculiarities and particularities that beings like us so innovatively and endlessly exhibit. I worry that we work against ourselves in a very basic respect by a continued a failure to appreciate that narratives explain.

2

Problems for Narrative Explanations: The Case of History

Narratives are stories, a telling that something happened. A narrative explanation presumably presents an account of the linkages among events as a process leading to the outcome one seeks to explain. Examples of explanations in a story-like format are readily found in history books, certain anthropological accounts, case histories in psychoanalytic writings, and the sort of stories one hears daily from students and colleagues as to why this paper was not done or that committee meeting was not attended. The use of narratives to explain is unquestioned; what is subject to philosophical dispute is whether this habit is to be tolerated or condemned. Objections arise because the notion of explanation is deemed by some clear enough to rule out any category of narrative explanation, no matter how 'narrative' is to be understood.

The question of what to count as an explanation becomes, in part, a question of the use of this term. The methodological objection assumes that a proper subset of disciplines ought to serve to define for the rest what this standard is. This debate on explanation has interesting parallels to the problem I have elsewhere termed the *Rationalitätstreit* (Roth 1987). That problem concerns whether standards of rationality vary radically or whether one may insist, following Martin Hollis, on the "epistemological unity of mankind." Each side of this debate, I maintain, is committed to a view I dubbed "methodological exclusivism." Exclusivists (of whatever stripe) presume that there is exactly one correct methodological approach to a subject. Yet once the philosophical presumptions of methodological exclusivism are exposed, exclusivism loses its appeal. As to explanation, it is worth reminding ourselves that there is no good reason to believe there is just one correct explication of the notion of explanation. Such claims to explication come to have a purely stipulative or legislative force in the absence of some notion of analyticity.

The three defining features of narrative explanations identified in the previous chapter—nonstandardization, nondetachability, and nonaggregativity—help to sharpen reasons for philosophical unhappiness with the very idea of a narrative explanation. This can be put in terms of three interrelated problems. The first two I term methodological because they concern questions of logical form. One I term the problem of *logical formlessness* and the other the problem of *evaluative intractability*. Hempel's (1942) proposal regarding historical explanation nicely illustrates the logical quandary at the core of both problems.[1] Hempel's model of explanation represents a textbook instance of explication inasmuch as it assimilates explanatory form to a type of argument form. The problem of evaluating explanation here becomes one with that of assessing the inference from explanans to explanandum. Formal and semantic considerations—validity and soundness—suffice on this model for purposes of evaluating the move from explanans to explanandum. And while Hempel's specific explication may be regarded as philosophically passé, the view that evaluating any candidate for explanation requires identifying its inference license remains entrenched in philosophical consciousness.

But especially in light of their three defining features, historical narratives simply do not appear to instantiate any logical form recognized as inference licensing. These considerations would seem to clinch allegations of logical formlessness. Yet absent any usual formal features for identifying inferential links, what then could justify connecting explanans and explanandum? Logical formlessness thus appears to preclude identifying and so assessing what links explanans and explanandum. Evaluative intractability seemingly has to be a direct consequence.[2]

Notice that the objections require only the assumption that history is a nonfiction discipline. This hardly seems disputable. Yet, if nonfiction, history either is a science or it is not. If it is, then narrative explanations will not do, for reasons just rehearsed. But suppose, if you wish, that history is not science-like. Perhaps the nature of historical inquiry is only to provide an understanding of events. To invoke a traditional distinction, history is an idiographic and not a nomothetic discipline. Historians, on this account, study unique and nonrepeating occurrences, or, at least, what is unique about events.[3]

Yet even on this conception of history, methodological objections remain concerning how to evaluate a narrative. For issues of evaluation do not intersect, in any obvious or interesting way, with those of narrative form. The extent to which history respects canons of narrative construction might influence the literary merit of that history. But it hardly seems relevant to determining the conditions for judging the explanatory merits of that history. Thus, whether the emphasis of a historian's task is taken to be explanation or is defined as understanding, normative concerns, at least those of interest to philosophers, seem to rule out the relevance of narrative form.

Both of these methodological objections, I shall argue, are ill-founded. Yet without some sense of what the logical form is, determination of truth conditions—however those are to be spelled out—and of implication remain obscure. And to the extent they remain obscure, the rational evaluation of issues is frustrated or precluded. I challenge the view that precisely one logical form is appropriate to explicating the notion of explanation. A positive case for a category of narrative explanation requires, inter alia, exposing enough formal properties of narrative accounts to establish how such explanations are viable candidates for objective evaluation. Answering them directly awaits chapter 4.

I focus in this chapter and the next on a third objection, primarily because I suggest it serves to legitimize and so make plausible the first two. Addressing it will help to properly motivate my account in chapter 4. This third objection proves very subtle and stubborn, and I term it *metaphysical*. Resolving this metaphysical objection in this chapter and the next will be a prolegomenon to undertaking the task of specifying an account of the logic of narrative explanations, for that account requires that certain assumptions about history first be rejected. In particular, the methodological objections do not take into account what histories seek to explain, and they fail to do this because, I suggest, of an assumption that there exists only a single past calling for explanation. But by giving grounds for rejecting this assumption, those methodological features of narrative explanations that I identify become justifiable and comprehensible. What makes this third objection metaphysical is that it assumes something like a correspondence theory of historical knowledge. This assumption, I hope to show in this chapter and the next, is incoherent. In rejecting realism about history, what results turns out to be not antirealism about the past but irrealism. But the case for irrealism must be deferred to chapter 3 in order to dispense with a type of commonsense metaphysics of history.

A version of what I have in mind here can be found in Maurice Mandelbaum's (1977) *The Anatomy of Historical Knowledge*. Mandelbaum deems the impulse to link history and narrative "unfortunate," because it emphasizes what he regards as, strictly speaking, a purely incidental aspect of historical inquiry. Narrative structure, on his view, represents a mere stylistic device. Whereas the methodological objections center on satisfying certain formal constraints, the metaphysical objection emphasizes the relation of what is written to what is being written about. Indeed, Mandelbaum invokes an almost Rankean image of the historian recounting the past "as it actually was":

> Describing history as narrative suggests—and I assume is meant to suggest—that historiography is to be compared with telling a tale or

> story. This is misleading even when applied to the most traditional histories. A historian dealing with any subject matter must first attempt to discover what occurred in some segment of the past, and establish how these occurrences were related to one another. Once this research has been carried forward to a partial conclusion, he must, of course, think about how he will best present his findings, and this . . . may be regarded as "constructing a narrative." Such a narrative, however, is not independent of his antecedent research, nor is that research merely incidental to it; the historian's "story"—if one chooses to view it merely as a story—must emerge from his research and must be assumed to be at every point dependent on it. It is therefore misleading to describe what historians do as if this were comparable to what is most characteristic of the storyteller's art. (Mandelbaum 1977, 25)

Mandelbaum's artless Baconian conception of historical research stops just short of endorsing what might be called a correspondence theory of historical truth and objectivity. The reluctance to endorse directly a correspondence theory is a consequence of contrasting the complexity of the "full" historical picture and any historian's necessarily limited depiction of it.

His version of the sort of metaphysical picture I ultimately want to reject has it that events enter into processes by some natural *historical* dynamic inherent in the events and processes of which they are parts. He argues:

> From what has been said it can be seen that the events with which a historian deals in tracing a process may belong together either because they are, quite simply, constitutive parts within that process, or because they have entered it through influencing one or more of these parts. In speaking of the constitutive parts of a series of events, I refer to the fact that when a historian seeks to understand the nature of and changes in a society . . . he is dealing with a complex whole, some of whose parts he already knows. It is these parts—and any others whose existence he uncovers—that are parts of the whole. . . . Thus, one can see that whenever a historian correctly analyzes the structures present in a society, or whenever he gives correct information as to the sequence of changes that it . . . has undergone, he has dealt with events that belong together because they are the parts of the continuing whole.
>
> Such a whole is not formed merely because the historian has defined his subject matter in a certain way and has confined the scope of his inquiry to what occurred with respect to that particular subject matter. . . . Rather, the events that he includes as belonging within the series

of occurrences with which he is to deal are those between which he finds inherent connections because they have influenced one another. (Mandelbaum 1977, 126–27)

Mandelbaum's guiding analogy likens history to mapmaking. Both maps and histories may differ in terms of scale, scope, and detail. Both may be subject to change over time. However, histories, like maps, are guides over existing terrains:

> One may hold that a basic structure is imposed on a historical account by the evidence on which it rests; the existence of lacunae in that evidence, and the new questions that are present in it, direct the historian's attention to the need for further evidence of a specific kind. . . . Thus, whatever evidence is originally available to a historian will not be an inchoate mass, and the more evidence there is, the less choice he will have as to the alternative ways in which he may reasonably structure his account.
>
> It is on the basis of the connections inherent in the evidence with which historians work that they can propose concrete causal analyses of the events with which they deal. (Mandelbaum 1977, 192–93)

Historical pictures are successively filled in by collecting more evidence concerning the events of interest. The picture is always partial, but what history provides is an ever clearer picture of things as they actually were. This expresses, of course, a version of a commitment to a Universal History of the sort considered and rejected in chapter 1, what Mink (1987, 201) terms the view of the past as an "untold story." Mandelbaum, in short, denies the nonaggregativity thesis. The work of a historian, on Mandelbaum's conception, is more like that of a scribe than an author.

The sort of metaphysical assumption that underwrites Mandelbaum's rejection of narrative, however philosophically tenuous his own exposition of it, has, as noted in chapter 1, deep intuitive roots. It is anchored in a presupposition that, as Mink (1987, 188) puts it, "the story of the past needs only to be communicated, not constructed." What needs to be rejected is the picture of a past that is simply there waiting for a historian to come along. Construing history on the model of narrative appears *inappropriate* so long as the historian's art is assumed to consist in chipping off the excrescences of time so that the past can stand revealed.

The aggregativity assumption on which the metaphysical objection is predicated is difficult to attack because it is most commonly implicitly assumed rather than articulated. As Mink (1987, 188) notes, "But that past actuality is an untold story is a presupposition, not a proposition which is often consciously asserted or argued. I do not know a single historian, or indeed anyone, who would subscribe to it as a consciously held belief; yet if I am right, it is implicitly presupposed as widely as it would be explicitly rejected." No sophisticated person, I presume, doubts that stories about the past can be constructed in many ways. But this belief is consistent with an assumption that the past is a *Ding-an-sich* at a temporal remove.

The metaphysical objection to narrative explanations in history presupposes the cogency of conceiving of a past that exists as (to recall Mink's phrase cited in chapter 1) "a single and determinate realm of unchanging actuality." What I propose to do in this chapter is to give this metaphysical assumption of the objective past the most plausible form that I can, and then show that the assumption is untenable.

Critically examining this metaphysical presupposition returns discussion to Danto's device of "narrative sentences" introduced in chapter 1. This device, I noted there, manifests a fundamental insight on Danto's part by making vivid and logically explicit why retrospective characterizations of the past add truths to past times not knowable at those times. To elaborate on this further, I examine in more detail how Danto develops his account.

Danto introduces as expository devices the notions of an Ideal Chronicle and, correlatively, an Ideal Chronicler. The purpose of these devices is to suggest a case in which the factual record of the past is as complete as can be imagined *at the moment at which events occur.*

> We can imagine a description which really is a full description, which tells everything and is perfectly isomorphic with an event. Such a description then will be *definitive*: it shows the event *wie es eigentlich gewesen ist*. . . . I now want to insert an Ideal Chronicler into my picture. He knows whatever happens the moment it happens, even in other minds. He is also to have the gift of instantaneous transcription: everything that happens across the whole forward rim of the Past is set down by him, as it happens, the way it happens. The resultant running account I shall term the Ideal Chronicle. (Danto 1965, 148–49)

Having assumed for the sake of argument that such a complete record exists, Danto then demonstrates that there are statements true of some time *t* in the past which cannot have been known to be true at that time. These statements will not appear even in an Ideal Chronicle. Examples are easy to generate. Simply formulate descriptions known to be true of persons at a time later than *t* and use them to refer to those persons at *t*. The result—what Danto calls "narrative sentences"—will be sentences true at *t* but which could not have been known at *t*, and so escape even the Ideal Chronicler.

Consider, for example, someone who viewed *Bedtime for Bonzo* when it was first released (1951). That person could not say truly, at that moment, that he had just seen a movie starring the fortieth president of the United States. But we can describe the matter in that way; we can give a true description of what happened at time t that is missing from the Ideal Chronicle. Danto's device vividly illustrates that what is interesting and important about events, what is of historical interest, is characteristically known only retrospectively. A perfect witness to a specific moment in the past cannot pick out or observe all there is to be known about that moment. Danto's narrative sentences are sentences true of a moment in the past but not knowable just then. They "belong to stories which historians alone can tell" (Mink 1987, 138–39). Danto (1965, 151) nicely summarizes his own point as follows: "There is a class of descriptions of any event under which the event cannot be witnessed, and these descriptions are necessarily and systematically excluded from the I.C. The whole truth concerning an event can only be known after, and sometimes only long after the event itself has taken place, and this part of the story historians alone can tell. It is something even the best sort of witness cannot know." Danto's characterization of narrative sentences is ingenious and, I believe, correct.

But how does any of this bear on the metaphysical objection with which I began? It is relevant in the following way. Recall that I claimed that this objection to narratives as a form of explanation takes its force not from the sort of flat-footed exposition one finds in Mandelbaum but from the intuition behind that exposition, the sort of intuition captured in Nietzsche's remark that the past is a rock you cannot move. The past is there. But if the fixity of the past is a coherent notion, as it seems to be, then this implies that there could be an Ideal Chronicle. Danto, for one, explicitly draws this conclusion in a passage I cited above. And even Danto betrays more allegiance to this notion of a fixed past than he otherwise claims to have by suggesting, as noted above, that the whole truth of an event might be known.

No matter that an Ideal Chronicle lacks narrative sentences; that issue does not now concern us. If the past is fixed, if it is a story waiting to be told, then it must be logically possible to have some chronicle of it of the sort Danto imagines. What I argue is that the notion of an Ideal Chronicle is *not* coherent, and so we must reject as well any metaphysical picture that implies it.

The critical difficulty with the notion of an Ideal Chronicle is hinted at in the following passage from Mink (1987, 195): "I refer to the Ideal Chronicle . . . to point out, merely, that we understand the idea of it perfectly clearly. And we could not conceive or imagine an Ideal Chronicle at all unless we already had the concept of a totality of 'what really happened.' We reject the possibility of a historiographical representation of this totality, but the very rejection presupposes the concept of the totality itself. It is in that presupposition that the idea of Universal History lives on." Mink is, I suggest, right in sensing a difficulty, but he does not develop an argument. In order, then, to make the problem explicit, imagine the Ideal Chronicler at work. What does the Ideal Chronicler record? Danto's suggestion is everything, and at once at that. But in agreeing that the Ideal Chronicler can write anything at all, we have, in a Wittgensteinian sense, been tricked; the very first step is the fatal one. *The conjuring trick is complete once one concedes that there is anything for an Ideal Chronicler to record.*

What is the basic unit of the posited perfect record? It is events of every sort: visits home, heartbeats, a first kiss, the jump of an electron from one orbital position to another. But, as we know, events may be sliced thick or thin; a glance may be identified as an isolated event or as an instance in an event. What the unit-event is depends on the telling of it. Given the instructions to record "everything that happens, as it happens," the problem is not that there is too much for an Ideal Chronicler to record; the irony is that there are no things in the abstract to be recorded. *An Ideal Chronicler never gets started because there are no ideal events to chronicle.*

What sort of things are events? On one standard account, events are identified only under a description. A reason for worrying whether events exist in some philosophically relevant sense of that term—that is, whether they count as legitimate objects of discourse—is that assuming their existence proves a convenience for the purposes of explicating the logical form of sentences about actions. Countenancing events facilitates the ability to draw permissible inferences which otherwise cannot be readily managed if events are ruled out as individuated objects.

To show, then, that my claim of a paragraph back does not simply beg the question against events as objects, consider someone such as Davidson, who has argued for tolerating such an ontology (see, e.g., Davidson 1980, essays 1, 6–10). But a Davidsonian ontology does not help the Ideal Chronicler with her task. Without some description or other, there are no specific events; with an identifying description, we still do not know if the event is of the requisite ideal sort—that is, not primarily of our making.

The specification of identity conditions does not solve the problem of underdetermination which has bedeviled philosophers of science. There is no unique physical theory entailed by the available evidence; incompatible theories can be formulated compatible with whatever data are at hand. My point about putative "ideal events"—those recounted in some Ideal Chronicle—is that treating such events as objects independent of our object (and event) positing scheme of things runs afoul of what we know about the relation of evidence to theory. The very possibility of an Ideal Chronicle presumes not just identity conditions for events but their existence apart from our theoretical specification of them. But it is precisely this realist inference which is unjustified by any set of identity conditions for events and which, given the problem of the underdetermination of theories, is patently unjustifiable.

The problem is, of course, not ameliorated by shifting to some set of identity conditions for events other than Davidson's. Let events be as well individuated as you please; as noted, I grant we might even be allowed to quantify over them (meaning, in nonphilosophic jargon, that events are treated on a par with individual objects). This does not change the problem. The objection arose not because of some inability to identify events but due to a question about the status of these events apart from some object (or event) positing scheme or other. The issue is their metaphysical status, whether or not we may presume some correspondence between our talk of events and events-in-themselves. To assume that logically adequate identity conditions for events must exist is tantamount to postulating that this is how things must be with the world and that is, of course, to beg the question at issue.

Events simpliciter cannot be shown to exist; they are not known to be of nature's making rather than of ours. Events exist only by proxy. This is why one cannot presume that there are any ideal events for our erstwhile chronicler to chronicle; knowledge of events is restricted to happenings isolated under descriptions provided by interested parties.

Can this problem be solved by augmenting the Ideal Chronicler with a complete set of descriptions? (I continue to exempt, for the sake of argument, the type of descriptions used in Danto's narrative sentences.) Does the notion of completeness make sense here? The metaphysical assumption requires that the completeness be of the past *wie es eigentlich gewesen ist.* The Ideal Chronicle is an objective record, a transcribing of all that has come to pass.

All statements of events appearing in the imagined chronicle are true. Therefore, they must be consistent with one another. But if all descriptions are allowed in, inconsistencies will cloud the chronicle. Consider the events depicted in Kurosawa's film *Rashomon.* The story of what happened in the forest is successively retold from the perspectives of the husband, the wife, and the robber. None tells the same story; indeed, their stories are inconsistent. One tells a tale of rape and humiliation and a husband's cowardice; in other tales, one or more of these descriptions is contradicted. The audience sees what happens each time through the narrator's eyes; it is just that the narrators see different things. Events off the screen certainly have this quality as well. If the conjunction of all possible descriptions is included in the chronicle, the imagined purpose of the chronicle is defeated. Since it contains inconsistencies, it is no longer the hoped-for objective record of what actually happened. But if some descriptions of events are excluded, then the chronicle is incomplete, contrary to its intended purpose. Hence, if complete, then inconsistent, and if consistent, then incomplete. There can be no Ideal Chronicle.

My argument, so far, assumed the premise that events are not natural entities; they exist only under a description. I then argued for the premise that the varying ways of individuating events are not always mutually consistent. Granted these premises, Roth's incompleteness theorem for Ideal Chronicles follows.

But let us make another pass at attempting to fill out the notion of an Ideal Chronicle. Perhaps what I have shown is that it is futile to imagine that there could be an Ideal Chronicle if such a chronicle requires a summing of all descriptions of events as various individuals perceive these matters. But an Ideal Chronicler need not proceed in this way. The charge of the Ideal Chronicler is not, after all, to be faithful to this or that perspective; the task is to record what happened, individual perspective be damned.

This way of putting the matter is tantamount to denying my first premise, the claim that events are not natural entities and exist only under a description. The problem, as I originally developed it, does not assume that some fact is left out; the problem is a failure of people to agree on what counts as the event to be described. Is there a way to include all events and exclude the descriptions of human agents?

Boethius imagined that God saw everything at once; all actions at all times stood revealed simultaneously to God. Certainly this is a way of capturing all that happens. Moreover, the advantage of a Boethian Chronicler is that this person need not rely, or so I shall assume, on potentially conflicting descriptions. This account, however, still will not do, not even if we cut it down so that at time t, everything up to and including what is happening at t stands so revealed to the Ideal Chronicler. The problem is that the Boethian vision, though comprehensive, still does not contain events, or, alternatively, it contains just one event, the total picture at t.

The past so pictured presents not a chronicle, moreover, but a Jamesian buzzing, blooming confusion. Put another way, the identification of events from the Boethian tapestry of the past requires separating the simultaneous presentation of happenings which Boethius imagined into particular strands, the ones that interest us. God may see everything at once; an Ideal Chronicler, within a temporal limit, may do the same, or so I asked you to imagine. But this chronicle gives us less than we have even now. It is not just that there might be a need to factor in cultural conditioning and personal quirks when discussing what we see; seeing is just not perceiving, not in any simple sense. The basic problem is more elementary than that. When we view a snapshot or read a page of a book, if the object is not at the proper distance from our eyes, in appropriate light, and so on, we cannot see what we want to see. If someone pushes the book or picture up so it touches our nose, we see something—but not, for example, the picture of the picnic or the story of the latest political gaffe. Given the Boethian view, the Ideal Chronicler is in just this position, or leaves us in this position when consulting the resulting tapestry of happenings. The Boethian Chronicler has no natural point of focus. But without a focus, either nothing appears—the blooming, buzzing confusion—or God-knows-what looms before us, like the photo pressed too close for one to view. Total information gives us less than we need to know.

Given the Boethian picture, it does not follow that human beings could say anything about it at all. Chronicles presuppose categorizations of time and events, and there is no reason to believe the Boethian account could be a chronicle. Nothing in that account, filled though it is with every conceivable happening, entails that there are humanly identifiable events arranged in recognizable order. If events are picked out by human agents, the chronicle is not ideal; if the world is viewed from the eye of God, there is no chronicle. A Boethian chronicle cuts things too coarsely to solve the problem of identifying events in an objective way.

The point at which the discussion has arrived is this: If events are individuated by some favored set of identity conditions, the notion of there being an ideal chronicle self-destructs; such a chronicle is logically impossible. If we imagine the chronicle along Boethian lines, the notion still cannot be made cogent, for the Boethian image cannot be translated into the form of a chronicle.

But perhaps the Boethian picture is a start. It is, at least, complete. The problem is to find a finer-grained description of matters uninfected by conflicting descriptions; this would preserve the metaphysical assumption that the past exists objectively as an untold story.

Problems arise, we just noted, if there is total information and no categories by which to organize and focus viewing. Perhaps a solution to this problem is a Carnapian Chronicler. The Carnapian Chronicler, let us imagine, defines a language—Ideal-in-L—which contains rules and definitions such that, given certain state descriptions, Ideal-in-L permits the derivation of the event that took place. Consistency is thus assured and no ambiguity threatens. But this is no Ideal Chronicle in the desired respect. The question of which events exist has now been relegated to the status of an internal question; the existence of events is explicitly relativized to a particular set of rules. This preserves consistency, but it defeats the purpose of positing the chronicle. The purpose is to explicate how to construct a complete and objective record of the past. The correspondence theory of historical truth remains unvindicated by appeal to a Carnapian Chronicler.

The only refinement on the matter I have left to suggest would be to limit the Ideal Chronicler's task. Do the problems abate if we imagine an Ideal Boswell? The task is cut down by giving the Ideal Boswell the more modest task of compiling a complete record for a single individual. If history is, as Carlyle claimed, but so many biographies, then the Ideal Boswell would preserve the metaphysical assumption. But, alas, the Ideal Boswell too produces only a blur. The root of the problem is not in the scope of the enterprise but in its completeness. Unless we equip the Ideal Boswell with our categories, there are no recognizable events. But if equipped with our categories, he ceases to be ideal. He is just one of us, albeit a tad more compulsive. I conclude that the notions of an Ideal Chronicle and an Ideal Chronicler cannot be coherently fleshed out, and so the metaphysical objection fails.

Viewing the world sub specie aeternitatis, an Ideal Chronicler is imagined to see events bare, shorn of the misperceptions and oversights to which mere mortals are prone. In particular, historical events are conceived as having their own pristine ontological integrity. Caesar crosses the Rubicon in 49 B.C. or he does not; if true, the chronicler notes it and if not, not. (The dating here makes this a narrative sentence, but this complication can be ignored.) A disinterested chronicle seems impossible. The core of my complaint has been that it is the pretense to disinterestedness and completeness that makes Danto's fiction ultimately incoherent. Given the lofty God's-eye perspective, no events appear. A less lofty perspective defeats the purpose of the literary conceit. The philosophical moral is one pressed by philosophers from Kant to Davidson. We may query the world and learn a great deal, but it is a confusion to think that the categories in which the questions are posed and the answers framed constitute, to paraphrase Richard Rorty, History's Own Vocabulary.

My primary concern throughout has been with a prima facie objection—what I have termed a metaphysical objection because it assumes a certain view about what must be real by way of history—to the notion of a narrative explanation. If there is a historical reality, then narrative form appears not simply incidental but fundamentally unconnected to explaining that history. My handling of this objection, with its challenge to the notion of a comprehensive or ideal perspective, even if

CHAPTER 2

convincing, is as yet no delineation, however, of what counts as a proper narrative explanation. Surrendering a belief in a God's-eye chronicle, and so a metaphysical commitment to the past as an untold story, does not impugn ties of historical inquiry to the world. Rather, rejecting any "commonsense" metaphysical understanding of how to account for what happened helps clear the philosophical stage for a satisfactory account of how narratives explain. The next chapter undertakes some further stage clearing and setting before introducing in chapter 4 my positive account of narrative explanation.

3

The Pasts

This chapter develops further challenges to the metaphysical objection to narrative explanation, an objection I take to be based on a view of history that takes past events to exist as fixed. One challenge to this view has been scouted in the previous chapter. This metaphysical presupposition, I suggested, underlies skepticism about the very possibility of a category of narrative explanation. For imagined as timelessly fixed and unchangeable, i.e., a past composed of a determinate inventory of events, there appears to be no reason why histories should necessarily have any of the distinctive qualities argued for in chapter 1. That is, a fixed past should plausibly contain, contrary to the characteristics identified in chapter 1, explanatory sequences that aggregate, standardize, and detach. *But insofar as any metaphysical assumption regarding a fixed or determinate inventory of what has past can be problematized, then this removes a seemingly important reason for assuming a form of explanation tailored to an ontologically or theoretically well-defined world.* A consequence of establishing the implausibility of any realist-inflected metaphysical assumption would be to help reopen questions of how historical events do become candidates for explanation. Put another way, realism deflects serious consideration of the special nature of historical explananda, and so what form their explanation can take. This chapter moves beyond the critique begun in chapter 2 by offering a positive argument for what I term *historical irrealism.*

My rejection of a metaphysics that posits a determinate past in favor of an irrealist view proceeds in this chapter in two general steps. Part I begins by examining important and innovative work by Ian Hacking (1995b, ch. 17) that leads him to conclude that there may be "indeterminacies" in the past. But Hacking does not recognize the full generality of the problems that he identifies because, I suggest, he never connects his analyses to those of Danto and Mink. Part II then develops and expands Hacking's insights by making these connections explicit and showing how his tentative thoughts about "indeterminacies" can be given both a greater generality and more significance than he appreciates. This vindicates an irrealist view of history, and so sets the stage for the analysis of narrative explanation in chapter 4. In particular, irrealism establishes why what histories attempt to explain have a uniquely important and special characteristic, viz., they come to be known only retrospectively. This feature necessitates employing what chapter 4 develops as "essentially narrative explanations."

I

> Worldmaking as we know it always starts from worlds already on hand; the making is a remaking.
> —Nelson Goodman, *Ways of Worldmaking*

Riddles of induction—old or new, Hume's or Goodman's—pose unanswered challenges to assumptions that experience logically legitimates expectations or classifications. The challenges apply to beliefs both folk and scientific. In particular, Goodman's "new riddle" famously confounds efforts to specify how additional experiences confirm the rightness of currently preferred ways of organizing objects, i.e., our favored theories of what kinds there are (see Goodman 1978, 1979). His riddle serves to emphasize that neither logic nor experience certifies accepted groupings of objects into kinds.[1] Hacking (1992c, 181) strongly endorses Goodman's riddle and what he takes to be its chief consequences: nature does not dictate any organizing scheme to us, and different schemes need have no connection to one another:

> It [Goodman's new riddle] shows that whenever we reach any general conclusion on the basis of evidence about its instances, we could by the same rules of inference, but with different preferences in classification, reach an opposite conclusion.
> ... There is no general solution to his new riddle. Its scope goes far beyond induction and other trifling modes of reason. It confirms his doctrine ... that we can and do inhabit many worlds.

No one organizing scheme can claim primacy; different organizing schemes need not be compatible with or reducible to one another. Hence, different "worlds" thrive and grow (Goodman 1978, 4–5).

Yet tolerating a pluralism of worlds does not sanction sacrificing rigor.[2] Goodman's (1978, 5) approach to exploring different worlds—painting, physics, literature, etc.—"is rather through an analytic study of types and functions of symbols and symbol systems." But where Goodman talks of symbol systems and worlds, Hacking writes of "styles of reasoning" and corresponding kinds. Hacking's position might be characterized as follows (paraphrasing Frege): Only within a style of reasoning does a sentence have a truth-value.³

Each style of reasoning, in turn, has a characteristic manner of constituting the kinds of objects reasoned about. Indeed, styles of reasoning themselves depend upon the recognized kinds about which to reason. In what follows, I explore Hacking's notion of "dynamic nominalism" and its place in and implications for constituting various kinds of persons and related categories of events. In particular, I explicate and defend Hacking with regard to how some Goodman-inspired problems destabilize the foundations of any historical knowledge-claims and what all this, in turn, implies for thinking about and constituting ourselves and others, as agents and as beings with a past. Emphasis on Goodman (and Wittgenstein and Foucault) helps make intelligible the notion of a past as something made, remade, and inherently open to being systematically changed.

Hacking (1999, 130 [191]; see also Hacking 1990)⁴ generates important insights by innovatively applying Goodmanian (and Quinean) skepticism about kinds to knowledge-claims about the past:

> We can well understand how new kinds create new possibilities for choice and action. But the past, of course, is fixed! Not so. As Goodman would put it, if new kinds are selected, then the past can occur in a new world. Events in a life can now be seen as events of a new kind, a kind that may not have been conceptualized when the event was experienced or the act performed. What we experienced becomes recollected anew, and thought in terms that could not have been thought at the time. Experiences are not only redescribed; they are refelt. This adds remarkable depth to Goodman's vision of world-making by kind-making.

In particular, skepticism and indeterminacy regarding *present* kinds apply to past schemata as well, particularly actions qua kind of behavior—a kind distinguished by an imputation of intentions.

A primary objective for Hacking as I understand him is to move away from an empirically sterile and unhelpful traditional debate between advocates of natural kinds (those who see essences defining what's what) and nominalists (those who see no more in kinds than habits of speech). He wishes to recognize both the fact that some groupings of things into kinds do function well for us, and that yet we do the groupings.

> How do such questions about human kinds compare with questions about natural kinds? Astrophysicists do ask: are quasars a (natural) kind of extragalactic object? Physicians and social workers do ask: are

> child abusers a kind of person? The similar form of the two questions
> may mislead us. A clearer understanding of our instinct for sorting into
> natural kinds may help diminish our confusion about human kinds. ...
> Those of us offended by an essentialist metaphysics of natural kinds
> need not abandon natural kinds out of spite for that philosophy. Just
> as the chief nineteenth-century interest in natural kinds was biological,
> so in the near future it will be socio-historical. How do we construct
> kinds? Under what constraints? With what effects? This type of concern
> with natural kinds spills over to problems about every kind of kind:
> Goodman's kinds, artifactual kinds, human kinds, and the differences
> between making up kinds of people and making up kinds of things.
> (Hacking 1990, 140; see also 135)

For example, laboratory-generated phenomena such as the photoelectric effect Hacking regards as a "manufactured" yet robust kind. Racial categories exemplify groupings that typically require substantial institutional underpinning to be sustained, in large part because people resist efforts to sort them in such ways. Hence, he proposes to look at what factors sustain groupings, both in terms of utility and in terms of social resources required to keep a grouping in place.[5]

Stability over time helps to determine whether "styles of reasoning" and "kinds" endure. Resilience of kinds manifests itself in their persistence even in the face of changing social circumstances. Hacking notes that some things are indifferent to how we classify them, e.g., microbes and acids, and some not, e.g., people. When things do *not* respond to being classified by us in one way rather than another, Hacking terms such kinds "indifferent." However, as numerous experiments in social psychology show, people do respond differently depending on how one classifies them. Such classification-sensitive responses Hacking terms "interactive" kinds.[6]

> My contrast with the social sciences is as follows. In natural science
> our invention of categories does not "really" change the way the world
> works. Even though we create new phenomena which did not exist
> before our scientific endeavours, we do so only with a license from
> the world (or so we think). But in social phenomena we may generate
> kinds of people and kinds of action as we devise new classifications and
> categories. My claim is that we "make up people" in a stronger sense
> than we "make up" the world. The difference is, as I say, connected
> with the ancient question of nominalism. It is also connected with history, because the objects of the social sciences—people and groups of

> people—are constituted by an historical process, while the objects of the natural sciences, particular experimental apparatus, are created in time, but, in some sense, they are not constituted historically. (Hacking, 1985, 115)

Hacking's distinction here provides a new and important twist on an old suggestion regarding how to distinguish the natural and the human sciences.

At least since Weber it has been held that the notion of understanding applies to the social but not the natural world; as the old saw has it, nature we explain, human life we understand. But the drive to understand exists not just because we imagine reasons to figure into a proper explanation of human action but also because humans, by reflecting on their reasons, can supposedly change them.[7] We may be creatures of habit, but we can also be creatures who, by reflecting on their habits, change them. Moreover, the stock of socially available ways of thinking about oneself shape and influence both of these causal processes—acting because of reasons, changing reasons by reflecting on them. Hacking's contribution to the debate here consists not in drawing the distinction between natural and social sciences in terms that reflect these factors, but in his brilliant depiction of why certain interactive kinds prove "unstable," i.e., do not identify a phenomenon that allows of ongoing duplication and experimentation.

Hacking's notion of "dynamic nominalism" I take to be an elaboration of his account of interactive kinds, but one that cross-cuts the distinction between stable and unstable. Some classifications of people into kinds prove relatively robust and stable (for better or worse), e.g., male and female as kinds. Some classifications, e.g., homosexual, Hacking suggests were "socially constructed" but then became the basis for stabilizing and forming a distinct social identity. In this regard, some labels become a type of self-fulfilling prophecy. By creating a social and conceptual space for a type of behavior or person, people invariably come to fill that space in a way that both defines and is defined by the label.

> A different kind of nominalism—I call it dynamic nominalism—attracts my realist self, spurred on by theories about the making of the homosexual and the heterosexual as kinds of persons or by my observations about official statistics. The claim of dynamic nominalism is not that there was a kind of person who came increasingly to be recognized by bureaucrats or by students of human nature but rather that a kind of person came into being at the same time as the kind itself was being

invented. In some cases, that is, our classifications and our classes conspire to emerge hand in hand, each egging the other on. (Hacking 1986b, 228)

Dynamic nominalism seeks to capture two important vectors shaping who we are. First, socially available roles define our conceptions of ourselves; this Hacking refers to as determination from above. But then there exist individual vagaries of behavior, variations on the life-themes the available roles provide. This points to an element of choice and innovation (Hacking 1986b, 234). But while the notions of split or multiple personalities, on the one hand, and homosexuals, on the other hand, are both products of dynamic nominalism, they do not stand on equal footing. For one—homosexuality—displays a conceptual robustness and stability that the other does not. Multiple personality syndrome has proven to be a tenuous phenomenon and a much-contested concept; homosexuality, in contrast, has flourished as a form of self-identification and institution-building.

Not all kind-making, then, is of a kind. Some of our efforts latch more successfully than others onto features that prove stable and enduring. Just as in his philosophy of science, Hacking emphasizes the primacy of experimental and laboratory work over theoretical elaborations. Stability and utility determine ontological status—"If you can spray them then they are real" (Hacking 1983, 23). That is, Hacking shuns theory as his guide to reality. He finds no substitute for examining the factors that help create, then sustain, and perhaps finally undercut ways of categorizing people in practice. "I do not believe there is a general story to be told about making up people. Each category has its own history" (Hacking 1986b, 234). In short, not even all interactive kinds are alike.

Hacking's account of intentional action involves both of the action vectors mentioned above: social availability and individual variation. He links his analyses of actions and kinds (Foucault and Goodman) in the following way. Like Alasdair MacIntyre and Erving Goffman, Hacking (1986b, 229) maintains that the roles available for people to assume define who any of us can be: "Making up people changes the space of possibilities for personhood."[8] But what bounds or defines the "space of possibilities"? To this critical question Hacking fashions a powerful and insightful reply. "We have," he astutely suggests, merely "a folk picture of the gradations of possibility" (229). But what determines the "gradations of possibility" for actions must be carefully examined. For, it turns out, the logical possibilities for action link more to what we say about them than, for example, the behavior of microbes or the possibility of a five-sided square.

The relevant sense of "action" here is intentionally directed behavior, i.e., behavior described using a particular vocabulary. Now Hacking (e.g., 1986b, 230) throughout his writings attributes this approach to G. E. M. Anscombe and her famous formula that intentional actions are "actions under a description." This tie to Anscombe provides an interesting connection, as we shall see, back to Danto and narrative sentences. But although this is, as far as it goes, an accurate characterization of the position Hacking consistently espouses, it fails to emphasize the philosophical points at issue (points Hacking knows quite well, but not ones apparent to all of his readers).

If the concern is to understand how people communicate, adverting to processes in the head looks the wrong way. The point that Anscombe and Hacking emphasize is that intentionality cannot be explicated in terms of a private mental state. Rather, as Hacking (1995b, 235) reads Anscombe, references to intentional acts reflect socially sanctioned way of describing what we or others sometimes do, i.e., how we characterize certain behaviors: "I should also say that Anscombe, much influenced by Wittgenstein, crisply argues that an intentional action is not, for example, an organized sequence of doings plus an inner, private, mental intention. The intention under which an event is done does not refer to some entity in the mind."[9] In this regard, attributions of intentionality also become a study of the use of "words in their sites."[10]

Having affirmed that the *kinds* of actions or social roles available to people connect to the kinds of descriptions possible, the question then arises for Hacking (1986b, 231) of how this impacts on the space of possibilities of accounting for or describing past behaviors: "What is curious about human action is that by and large what I am deliberately doing depends on the possibilities of description." But what sense can be given to the declaration that "the possibilities for what we might have been are transformed"? Hacking illustrates his point here by briefly noting how the use of the category of suicide evolves over the nineteenth and early twentieth centuries.[11] As much as almost any other concept of the sort that interests Hacking—ones that involve the determination for purposes of medicalization of "states of mind"—suicide enters the realm of what can become "medicalized" once statisticians begin to count and classify kinds of deaths.

Any number of people have over the course of history had a hand in actively bringing about their own demise. But what interests and concerns Hacking (1986b, 234) is the emergence of a special notion of suicide, one that classifies a suicide, any suicide, as a type of insanity. Suicide thus becomes an index of mental health for individuals, and the rate of suicide becomes a corresponding index for that of national groups.

This connects, Hacking suggests, Foucault's "two poles of development," one centered on how to classify individuals—his "anatomo-politics of the human body"—and the second that characterizes the "biopolitics of the population." Durkheim's (1951) *Suicide* virtually creates a discipline, or at least a paradigm for one, by forging one of the first suggested links between these two poles. This link would have been impossible but for the statistics collected over the previous years, and the statistics required a prior commitment to counting and classifying the intention leading to death. But the intention here can be for Hacking nothing other than a piece of behavior we choose to describe in a particular way. "Even the unmaking of people has been made up" (235).

Changing the past by changing the descriptions available works, then, for Hacking in at least two different ways. Reclassification can change the past impersonally, i.e., in ways regarding others but not oneself, or it can change one's own past, that is, with regard to oneself. Hacking's discussion of the notion of suicide illustrates the first case. Although brief, his account of suicide shows how reclassification changes the past because a description of action introduced later—the medicalized notion of suicide—literally changes what someone previously did. *How could it not? What other kind of thing could it be?* If what happens in the world is at least in part a function of human actions, and if Goodmanian kinds, i.e., exemplifications of ways a given community descriptively collates behaviors in particular ways, are what actions are, then when new descriptions, new ways of collating physical doings become available, this changes what actions happened, whenever they happened. Only descriptions create a past in which human actions have meaning. For meaning requires ascribing an intention, and such ascription depends on what categories humans have forged and when.

Hacking develops his take on the Anscombian point by pushing characterizations of intentional doings as a kind into a problem area he perceives as one characterized by a confusion of causal and definitional aspects. For example, in chapter 6 of *Rewriting the Soul*, Hacking (1995b, 82) traces out how confusion of cause and concept lies at the heart of the now accepted etiology for multiple personality disorder: "We should not delude ourselves into thinking that we first defined the disorder and then discovered its cause." The problem here involves failing to distinguish between suggesting a name for a particular type of childhood trauma and presenting, "as if it were a discovery, that multiple personality is caused . . . by childhood trauma" (82). For when presented as a cause, it invites patients classified on the basis of certain symptoms (they have multiple personality disorder) to discover and attribute a corresponding sequence to their own history.

It is at this point that the confusion of intentions and causes becomes germane, for it turns out to be a special case of people's getting made up, by themselves or by others. Here the Goodmanian considerations on kinds come full flower for Hacking (1995b, 89; emphasis mine), for his account reveals that these considerations extend to our self-understanding and our understanding of others:

> A certain picture of origins is imparted to disturbed and unhappy people, who then use it to reorder or reorganize their conception of their past. It becomes their past. I am not saying that their past is directly created by doctors. *I am saying that this picture becomes disseminated as a way of thinking of what it was like to be a child and to grow up. There is no canonical way to think of our own past. In the endless quest for order and structure, we grasp at whatever picture is floating by and put our past into its frame.*

We have no choice but to "make up" a past, to impose an order on what we take to have happened. If we did not, there would be no cohering scheme to refer to by "the past," no way of sequencing events that account for how things are now based on how they were. (See Roth 1998 for further development of this line of thought.)

For example, once patients diagnosed as multiples assimilate a confusion of definition and cause into their own self-understanding, they set about becoming the people they are told they are.

> I suggest that we have not found any ordinary etiology of this illness.
> We should not think of multiplicity as being strictly caused by child abuse. It is rather that the multiple finds or sees the cause of her condition in what she comes to remember about her childhood, and is thereby helped. This is passed off as a specific etiology, but what is happening is more extraordinary than that. It is a way of explaining oneself, not by recovering the past, but by redescribing it, rethinking it, refeeling it. (Hacking 1995b, 93–94)

At least part of the significance of the distinction here as Hacking deploys it concerns how people make themselves into the kinds of people a therapist describes by internalizing and then acting in accord with certain descriptions of themselves. This is how multiples or abused children behave, one learns, and then other people take it from there.[12]

Perhaps the most important aspect of Hacking's embrace of the Anscombian account of intention, and one that he himself does not stress enough, is how it shifts the question that sometimes bothers Hacking himself: What can it mean to say that the past changes, that actions done

CHAPTER 3

possess an "indeterminacy" with regard to how they can be characterized? The past, a strong intuition suggests, is fixed, closed.

But just here it pays to press Hacking's own suggestion that we push past any folk understanding of "the possible." Hacking's account reveals the relevant question to be *What supposedly stabilizes or fixes what happened previously?* It—what is past—should prove no more (or less!) changeable than the processes comprising it. A past that depends for its coherence on contingent concepts or processes, kinds that themselves lack any particular stability, proves open and subject to change.

I emphasize here that I do not mean just or exclusively our "understanding" of the past, whatever one takes that to be. Changes of understanding might be construed so as to imply that such "change" does not alter "the past itself" but just alters, so to speak, one's appreciation of what went on. Rather, my claim, following from my reading of Hacking, is that some categories used to constitute the past, including especially human actions, possess nothing that intrinsically stabilizes them. In this regard, past actions may change because intentional kinds have no stability or essence beyond the contingencies of community-sanctioned descriptions used to characterize them.[13]

This is particularly true of how we think about ourselves, as noted above.[14] The indeterminacy of the past consists of the fact that we make all kinds, and that human-action kinds in particular are bound only by our ways of describing them. Narrowly bound, behavior construed as intentional may encompass a limited time slice (a wave or a wink to a friend) or it may extend over longer stretches of time and many individuals (how the atom bomb came to be built or the human genome unraveled). "The best analogy to remembering is storytelling. The metaphor for memory is narrative" (Hacking 1995b, 250). *Although Hacking never draws this conclusion, his own argument for an indeterminacy in the past points to just this "narrativizing" feature as constitutive of the past, and so as the reason for its indeterminacy.*

We make, unmake, and remake the past not out of ignorance but because, regarding human actions, a past consists of just such makings and remakings. Talk of changing "the past" rings odd only because we (wrongly) attribute to interactive and intentional kinds the robustness possessed by some indifferent kinds. In this regard, Hacking (1996, 73) stresses that a hallmark of humanistic thought is its lack of those features that make for stable scientific knowledge: "A happy by-product of my analysis is not only that each style has its own self-stabilizing techniques, but also that some are more effective than others. The taxonomic and the historicogenetic styles have produced nothing like the stability of the laboratory or the mathematical style, and I claim to be able to show why." Hacking (1993, 303) looks askance at putative sciences whose identity conditions for entities stand only because "clamped to taxonomic trees."

Hacking takes two tacks in showing why what he terms "historicogenetic" and "taxonomic" styles lack stability. They are related in the ways already sketched. In the taxonomic case, there exists the confusion of definition and cause. A definition is stipulated and reemerges as the announced discovery of the cause. The historicogenetic exemplifies the Goodmanian concerns with which I started.[15] We project some predicates rather than others, but what we take to be stable features turn out to be socially entrenched practices which have become, in the fullness of time, taken for metaphysical verities.

To change slightly Hacking's (1993, 304) order of exposition, his argument is that, first, "kinds are at the heart of all knowledge," and, second, with regard to the human psyche, "our very classifications change the people and behaviors classified." The argument for the second premise rests on Hacking's extended case studies of how psychological taxonomies get created and made canonical. Taxonomies rely, he suggests, on explicated and unexplicatable notions of kinds, i.e., appeals to intuitive notions of similarity. But the legitimacy of such intuitive appeals he finds Goodman to undercut. Such taxonomies, including taxonomic classifications of behaviors into actions, have no joints at which to carve. They exist only insofar as community-sanctioned practices of projection maintain them.

> When it comes to retroactive redescriptions of the past, political rhetoric will influence many people more than argument and reflection will. I do not want to convince anyone to draw the line, in retroactive redescription, at any particular place. Rather I would urge that it may simply not have been very determinate, in the past, that certain future descriptions of past intentional action would apply or could be applied. . . .
>
> Old actions under new descriptions may be reexperienced in memory.
>
> And if these are genuinely new descriptions, descriptions not available or perhaps nonexistent at the time of the episodes remembered, then something is experienced now, in memory, that in a certain sense did not exist before. The action took place, but not the action under the new description. Moreover, it was not determinate that these events would be experienced in these new ways, for it was not determinate, at the time that the events occurred, that in the future new descriptions

> would come into being. . . . Thus I am suggesting a very difficult view about memories of intentional human actions. What matters to us may not have been quite so definite as it now seems. When we remember what we did, or what other people did, we may also rethink, redescribe, and refeel the past. These redescriptions may be perfectly true of the past; that is, they are truths that we now assert about the past. And yet, paradoxically, they may not have been true in the past, that is, not truths about intentional actions that made sense when the actions were performed. That is why I say that the past is revised retroactively. I do not mean only that we change our opinions about what was done, but that in a certain logical sense what was done itself is modified. As we change our understanding and sensibility, the past becomes filled with intentional actions that, in a certain sense, were not there when they were performed. (Hacking 1993, 244, 249–50)[16]

> The old, and valuable, Freudian insight is that scenes that are recovered, whether it is in flashbacks, or through memory therapy, or through more ordinary reflective but unassisted recollection, become invested with meanings that they did not have at the time that they were experienced. Let me add that in our days of inflated psychological verbiage, the human actions which occur in those scenes are very often retroactively redescribed. That is, they become actions under descriptions that were not available at the time the actions were first performed. (Hacking 1995b, 254)

The conclusion from these premises is that the past is indeterminate, insofar as what constitutes the past results from a particular narrative, certain ways of classifying and sequencing behaviors so as to depict them as actions of particular sorts. Changing classifications changes groupings, and so literally alters the actions ascribed and so reconfigures accounts of causes and consequences of such actions.

In remarkable, consistent, and insightful fashion, Hacking relentlessly follows out Foucauldian insights in work that spans more than twenty years. Turning inward Foucault's denial that "the human sciences have a genuine object to talk about," Hacking (1986a, 32) worries about the concepts we are "given" to think about ourselves. He worries not because they might still the voices of a "true self." Like Foucault, he harbors no such romantic illusions.[17] Rather, it is precisely because whatever sense we can make of human agency, for moral purposes or otherwise, depends so critically on what categories are made available to us that we must exercise constant vigilance over invitations about how to think about ourselves.

II

Ironically, as fond as Hacking proves to be of utilizing historical examples, and despite the implications of his account for historical understanding, he says nothing about what makes for historical explanations, much less good or bad ones. Nonetheless, his use of Goodman and his own tentative discussion of indeterminacies in the past point to implications beyond those he explicitly considers. Indeed, by linking Hacking's insights regarding the historical and dynamic character of kinds and categories and considerations by Danto, Mink, and others on narrative sentences and their role in constituting a past, a much more general critique can be formulated of a notion of a determinate past.

I begin by noting that Danto's analysis of narrative sentences might itself appear to leave undisturbed a commitment to a type of realist metaphysics with regard to past states. The imagined realist holds that although new descriptions of the past may later become available, there can exist exactly *one* immutably real past. From the standpoint of subsequent times, all statements about the past, even if they are evidence-transcendent, have a fixed truth-value. As Crispin Wright (1993, 148–49) observes, realism makes historical truth "investigation independent," that is, "that what judgments are correct in particular circumstances is something determined quite independently of human reaction to those circumstances." Wright importantly notes as well that this view implies an indifference of truth to the passage of time. "But this natural thought is simply tantamount to the assumption that the passage of time should have no part to play in determining our conception of what states of affairs may coherently be conceived as possible. . . . And this assumption, of course, is here at issue" (187).[18] A past so conceived must be changeless. Otherwise, truth-values would not be timeless.[19]

Antirealism "takes more seriously the fact that we are immersed in time; being so immersed, we cannot frame any description of the world as it would appear to one who was not in time, but we can only describe it as it is, i.e., as it is now" (Dummett 1978, 369). As Michael Dummett imagines it, antirealism allows for truth-value gaps; some statements about the past might lack a truth-value, a position that realism denies. Each position captures opposed intuitions about the past; each offends against intuition in its own way. The problem here lies in the implication that realism and antirealism about the past constitute the sole metaphysical options, and so one has to make a forced choice between them.

But much rides on this metaphysical debate. For one, it subserves a theory of understanding, i.e., an account of how sentences (including tensed ones) could be learned and shared. Epistemology and logic have traditionally featured in this debate only insofar as certain types of statements represent a canonical form of verification (for example, perception and implication). Implication flows on this view from observational statements taken as semantic atoms to statements about unobservables. Dilemmas generated by current metaphysical debates about the reality of the past reflect, on my view, a misplaced emphasis on the nature of canonical verification, one shared by realists and antirealists alike. A fundamental aspect of my critique focuses on the assumed canonicity of observational statements as a prototype of knowledge and associated views regarding the type of logic needed to account for how language functions.[20]

The philosophical critique of current metaphysical views about historical reality that animates this essay emphasizes instead how holism and naturalism reconfigure the issues regarding the epistemology and metaphysics associated with historical knowledge. The "reality of the past," I argue, proves to be no more (or less) problematic than our account of any other aspect of reality, and so historical claims ought to be treated as subject to the same conditions and caveats that apply to any theory of empirical knowledge.[21] Empirical knowledge, in turn, on the view defended here requires some general beliefs about the world—a theory in an extended sense of that term—in order for anything to emerge as an event from the flux of experience.[22]

Most important, insofar as a primary motivation for exploring the existing metaphysical options involves determining which offers a workable basis for an explanatory account of history, neither does. Rather, I use Danto's early insight to motivate irrealism about the past.[23] On my revised view *nothing* answers to "The Past." Absent a "view from nowhere," no good reason exists for asserting either verification independent truth-conditions or truth-value gaps. That is, realism requires a framework-independent view of reality of the sort denied in chapter 2. Likewise, antirealism too turns out to depend on just this sort of metaphysical determinism, for otherwise the problem of truth-value gaps could not arise. Irrealism, that is, does not require a semantic structure that assumes either a perspective out of time or one where meaning requires verification conditions dependent on what might be available now. Since there will be narrative sentences true of any particular time t but not knowable at t, these could not be verified at just that moment. Thus, contra Dummett's version of antirealism, there can be true but in principle unverifiable sentences at a given time even absent the assumption of realism.[24] Irrealism results by acknowledging that one's own history must play an important and ineliminable role "in determining our conception of what states of affairs may coherently be conceived as possible." Irrealism as I develop it also implies that how earlier and later times may influence one another remains at least partially indeterminate. Indeed, a coherent account of why our future remains undetermined at least in some respects also presumes a past that remains open.[25] In particular, irrealism helps account for why historical explanation involves a retrospective perspective, one that in turn requires a narrative form.

Against, then, a tradition within analytical philosophy regarding knowledge of the past from Danto to Dummett that emphasizes analyses of statements, I develop an alternative account of historical knowledge owing to Leon Goldstein and Ian Hacking, one that eschews the metaphysics of both realism and antirealism. Goldstein's account of historical knowing utilizes important but overlooked forms of holism and nominalism. This position has the advantage of taking seriously issues arising from historiographic, scientific, and epistemological considerations of knowledge about the past.[26] However, Goldstein's formulation suffers because it permits an unreasonable proliferation of historical "knowledge." If a historian constitutes a past, how could a past so constituted fail to represent? What would it be, in other words, for an act of historical constitution to go wrong?

Separating Goldstein's valuable account of historical constitution from this untoward implication requires developing an aspect of his position at which Goldstein himself only hints. This feature, as I argue below, links to the earlier discussion of Hacking's innovative application of Goodman's irrealism to historical analysis. The view that results I (following Goodman) term an irrealist view of history. This displaces the metaphysical assumption of a fixed or determinate past.

Goldstein (1976, xxii) defines and develops his signature doctrines of historical constitution and historical knowing by contrasting them to a doctrine he labels "historical realism": "By *historical realism* I mean that point of view according to which the real past as it was when it was being lived is the touchstone against which to test for truth or falsity the products of historical constitution." Realism as Goldstein opposes it treats "the historical past on the model of the experienced present; it is an extension of our everyday attitudes to the world of past events" (38; see, e.g., Ayer 1952, 9). But Goldstein (1996, 154) terms realism so conceived an "absurdity," a doctrine "utterly false" (Goldstein 1976, xxii) to those processes that make historical knowledge possible and a subject of rational evaluation.

Goldstein (1976, xxiv) finds historical realism operating more as an unquestioned assumption in writings about history than as a doctrine explicitly advocated: "Historical realism is a habit of mind—not a refined doctrine—which inclines those possessed of it *simply to assume* that the conceptions of factuality, truth, or reference which apply when we speak of the natural world in the natural present must apply when we speak of the historical past, that, indeed, they must apply to any realm of discourse to which considerations of truth and falsity obtain." Goldstein (1996, 243) protests throughout his writings against conceiving of the past as an independently subsisting "touchstone," as something fixed and therefore prior to historical research that true histories represent.

Writing in a similar vein and at about the same time of the publication of Goldstein's book, Mink also focuses on the plausibility lent to the idea of a historical realism—"the past as an untold story"—by the assumption that the past, as past, was fixed, immutable, not open to change (recall Mink 1987, 194). Indeed, the core of historical realism consists of the belief that *histories are found, not made.* What determines the truth-value of statements about the past does not depend on available evidence or human judgment.[27]

Although he claims to find everywhere thinkers implicitly assuming historical realism, Goldstein (1976, 38) remarks that he knows "of no attempt to explicate and defend historical realism." I do. William Dray, for one, insists on this view. For Dray, the past so conceived constitutes a type of permanent possibility of narration—a "tellable."[28] Dray (1989, 162–63) succinctly puts the case against antirealism, a view he attributes to thinkers as otherwise diverse as Goldstein, Mink, and Hayden White, as follows: "The separation [by White and Mink] of historical discovery from the aesthetic or moral task of 'writing up' what has been discovered in narrative form is based on a simple but serious error: it implicitly, but falsely, denies that part of what the historian discovers is the configuration the narrative displays. . . . But the form, the configuration, is itself the most important fact that historians discover. And facts can exist unknown." Note just that Dray straightforwardly asserts what Goldstein denies, namely, that historians discover *the* past, a "configuration" that exists prior to any activity of historical inquiry, a "tellable" as a "fact unknown."

Yet just what metaphysical status could such historical events have? On what basis could one hope to say that events qua kinds of human activities are found, not made? In speaking of the sort of events relevant for historical analysis, I focus on events characterized as intentional or purposive actions. Such events—behavior characterized "under a description" of a certain sort—prove central to Goldstein's account of what historical knowing constitutes as the historical past. An event "emerges" from all that remains available because some elements can be imagined as instantiating a purpose.

Goldstein's (1976, xxi–xxii) thesis of historical constitution invokes the methods specific to historical theorizing as simultaneously constitutive of the object of historical knowledge: "By *historical constitution* I mean that set of intellectual procedures whereby the historical past is reconstructed in the course of historical research." *An eventful historical past exists only as a result of human theorizing. History becomes an artifact of a disciplined disciplinary imagination.*[29]

Goldstein's formulations underline a point noted from Danto, namely, that historians characterize events at a time—for example, "pre-Columbian Nordic excursion"—under descriptions not available at that time although now true of that time. What historians constitute when constituting a past might be thought of as a paradigm of a past resulting from present traces—an account that offers problem-solving potential with regard to what the traces trace.

The claim "No constitution, no reference" insists that only in the context of a theory do historical questions have a meaning (see also Lorenz 1998). For example, questions regarding the Dead Sea scrolls or pre-Columbian Nordic excursions in North America can be asked only within a prior context that provides these phrases with their meaning. "It seems clear that everything that we can come to say about the historical past emerges entirely within the framework of historical knowing. Every attempt to subject to verificational test the claims that historians make requires that the procedures which led to the claims in the first place be repeated. There seems to be no way to the referent of a historical assertion except by means of the procedures of historical constitution themselves" (Goldstein 1996, 168–69). The real—truth-makers for statements about the past—emerges from *within* a constituted past. Items appear as candidate truth-makers by virtue of their location within a constituted framework. Goldstein's (1976, 127) historian, speculating on the origins of the Dead Sea scrolls or pre-Columbian Nordic excursions into North America, shapes explanatory events: "In sum, the relation of the historical occurrence to the evidence upon which it is based is not one of logical entailment of the occurrence from the evidence, but the occurrence is offered hypothetically as what would best make sense of the evidence."[30] Historical events emerge abductively, as part of an inference to the best explanation, retrospectively conceived.

Again, the inert and fragmentary remains of a second-century construction can be characterized under multiple descriptions. "Even to know that it was built during the reign and, presumably, upon the instruction of Antoninus Pius is not really to know what it is. . . . To know what it is as something historical is to know what purpose it served, what thoughts—policies—it embodies" (Goldstein 1996, 319–20). Although he speaks here of Collingwood, I take Goldstein to be expressing his own view as well. In order for remains (traces of the past) to be evidence

CHAPTER 3

for something, they must be categorized in a certain way. Categorization will often require attribution of a certain purpose. The assumed purpose configures artifacts as instantiating a kind or an event.

Similarly, the notion of a career represents a constituted category. What makes for a career, and where is it located? Pressing these questions, Goldstein (1996, 154) maintains, reveals once again the deeply problematic assumptions made by historical realism:

> The absurdity [of realism] emerges from the view that the events of human history are located in the past. It depends on taking literally the metaphor of temporal location. . . . Franklin-Roosevelt-being-elected-in-1932 occupies one span of time; Franklin-Roosevelt-being-inaugurated-in-1933, another span of time; and so on until Franklin-Roosevelt-dying-in-1945, which occupies still another. . . . In my view, the "unity" of all these disparate Franklin Roosevelts is simply a consequence of the fact that it is one career which emerges from the attempt of historians to deal with the relevant period of American history. In fact, there is no problem of unity. . . . What is closer to the truth is that they constitute a course of events or the course of a life. The continuities are built into the historical constitution itself. (cf. Danto 1965, 149/146)

Roosevelt's career does not exist until constituted by a historian. The grouping represents an artifact, a colligation by historians studying a particular person or period.

Goldstein registers an appreciation of the seemingly ineliminable tension between a sort of commonsense realism about the past as opposed to the "ways of pastmaking" that his own account of historical knowing allows. He quotes with hearty approval, in this regard, the following remark by G. H. Mead: "The estimate and import of all histories lies in the interpretation and control of the present; that as ideational structures they always arise from change, which is as essential a part of reality as the permanent, and the problems which change entails; and that the metaphysical demand for a set of events which is unalterably there in an irrevocable past, to which these histories seek a constantly approaching agreement, comes back to motives other than those at work in the most exact scientific research" (Goldstein 1996, 245, quoting Mead 2002, 28). Goldstein (1996, 246) then remarks, in keeping with what I earlier (see fn. 43) identified as his Russellian view of knowledge, that the "quotation from Mead makes its point with respect to the past, but his point is quite general. Any attempt to take one's stand on reals which are alleged to be independent of inquiry is motivated by commitments which are independent of the systematic quest for knowledge." He goes on to reflect on what his position implies with regard to, for example, conflicting interpretations of the Holocaust (a favorite bogeyman for all those who view failure to subscribe to historical realism as tantamount to a moral failing). Although he recognizes and sympathizes with the realist desire to have a metaphysical club with which to beat down revisionists and others, he observes that however "worthy such a goal, in the end it cannot be realized. . . . The only past we can talk about is the past as it is known to us" (252).

The contrast here between Goldstein's view and Dummett's reflections on realism and antirealism proves instructive. All the metaphysical options as Dummett conceives them assume observation-like sentences as a model of verification. All statements about nonobservables, including statements about the past, build inferentially on these. But Goldstein's considerations bring to the fore how radically naïve and inappropriate this model turns out to be for statements about the past, and especially ones at any significant historical remove. One might easily miss what remains of live interest in Goldstein's philosophy just because the account of confirmation on which he relies ignores the holist constraint on which he otherwise insists.

Goldstein's discussion has, then, the virtue of highlighting what sorts of inferential practices actually come into play in constituting the past. *The perspective from which a historian makes statements such as those found in histories typically does not consist of a perspective that could have been had by any observer at that time.* Even if what a historian reports appears to be a matter of fact, no observer at that time could likely have described the event in that way. The "logic" used to constitute the past resembles *not* a recursive structure built on observation. Rather, the structure given to time and memory reflects a significance that emerges regarding what happened when viewed looking backward.[31] Relatedly, appreciating that observability itself becomes identified intratheoretically, Goldstein's account of the interpretive element in the constitution of evidence ceases to mark history off from other forms of inquiry.[32] Further issues regarding evidence and inference emerge below. But for now, the point of note concerns how a prior theoretical structure determines the semantics of statements about the past.

Yet Goldstein's version of antirealism has its costs. If the *activity* of historical knowing constitutes the very objects of historical knowledge independently of perception,[33] then Goldstein leaves unclear just how, on his account, any activity of historical knowing *could fail* to produce knowledge. Since Goldstein's antirealist constitutes the past, how can there be any error in representation? There seems no way for a historian to go wrong. Thus, an ironic consequence of Goldstein's antirealism would appear to be not a lack of historical knowledge but its proliferation. Historical knowledge so conceived seems to be knowledge too easily had. Knowledge proliferates because nothing on this account appears to remain by which to drive a wedge between representations of the past and its putative object—"The Past."

Interestingly, a very different way of answering this vexed question—What limits the process of historical construction?—can also be found in Goldstein's writing. On the alternative formulation he offers, historical knowledge stands as *prototypical* of empirical knowledge. All knowledge, Goldstein says in this other mood, turns out to be constitutional in something like this broadly naturalistic way. Knowledge becomes understood as an artifact of a particular approach within which interrogation of nature proceeds and through which one interprets its answers.

In this regard, nothing marks off the intratheoretical methods and practices constitutive of what Goldstein terms historical truth or historical objectivity[34] from any other form of scientific inquiry. "I want my remarks to be general, since I believe that the primacy of knowing is a generally sound epistemological stance, though I do not want to stray too far from philosophy of history" (Goldstein 1996, 163; see also Goldstein 1976, 89–91). Historical constitution preserves bivalence just as Dummett's limited antirealism did, by making sentences true or false relative to a model. "The description is historically true not because it corresponds to an actual event as a witness may have observed it, but rather because given the evidence in hand and the ways in which historians deal with and think about such evidence it is reasonable to believe that some part of the human past had such-and-such characteristics" (Goldstein 1996, 117–18). This emphasis on the role of prior beliefs and a disciplinary matrix has the great merit of bringing into high relief a feature common to both historical realism and antirealism. Each explicitly utilizes current habits of categorization in its characterization of past events and actions (Goldstein 1976, 38).[35] Absent some magical ability to reproduce a bygone *Weltanschauung* (with no small part of the magic residing in the belief that there exist such determinate and shared mind-sets to reproduce), what historians do is to use resources available now in an effort to reconstruct prior patterns of categorization.

One final consideration here is how realism and antirealism have been treated as the only available options for conceiving of the reality of the past. Realism demands that all sentences about the past now have a determinate truth-value. Dummett's global antirealism allows sentences to have a truth-value based only on what can be known now; consequently, there will be truth-value "gaps." Some sentences about the past will be judged neither true nor false. Finally, what Dummett terms "limited antirealism" and Goldstein dubs "historical constructivism" have truth or falsity relative to a model of historical knowledge. In this regard, Goldstein's animus toward realism appears tempered by a type of Peircean faith in the convergence of inquiry. That is, both Goldstein and Dummett hold out for notions of truth that transcend relativity to a model. To the extent that each does, each remains committed to a traditional metaphysical picture of a structured past prior to any constitution by human categories.[36]

Danto, however, offers a sophisticated analysis of the problem of attaching truth-values to sentences about the past that shows that the variants canvassed by Dummett and Goldstein do not capture the full complexities. Bringing this complexity into view reveals a sense in which knowledge of the past remains contingent, but a contingency that does not arise because of any lack of evidence about the past. Contingency so conceived offers a counter to an antirealist view of the past without yet being realism.

I begin by developing an example from Danto (1965, 195; see generally his discussion on 193–96):

> (1) "Talleyrand begat Delacroix and Delacroix painted the *Mort de Sardanapale*."

This sentence has the following interesting logical feature: although both its conjuncts are now true, they were not always simultaneously true. Some years passed between the state of affairs described in the first conjunct and that described in the second conjunct. This generates the following puzzle. Sentence (1) is a conjunction, and so formally its truth-value should be a function of the truth-values of its conjuncts. But the conjuncts are indexed to different times. So, depending on the time of the statement, the first conjunct may be true and the second false. In order to capture the cases when just (1) would be true (Danto calls this "time-true"), Danto maintains that the time-true version of (1) is:

> (2) "Talleyrand begat Delacroix and Delacroix will paint the *Mort de Sardanapale*."

But although (2) may be time-true, is it true? If true, (2) entails

> (3) Delacroix will paint the *Mort de Sardanapale*.

Yet (3) is a paradigm instance of a sentence without a truth-value, since it speaks of what will be, not what is or was. Danto takes this to show the nonequivalence of "time-true" and "true." His "narrative sentences"—sentences that mention events standing in a determinate relation in time but that utilize a later event to describe the earlier, for example, "Pier da Vinci begat a great genius"—will typically be analyzable as containing a time-true part. This creates a logical puzzle. Future-tense statements like (3) conjoined with any true statement should yield a statement without a truth-value, but (2) proves otherwise.

Moreover, since we take the logical relation of time-dependent events such as those in (2) to be contingent, Danto (1965, 196) notes "that when any such compound proposition *also* contains a time-true, past referring, singular proposition, the entire compound proposition [such as (2)] expresses a *past contingency*. So not every time-true sentence about the past is true or false." This analysis of narrative sentences therefore yields time-true sentences, not sentences true or false absolutely. Simply put, narrative sentences that have determinate truth-values relative to a model (that is, are time-true) do not allow for the usual inferences regarding the truth-values of their constituent statements.

Call such sentences "inferentially opaque," meaning that without the relevant model, uncertainty exists regarding whether or not the usual deductive inferences can be applied. The source of opacity resides in what Danto terms their past-contingency; some passage of time must be assumed in order for both conjuncts to be true. How matters turned out for this child of Talleyrand illustrates in turn how future events lead to a redescribing of a past event.[37]

It is important to note that Danto (1985, 341) recognizes that insofar as what happens later leads to redescriptions of what happened earlier, changing the past can change the present as well:

> But for the rest, I think, it may be said that to the degree that our past is in doubt, our present—the way we live in the world—is no less in question. And indeed, our very actions inherit these margins of incertitude, for what we do can only have the meanings we suppose it to have if is located in a history we believe *real*. . . . The present is cleared of indeterminacy only when history has had its say; but then, as we have seen, history never completely has its say. So life is open to constant re-interpretation and assessment.

But now tensions within Danto's position emerge full flower. On the one hand, Danto's account of narrative sentences denies a key realist doctrine regarding all sentences having their truth-values timelessly. But, on the other hand, he endorses the arch-realist doctrine that true sentences are, in Wright's earlier quoted phrase, "investigation-independent."[38] He does this because, like Dummett, he assumes a deep link among meaning, truth, and logical structure. But Danto's (1985, 320–21) own analysis of narrative sentences makes problematic that such a formula applies as an analysis of statements about the past.[39]

More generally, what Goldstein and Danto show each in his own way is that questions of the reality of the past turn out to be anything but investigation-independent. Goldstein highlights the roles of prior theoretical beliefs and abductive inference. Danto demonstrates that narrative sentences will generate the type of "truth-value gaps" in statements about the past that Dummett takes as a hallmark of an intuitionist approach to understanding and a type of antirealism about the past. But these logical problems turn out to connect to a yet more general logical problem regarding the constitution of kinds, events, and intentional actions. Hacking develops and exploits this.

Keep in mind that metaphysical issues remain tied to questions of how language can be learned and shared—what Dummett terms a "theory of understanding." Although I have no such theory to propose, my arguments do show that whatever logic drives such a theory needs to provide an account of how humans agree in judgment with regard to language use, in particular categorization. Emphasis on so-called canonical forms of verification presupposes agreement in judgment with regard to categorization rather than explaining it. By complicating any account of agreement through discussions of the reality of the past, a goal here is showing how much more interpersonal coordination a theory of understanding involves than is usually acknowledged.

I suggest that Goldstein's "historical knowing" or constructivism be understood as just a type of Goodmanian exercise, of organizing traces into kinds. Goldstein (1976, 133) read as a Goodmanian recognizes that "criteria for the grouping are drawn entirely from those intellectual operations which are the practice of history itself."[40] This point applies quite generally. What is the case for historical knowing as a type of constituting extends to all forms of knowledge. What counts as evidence, and for what it counts, turns out to be a product of practices of inquiry as informed by the use of predicates (past or present). Training, feedback, and group reinforcement anchor words to the world. The features that Goldstein identifies as central to historical knowing turn out to be generic features of empirical knowledge.

This allows Goldstein's account of historical knowing to connect with considerations that Hacking's work brings into high relief. Hacking's interpretation of Goodman's riddle and his account of kinds discussed in part I bears directly on issues central to a theory of understanding that so concern Dummett and his interlocutors. For there to be communication, a linguistic community requires, as Wittgenstein famously remarks, agreement in judgment. This presupposes at least some agreement on how predicates can be applied or reapplied. So, learnability conditions must involve acquiring compatible standards of inductive inference, that is, classification. This suggests that these issues about how language can be learned and shared—the concern with a theory of understanding that motivates the metaphysical debate—should not take observation and deductive inference as basic. The perceptual and logical operations presuppose an understanding of classification but do not explain it.

This suggests that learning a language has important analogies to learning a theory or to processes involved in theory change. Hacking takes to heart Kuhn's observations on the training of scientists and applies them to linguistic communities generally. When individuals no longer receive training or guidance in the use of the categories that have fallen out of use, all criteria of correctness for application of them can become lost.

> The nominalist replies, (a) the world is a world of individuals; the individuals do not change with a change of paradigm. But a nominalist may add, (b) the world in which we work is a world of kinds of things. This is because all action, all doing, all working is under a description. All choice of what to do, what to make, how to interact with the world, how to predict its motions or explain its vagaries is action under a description; all these are choices under descriptions current in the community in which we work and act and speak. Descriptions require classification, the grouping of individuals into kinds. And that is what changes with a change in paradigm: the world of kinds in which, with which, and on which the scientist works. (Hacking 1993, 277–78)

An important historicist-like point, moreover, emerges just here. Once again, for habits of classification at any significant historical remove, claims to be able to use this language, absent a living core of users, become quite literally meaningless.

Hacking illustrates this point by reference to alchemical theory and Paracelsus. One can, he notes, read the words Paracelsus wrote. But the challenge of knowing what Paracelsus meant by the terms comes now in applying those terms to things in the world as they presumably were when Paracelsus and his contemporaries were alive. But how can one judge if one has the use right if there now exists no community to corroborate judgments regarding use? (Hacking 1993, 297).[41] For the reality of the past construed in terms of witnessing presupposes either magical access to what now no longer exists—a community of users who support and sustain patterns and habits of application—or assumes unjustifiably that present patterns of categorization suffice for the witnessing involved. But absent communities of past speakers or a fact of the matter with regard to meaning, neither assumption can be said to enjoy even the slightest plausibility.

As noted in part I, Hacking strongly endorses Goodman's riddle and its chief consequences: nature does not dictate any organizing scheme to us, and different schemes need have no connection to one another. No organizing scheme has primacy; different organizing schemes need not be compatible with or reducible to one another. Hence, different "worlds" come to be. These points bring together Goldstein, Goodman, and Hacking not only with regard to constituting a past but also with the most striking and remarkable consequence, that there must be a sense in which the past can be indeterminate, open to change. In particular, skepticism and indeterminacy regarding *present* kinds apply to past schemas as well, particularly actions qua kind of behavior—a kind distinguished by the presence of intentions. Recall the lesson Hacking (1999, 130) drew: "We can well understand how new kinds create new possibilities for choice and action. But the past, of course, is fixed! Not so. As Goodman would put it, if new kinds are selected, then the past can occur in a new world."[42] Goodman's riddle challenges the belief that the categories and classifications employed to name events also specify metaphysical essences. It suggests that identifying events proves no more fixed than current habits of classification. Insofar as actions appear immutable and their effects flow forward from this nature, the past appears fixed. In this respect, entrenchment goes deep; it fosters the illusion that the past consists of something more, by way of events, than contingent classifications.

The argument has been that antirealism still privileges a naïve notion of the observational, and so creates a false contrast between knowledge in the present and knowledge of the past. Damian Cox (2003, 37) suggests that one cannot "avoid a dichotomy between some version of metaphysical realism on the one hand, and some version of irrealism on the other." Cox explores senses in which worlds can, following Goodman, be said to be made and yet not fashioned from materials that, in the end, appeal to the very sort of metaphysical realism with which irrealism was to contrast. For example, it poses no particular affront to realism to suggest that before the stars were mapped in a particular way, the Big Dipper did not exist. But what of the stars the maps map? "If the Big Dipper doesn't predate our introduction of the 'Big Dipper Concept,' do the stars themselves predate our development of the concept of a star?" (Cox 2003, 40). But Goodman has a response. If the world made contains stars billions

CHAPTER 3

of years old, it poses no problem to the claim that we made that world that it has features not possessed by the version of the world we make. For example, one can make a two-dimensional representation of a three-dimensional object, or a black-and-white version of a colored object. A nominalist strategy focuses on what makes for categories and kinds; it does not conjure into existence something from nothing.

The making need not have every feature imputed to the made. As Cox (2003, 41) comments, "We make a starry past, in part, by making the spatio-temporal order of the past. Since there is no ready-made temporal order, we make a past by imposing a temporal order on things. We make stars in the remote past, but we shouldn't expect this making to have itself occurred in the remote past."[43] Once made, concepts do not remain in control of their makers. This implies, among other things, that whether there exist "traces" supporting the made-up world cannot be determined except by looking.

As a final illustration of an irrealist explanation, I consider an argument by a historian of science, Gad Prudovsky (1997), concerning the legitimacy of imputing to historical figures concepts they could not possibly have had. The particular case concerns Koyré's interpretation of Galileo, specifically the ascription by Koyré to Galileo of a conception of mass that Galileo did not possess. Prudovsky asks, "What can be the justification of *ascribing to* Galileo a terminology ('mass') of which he knew nothing? and second, can this type of ascription withstand the anti-anachronistic critique of recent studies in the methodology of historical writing?" (16). Without here examining the full complexity of Prudovsky's sophisticated defense of the concept of inertial mass that Koyré reads into his reconstruction of Galileo, the core point that emerges is a deliberate strategy to make the historical personage as rational as possible.[44] The justification maintains, unsurprisingly, that the concept or something like it exists already implicitly in Galileo's reasoning. This legitimates, Prudovsky argues, the imputation of the anachronistic concept.

What makes Prudovsky's (1997, 26) account of particular interest is the Goodmanian account that he (unawares) finds in the implicit yet still unarticulated notion of inertial mass that Koyré ascribes to Galileo: "Koyré wanted to argue that this is the first step in the development of the concept of inertial mass in the history of science. Such a step is obviously a preliminary move, not wholly clear to those who made it, and hence lacking the maturity of the later classical concept. Thus, the concept does not remain constant: it changes in the transformation from its implicit phase to its explicit one." That is, as Prudovsky reads Koyré, the concept of inertial mass does interpretive work, but what he employs is equivalent not to the contemporary concept but only to some indeterminate approximation of it. Like Kripke's "plus" and "quus," one cannot

THE PASTS

say that Galileo must have some particular function "in mind." This allows Prudovsky to explain how Galileo applies the concept to the cases without having to claim that Galileo has a "worked out" version of the concept and so knows precisely to which cases it extends and which not.[45]

One could say here, on Prudovsky's reading of Koyré, that by ascribing to Galileo a concept he could not have possessed Koyré constitutes a Dantoesque event—the moment in history when Galileo introduces what will become the concept of inertial mass—and then uses this to explain why what Galileo argues makes sense. No one could say or predict at that moment that this was happening, or that a certain concept would come to have a settled use in a future scientific community. The point rather is to illustrate how historical events may be constituted and explained in terms of concepts in some sense present in but not known to those to whom they are attributed.

At the most general epistemological and metaphysical levels, no principled distinction emerges between empirical knowledge generally and knowledge of the past. The forms of inference required to have empirical knowledge at all—inductive, abductive, and deductive—arise for all such cases of knowledge. *Once the presumption of givenness with regard to evidence or of shared conceptual schemes is renounced, the "shape of the past" and the "shape of the present" receive their form under fundamentally similar holist constraints.* Temporal distance may accentuate problems of making sense of others and what they did, but the problems posed turn out not to be at all unique. Only in a theory do things—for example, facts, events, kinds, actions—exist and have explanations.

The suggestion that people now decide what traces are traces of proves shocking only if one imagines that this attaches only to attempts to know the past. A persistent fear post-Kuhn has been that in erasing a clear line between experience and theory, nothing "real" remains to serve as a check on interpretations. What people imagined empirical evidence to be turns out to be theorizing by another name. Excesses of this sort do exist.[46] But this fear proves overblown inasmuch as the position developed here simply makes divides between theory and evidence or observables and nonobservables into a contingent fact and not a necessary or conceptual one.

More generally in the philosophy of science, problems arise concerning, for example, charting progress across incommensurable scientific theories where the events or facts described in one have no status in the theory that supersedes it. But for all such cases, no ultimate arbiter for what constitutes the reality of kinds and events exists.[47] Analogous factors in the philosophy of history have not been given the attention they deserve.

As noted in chapter 1 and the discussion of the nonstandardization thesis regarding narrative explanations, Mink comes closest to making explicit why reference to events in time—Danto-like narrative sentences—must make a difference to the form that historical representation and explanation take. And as discussed in that earlier chapter, Mink seizes on Danto's suggestion that historical events lack, and scientific events have, a "standard description" as what separates historical discourse from scientific discourse. A scientific theory specifies what features a description of an event must include in order to be considered complete; events in historical discourse remain descriptively incompletable (Mink 1987, 139n6; cf. Danto 1965, 176–77). Inasmuch as salient features of a situation continue to emerge only retrospectively, this fact logically precludes any possibility of stating (timelessly) what (for a particular time) will be of significance.

Mink published his review of Danto in 1968, when a symmetry of explanation and prediction was widely assumed. He uses this assumption to argue that Danto's account demonstrates why the lack of a standard description will make historical events unpredictable, and so inexplicable. For the view that a "standard description" would be possible would be equivalent to assuming the possibility of an Ideal Chronicle. But Danto's own analysis demonstrates that historical descriptions of earlier events often incorporate knowledge that comes later, either because the later event informs on the earlier or because the conceptual vocabulary comes later. In such cases, nothing known by anyone at the time could have been used to predict, and so explain, what lies ahead. "So," Mink (1987, 145) concludes, "the analysis of descriptions possible only after the event is also an argument against the *possibility* of covering-law explanations in characteristically historical discourse." But renouncing as necessary a symmetry between explanation and prediction might appear to deprive this argument of its force.

I draw a different lesson, for Mink's contrast between what would be required of an event in order for it to be fodder for a scientific theory—a "standard description"—and the absence of such a description for historical events remains an important and useful insight. Mink and Danto agree that "essentially historical discourse" requires expression through narrative structure. Moreover, that some events allow a scientific treatment in the most robust sense of the term, Mink (1987, 145) acknowledges, "is one thesis on which reasonable men will not disagree." But he then adds, "There is nothing wrong with being wise after the event; it is just that we can't be wise after the event, before the event." To be sure, what comes to be learned later just might reveal what could not possibly have been known earlier. Hindsight may teach that nothing could have remedied ignorance of what was to come.

But about which events can one be wise before the fact, and which only after? What shows that some historical event could not have been predicted at the earlier time? In order to avoid toy examples, consider the following: "'The long Second World War' commenced at the moment in which various states required that their peoples' liberties be subordinate to their nationality. No precise definition is possible, but 1922 would be a sensible starting point for Italy, 1931 for Japan, 1933 for Germany and perhaps 1929 for the USSR. . . . [The Munich agreement] sounded the final prelude to those actual wars which would break out in Europe and the wider world between 1939 and 1941 and which are known as the Second World War" (Bosworth 1993, 6–7). Danto (1985, xv) at one point speaks of philosophical analysis as revealing "a descriptive metaphysic," by which he means "a general description of the world as we are obliged to conceive of it, given that we think and talk as we do." Mink (1987, 145–46) agrees, but quickly makes the point that any such descriptive metaphysics will itself be subject to historical influence and change: "But one may still ask: could we think and talk differently? The answer must be yes, by the witness of history itself. . . . And to acknowledge this possibility is to bring our descriptive metaphysic under the category (itself historical) of history. Yet since our central concepts stand and fall together, change cannot be capricious, or fragmentary, or idiosyncratic." I do not endorse any suggestion that human cognition embodies functions that *must* be or even typically are "capricious, or fragmentary, or idiosyncratic." But the arguments of this chapter suggest that any "descriptive metaphysic" represents a historically fashioned imposition on the flux of experience and not a discovery of "categories in the mind" shared by all who communicate. Claims to conceptual necessity turn out to be just one more attempt to lay hands on the "really real." In addition, once belief in shared conceptual frameworks goes, so goes their explanatory utility. As Davidson (1973–74, 20) perceptively notes, "If we cannot intelligibly say that schemes are different, neither can we intelligibly say that they are one." The extent to which various ways of characterizing the world stand or fall together remains an open question.

This chapter has charted a course that began with Danto's insight that established that descriptions true of a past time cannot be determined at that time. What events can justifiably be said to have taken place at a time changes over time. Using Goldstein's account of historical constitution, I then argued that historical events said to occur at any particular time must be products of attributing some unifying theme or purpose. Events as usually discussed in human histories must be constituted at least in this sense. Finally, I developed this notion of historical constitution further by employing Hacking's view that what events can be said to exist depend on the stock of descriptions or categories available. In particular, I argued, when the stock changes, by addition or deletion, the extant events at a time do as well.

The overall import of these arguments has been to problematize the notion of an event in particular, and evidence in general, in relation to the construction of pasts, of histories. To speak of pasts as constituted and not found gives priority to modes of classification over perception in the order of understanding. Because nothing a priori anchors practices of classification, no sense can be attached to claims that some single structure must or does determine what events take place in human history. In addition, in the process of examining the arguments for rejecting the metaphysical assumption, rationales for the defining features of historical narratives—nonstandardization, nondetachability, and nonaggregativity—emerge as consequences.

Irrealism denies an assumption that both realism and antirealism turn out to share: an imagined view from nowhere, a past seen sub specie aeternitatis. In this respect, the arguments against an "ideal" perspective developed in chapter 2 can now be seen to draw support from irrealism. Given alternative modes for structuring what happens, changes in descriptions can alter relations among events imputed to a past, and so how a past thus structured impacts what becomes possible going forward. A plurality of pasts results because constituting a past depends to some degree on socially mediated negotiations of a fit between descriptions and experience. Even what we take to distinguish what can change and what cannot itself depends on the descriptions deployed. Unless for reasons now unknown there ceases to be a possibility of descriptive change or reclassification, human histories will continue to reveal a multiplicity of pasts.

This brings us back, of course, to the question of how rejecting a realist metaphysics relates to the methodological objections of logical formlessness and evaluative intractability that seemingly followed from the characteristics of historical narratives stressed in chapter 1—nonstandardization, nonaggregativity, and nondetachability. At a first pass, arguments against a realist view of history also provide reasons why the use of narrative form proves to be nonaccidental. The past has no form until given one by categories imposed on what we take to be evidence. But even renouncing realism does not yet show that narratives have title to being called explanations. However, the next chapter argues that, granting irrealism, one can recognize a category of what I call essentially narrative explanations. What these are, and how they serve to answer the methodological objections, is the focus of the next chapter.

4

Essentially Narrative Explanations

We can now return to considering the methodological objections to narrative explanation rehearsed in chapter 2, viz., the charges of logical formlessness and evaluative intractability. Understood from this perspective, philosophically situating narrative as a species of the genus explanation requires satisfactorily replacing the work done by validity and soundness in more traditional philosophical accounts.[1] Attention to narrative form, however, slights this critical point. Since analyses of narrative structure underline the parallels between history and fiction, the study of narrative is not going to illuminate the relevant differentia of historical explanations. The complaint, in brief, is that emphasis on narrative structure situates historical practice too close to the writing of fiction. So the category of narrative explanation must be rejected inasmuch as the analysis of narrative stands unrelated to the rational evaluation of historical inquiry.

In this regard, those features identified as serving replacement functions should be linked to one another at least insofar as whatever logic connects explanans and explanandum also helps underwrite claims to explanatory significance. Methodological naturalism[2] requires no more for scientific standing, i.e., establishing a "family resemblance" in these key respects between narrative explanations and other accepted forms of explanation. Thus, one goal of the next several chapters is to establish that evaluating narrative explanations turns out to be no more difficult or problematic than assessing other explanatory practices.[3]

Reasons for rejecting the methodological problems based on charges of formlessness and intractability emerge in the process of answering three interrelated questions. First, what determines that an explanation has in some critical or essential respect a narrative form? Second, how does a narrative in such cases come to constitute a plausible explanation? Third, how do the first two considerations yield a basis for evaluating an explanation offered as a narrative? Answers to each of these questions include illustrations of actual narrative explanations and also function to underline attendant dimensions of evaluation. Together these answers and examples will locate those features that mark narratives as explanations and correlatively identify the evaluative considerations that attach to them.

The view defended here will be that narrative explanations explain narrative sentences (i.e., an explanandum expressible as a narrative sentence). In particular, I show why only a narrative can explain some events formulated as narrative sentences. As a consequence, evaluating explanations that have narrative form essentially (in a sense to be clarified below) will primarily be a function of assessing competing explanations, and so draw on evaluative criteria more akin to theory appraisal than to hypothesis confirmation. But my case for identifying those dimensions of rational appraisal relevant to narrative explanations builds on features unique to having narrative sentences as explananda.[4]

What marks an explanation as having narrative form essentially? For purposes of identifying narrative explanations, the minimalist notion of what counts as a narrative sketched in chapter 1 will do. As given there, a narrative involves an "unfolding," sequencing of a series of events that accounts for a development. This indicates why many theorists hold that there exists a deep conceptual tie between narrative form generally and histories in particular. Psychoanalytic theorist Humphrey Morris (1993, 36) provides a succinct expression of this view: "A 'narrative' . . . is a particular language form that is organised according to a fundamentally temporal principle, that is, according to some variation on a 'beginning-middle-end' structure. Narrative, in this structural sense, is self-evidently 'historical.'" Related remarks offering a minimalist characterization can readily be found in writings of literary theorists (e.g., Miller 1990).

This minimalist approach to characterizing narrative results unsurprisingly in a liberal standard regarding what to count as a narrative. Yet for the purpose of getting clearer about narrative explanations, it matters not that by this criterion many works may qualify as narratives. Rather, what proves critical to clarifying narrative as a form of explanation involves whether or not an explanation in this form can also be nonnarratively structured. That is, does it allow for paraphrase into some other, nonnarrative explanatory form? For if so, then whatever explanatory import such a narrative seemingly possesses—revealing how things at the beginning of a series came to be what they later were—turns out to be inessential for purposes of explanation. Hempel's well-known example of a radiator bursting provides a case in point. A story explaining why it burst—e.g., one's failure to put in antifreeze—can be recast and given instead classic deductive-nomological form. In short, the core issue concerns whether or not some explanations must have narrative form essentially.[5]

Chapter 1 sought to establish that narrative explanations possess three key characteristics: (1) the nondetachability of the explanandum from the supporting narrative, (2) the nonstandardized character of event(s) explained, and (3) the nonaggregativity of narrative histories. (1)

follows from the fact that a narrative constitutes both the explanandum and its relations to the explanans—statements of the event to be explained and those that explain it. Jouni-Matti Kuukkanen (2012, 342; see also 355) rightly emphasizes this feature as the hallmark of the "narrativist turn" in historiography: "Narrativism sees historians as constructors of literary products—narratives—in the production of which they employ various rhetorical and literary techniques. Sometimes 'narrative' is understood as a story or story structure, but it may be better to understand it as any cognitive structure that connects individual statements and creates some general coherent plot, meaning, or interpretation of the past." A focus on the study of narrative construction as a defining feature of historiography reflects the ongoing influence of Hayden White's work. For what White emphasizes and what has guided discussion within historical theory for over four decades has been the historian's fundamental role as a creator of historical narratives. But where White typically focuses on narrative as a literary resource, the basic point at issue in this chapter is epistemological: what passes as historical knowledge. Historians sometimes write as if occupying a "view from nowhere," but my account follows White's by insisting that this represents only a rhetorical conceit and not a possible epistemic position.

The nonstandardized feature mentioned in (2) relates to (1) inasmuch as the sort of events to be explained—wars, revolutions, famines, and other typical foci of human histories—do not exist as "standardized" in some conventional theoretical sense, as the periodic table and related laws of compounding standardize elements and formulas in a natural science such as chemistry. There exists no settled theoretical "recipe" in historiography regarding how facts should or could be put together to make an event and which events they make. Insofar, then, as a history both claims to provide causal knowledge and yet has no scientific laws to cite, its theoretical underpinnings require special excavation and scrutiny. In this respect, (2) also underwrites (3), inasmuch as different narratives identify different events and so different causal sequences. These cannot be expected to aggregate, to yield some integrated account about what happens and why. Nonaggregativity denies the possibility of a Universal History—some single account that links all possible events under one explanatory rubric.

Further, for reasons discussed in chapters 2 and 3, it can now be appreciated how what Danto terms "narrative sentences" exposes an underlying rationale for all three characteristics. Such sentences express truths about past times that can be known only retrospectively, even though true at an earlier time. Narrative explanations I claim prove uniquely suited to account for those retrospectively knowable truths that narrative sentences express. *So, in addition to possessing the features of nondetachability, nonstandardization, and nonaggregativity, an essentially narrative explanation will also have a narrative sentence as a statement of its explanandum.* A narrative explanation will be a presentation of a temporal series that answers why the explanandum turns out to be as it is. For without reference to this retrospective stance, there would exist nothing to explain. And since what must be explained has no standardized format that explains it, a temporal sequence that cannot utilize laws or law-like generalizations will be required. If a narrative explaining a narrative sentence has narrative form essentially, then there exists no nonnarrative way of explaining just that event. That is, in those cases where the available antecedents provide no basis for rationally accounting for the outcome (e.g., assuming that in 1951 it could not be predicted that Ronald Reagan, who starred in *Bedtime for Bonzo*, would be elected the fortieth president in 1980), then a sequencing of events that has the later event emerge as a consequence of the earlier (i.e., a narrative) provides the only sort of explanatory account one could have for such cases.[6]

The issues here do not concern, e.g., ignorance at some moment or a lack of access to some relevant facts. That is, what makes narrative sentences possible turns out to be quite unlike cases where mere ignorance precludes knowledge—e.g., those who experienced the plagues that Europe suffered in the fourteenth century could not know exactly what beset them.[7] By contrast, in the case of an event such as the Black Death, the fact that it began some time in the fourteenth century simply could not be known then because the event so named emerges only later than when it first started. In other words, a narrative sentence *adds* a truth to an earlier time because related to some subsequent occurrence. By contrast, a statement to the effect that people at time *t* were sick with a particular disease at *t* does not expand a list of what could be said to be true of a moment at just that moment.

In this key respect, i.e., by creating a means to explain narrative sentences, narrativizing *enables* a historian's enterprise and constitutes no obstacle to it. Wallace Martin (1986, 73; emphasis mine) nicely summarizes this fundamental sense in which those conventions that constitute a possibility space for narrative form in turn make history possible:

> The conventions of narrative, as identified by Danto and [Hayden] White, are not constraints on the historian and novelist; *rather they create the possibility of narration*. Without them, and confronted with a sheer mass of facts, the historian would have nowhere to begin. Knowing what is of human significance, the historian has a subject; knowing something of human thoughts, feelings, desires, and the incredible variety

of their manifestations, and the social structures that mediate them he or she can form a hypothesis concerning why something happened as it did. This hypothesis determines which facts will be examined and how they will be put together.

More generally, any charge that narrative form (as determined by those conventions discussed by narrative theorists) imposes a fictionalized structure on history misses that fundamental epistemic insight narrative sentences reveal, viz., that human histories exist only as a product of a very special sort of retrospective description. This is why to say that events such as the beginning of the Holocaust or the onset of the Black Death emerge only from that sort of perspective in no way implies some lack of "reality." Rather, it acknowledges the unavoidable fact that such events exist only by virtue of humans who shape experience in certain ways for certain purposes.

> At their points of origin, historical and fictional narratives appear to be entirely different. . . . Despite these differences, the two narrators face the same problem: that of showing how a situation at the beginning of a temporal series leads to a different situation at its end. The very possibility of identifying such a series depends upon the following presuppositions, as Arthur Danto and Hayden White have shown: (1) the events involved must all be relevant to one subject, such as a person, a region, or a notion; (2) they must also be unified in relation to some issue of human interest, which will explain why (3) the temporal series must begin and end where it does. (Martin 1986, 72–73)

The point made in (2) above—the human interest in play—determines as well the subject (1) and the series to be studied and explained, i.e., (3).

Interestingly, Martin (1986, 74; emphasis mine) identifies narrative sentences (without naming them as such) as that which structures a narrative: "It is the end of the temporal series—how things eventually turned out—that determines which event began it; *we know it was a beginning because of the end.*" Martin neatly connects what defines a history as narrative—a beginning-middle-end structure unified by showing the development of a subject over time—and what a historical narrative contains that no other nonfiction inventory includes: an occurrence at an earlier time knowable only through and as constituted by a retrospectively available description.

But having suggested an answer to the first of my original questions, i.e., what determines that an explanation has narrative form, the other two initial questions remain: How do these factors ease worries tied to logical formlessness and evaluative intractability? That is, what makes narratives explanatory, and how do their structural features inform on standards of evaluation?

In particular, a serious obstacle to answering either of these questions arises from a belief that narratives typically seem to be descriptive, i.e., context-providing. And insofar as narratives develop context, what they offer seems to fall on the philosophically unhelpful side of any imagined descriptive/normative divide. How, then, could narrative form reflect or connect to any evaluative norms? As Allan Megill (1989) nicely put this issue, narratives seem to offer primarily recountings, i.e., detailed descriptions of a chosen subject over time. Descriptions to be sure can be judged according to standard canons to be correct or incorrect, justified or not, but such judgments would be informed by norms extrinsic to a narrative, and so not by features specific to narrative structure. Considerations of narrative form would thus remain extraneous to evaluation.

Megill develops an analysis of Fernand Braudel's (1976) *The Mediterranean and the Mediterranean World in the Age of Philip II* that provides a helpful initial approach to answering my remaining questions. Megill qualifies as a "narrative liberal" regarding how to interpret a text. For he maintains with reference to his chosen example that although Braudel does not position or understand *The Mediterranean and the Mediterranean World* as a narrative history, it nonetheless is. A primary reason for not classifying Braudel's classic as a narrative would be that it seems to lack a defining feature of a narrative: a focus on how a single subject develops over time in a way that accounts for why that subject is as it is at the end of the sequence.

Can the Mediterranean be said to change or develop, such that some germane features of it can be expressed in terms of a narrative sentence? Megill (1989, 646) maintains that Braudel does just this: "*The Mediterranean* tells us what 'the Mediterranean' was and, to some extent, still is." Or, as Megill notes quoting Braudel: "The Mediterranean speaks with many voices; it is a sum of individual histories" (646).[8] Indeed, in the sentence immediately following the one that Megill quotes from Braudel, Braudel (1976, 13) goes on to state, "If these histories assume in the course of research different values, different meanings, their sum must perforce change too." This sentence suggests a narrative sentence, a retrospective view of things past that adds a truth—"their sum must perforce change"—about that past not knowable at the earlier time.

Braudel's book repeatedly realizes this suggestion. Consider the following example: "To claim that there is a global Mediterranean which in the sixteenth century, reached as far as the Azores and the New World, the Red Sea and the Persian Gulf, the Baltic and the loop of the Niger, may appear an unwarranted exaggeration of its boundaries. . . . To meet the historian's demands, however, the Mediterranean must be accepted as a wide zone, extending well beyond the shores of the sea in all directions" (Braudel 1976, 168). The "demands" to which Braudel refers here are explanatory ones. He indicates this when he writes, "Politics merely followed the outline of an underlying reality" (137). In short, statements such as the one regarding the "global Mediterranean" express a narrative sentence, a statement knowable as true only in retrospect, and yet true of the Mediterranean at that earlier time.[9] The apparently descriptive statements—Megill's "recountings"—serve as Braudel's justification for his narrative sentence.

Megill (1989, 642) notes that in Braudel's epic work "explanations seem embedded in something much larger that is not explanation." He terms the "something much larger" the descriptive element. However, what Megill characterizes as the descriptive part dovetails with the claim just made that Braudel's narrative simultaneously constitutes and constructs both explanans and explanandum. Put another way, as previously noted, narrativists in historiography rightly emphasize that facts do not "speak for themselves." Accordingly, they have long insisted that both what gets described and how it gets described are products of normative considerations on the part of the historian. Reflection on essentially narrative explanations demonstrates exactly why, for these cases at least, there simply exists no separating descriptions of what happens and justifications of how a sequence accounts for an event, i.e., nondetachability. For if there could, that explanation would not have narrative form essentially. The descriptive and the normative, the contextual and the explanatory, must become of a piece in cases where only a narrative can shoulder the explanatory load. Narrative sentences in particular typically express truths that only narratives can explain.

The Mediterranean and the Mediterranean World in the Age of Philip II provides an explanation of narrative sentences such as, "A global Mediterranean Sea reaching as far as the Azores and the New World, the Red Sea and the Persian Gulf, the Baltic and the loop of the Niger existed in the 16th century." This in turn demonstrates how apparent agents (people of various times and regions) actually respond to an "underlying reality," i.e., the Mediterranean. But then all the elements needed for a conventional narrative turn out to be present, just as Megill (1989, 646) claims, with its chief "actor" being a protean geographic entity:

> *The Mediterranean and the Mediterranean World* is best seen, then, as a vast character analysis, in which Braudel broke down "the Mediterranean," which begins as an undifferentiated entity, into its constituent parts,

CHAPTER 4

> with growing attention over the course of the book to the human processes that are carried out within this geohistorical space. . . . *The Mediterranean* tells us what "the Mediterranean" was and, to some extent, what it still is. Braudel's explanations are contributions to this end. The work is a vast recounting, into which explanations are stuck like pins into a pin cushion. It is likewise a vast narrative, though more an anatomizing narrative of character than a sequential narrative of action.

This might appear to contradict the gloss on the notion of a narrative that, following Little, I earlier provided. But the problem is only apparent. For purposes of better understanding narrative explanations, Megill's analysis importantly illustrates how a narrative explanation can have a diffuse and dynamic subject as its focal element. *The "character" of a geographic entity exerts an influence that structures development over time.* As narrative liberals, we take an expansive view regarding what counts as a historical narrative. This liberality helps identify texts that expose, in turn, instances where only by describing a situation in a particular way can certain claims be justified.

This does not confuse description and justification. Rather, such cases exemplify why when a narrative sentence requires explanation, that distinction ceases to be relevant. Unlike Megill, I focus on narrative sentences and their special role in narrative explanations. Put in my terms, by identifying the fact that narrative sentences express that which Braudel seeks to explain, only a narrative can be marshaled to do the work of explanation. This forced use of narrative form for purposes of explanation collapses in that context any descriptive/evaluative distinction.

Consider in this regard the following remark by Raul Hilberg (1985, 1044): "The destruction of the Jews was thus no accident. When in the early days of 1933 the first [German] civil servant wrote the first definition of 'non-Aryan' into a civil service ordinance, the fate of European Jewry was sealed." Somewhat more prosaically, Hilberg's statement may be reworded as a narrative sentence: The Holocaust began in 1933. While one may of course dispute Hilberg's statement, it clearly can be construed as a narrative sentence, one stating what his vastly influential work explains. Much of Hilberg's "recounting," as Megill would have it, in that massive work consists of facts arranged, as Hilberg (1985, 993–94) himself so aptly puts it, so that, "in retrospect, it may be possible to view the entire design as a mosaic of small pieces, each commonplace and lusterless by itself. Yet this progression of everyday activities, these file notes, memoranda, and telegrams, embedded in habit routine, and tradition, were fashioned into a massive destruction process. Ordinary men were to perform extraordinary tasks." Although Hilberg does not credit himself as the one who deliberately and carefully crafts this mosaic, nonetheless he basically creates for scholarly study an event now known as the Holocaust.

The eminent Holocaust historian Christopher Browning offers the following appreciative assessments of the lasting impact of Hilberg's book:

> Hilberg's major contribution was to portray the Nazi destruction of the European Jews not as a giant pogrom, orgy of sadism or descent from civilization into barbarism, but rather as "an administrative process carried out by bureaucrats in a network of offices spanning a continent." (Browning 2007c, 10–11)

> In Hilberg's portrayal, this event was a vast bureaucratic and administrative process employing a cross-section of German society, not the aberrational accomplishment of a few demented individuals. The Holocaust comes to be marked as an *independent event*, one whose workings have implications that extend beyond situating it as a historical aberration, a freak, pathological event on the margin of German and European history. (Browning 2007a, 1; emphasis mine)[10]

A point I would emphasize here concerns the fact that Hilberg's narrative makes the primary actors bureaucracies and institutions (the institutional context for his "habit, routine, and tradition"), and the event explained exists in a very temporally and spatially diffuse sense: the destruction of the European Jews.

This event becomes true of those sites and times where exterminations occur, although no one site and no one time constitutes the event in question. Retrospectively naming that event makes it possible to identify other true statements about that event that would not exist absent that understanding. Moreover, no causal sequence exists to be fashioned until such an event needs explanation. *The causal sequence, in turn, can consist only in this case of seeing facts as ordered and so related in a particular way.* The description creates this event, and the event named by 'the Holocaust' becomes true of a collectivity of occurrences after the fact. This exemplifies not only an underlying irrealism of events but also all the characteristics of essentially narrative explanations.

In order to gain some appreciation of how Hilberg's narrative came to constitute this event, consider the remarks of H. R. Trevor-Roper, a prominent British historian who published a highly influential early review of *The Destruction of the European Jews*. Trevor-Roper begins by noting a point crucial for our purposes: what he finds to be new about this book does *not* consist primarily in the information it provides; it resides, rather, in Hilberg's structuring of that information:

CHAPTER 4

> This is a forbidding book. It is nearly 800 pages long. The pages are double-columned. It has nearly a hundred statistical tables. It is written in an austere style, without literary grace or emotion. And it deals with a subject of which, this year, we have already read a great deal. I hardly thought, on taking it up, that I should be unable to put it down . . . [that] I should have read it through, almost without interruption, and quite without skipping, to the end. For this is not merely a compilation or a recapitulation of the now documented facts. It is not yet another chronicle of horrors. It is a careful, analytic, three-dimensional study of a social and political experience unique in history: an experience which no one could believe possible till it had happened and whose real significance still bewilders us. (Trevor-Roper 1962, 351)

As Trevor-Roper (1962, 352) emphasizes in his review, by focusing not on the victims but on how the machinery of destruction came to be mobilized, Hilberg raises a question—the key question, I am inclined to say—regarding how perpetrators come to be recruited in order for something like this to occur: "The great interest of Mr. Hilberg's book is that he has faced this total problem. . . . While keeping to a narrative form, he has studied the social problem analytically: his narrative carries along with it a profound social content. That is why I call it 'three-dimensional.' It reveals, methodically, fully, and clearly, the development of both the technical and the psychological process; the machinery and the mentality whereby one whole society sought to isolate and destroy another which, for centuries, had lived in its midst." He clearly was not alone in experiencing a type of "gestalt-shift" upon reading Hilberg's work.[11] Browning (2007a, 1) observes that as late as 1969 his graduate student encounter with Hilberg's work induced "the equivalent of an academic 'conversion experience.'" Trevor-Roper's remarks bring into sharper focus the point made above regarding the narrative sentence that states Hilberg's conclusion and how his detailed recounting also functions as justification—showing how an act of institutionalizing anti-Semitism starts a nation down "the twisted road to Auschwitz."

The Destruction of the European Jews fits the mold of a narrative explanation developed above. Its conclusion can be stated as a narrative sentence, one that the text explains by providing a beginning-middle-end structure that presents a story line detailing the causes of that event, but where "causes" can be identified only by offering specific steps in an extended developmental sequence. No laws underwrite this sequencing. And while other genocides happen both before and after, "genocide" does not name a scientifically standardized event type. The result will be explanatory, an answer to an important "Why?" question that depends essentially (in my sense of the term) on a temporal sequencing of certain statements of fact. Here again no functional distinction exists between describing that sequence and justifying causal links. The event explained—what "the mosaic of small pieces" depicts—moreover cannot be detached from the narrative that presents it.

Indeed, as noted in the remarks by historians who first encounter it or who reflect on it even fifty years after its publication, that "event" became visible only after Hilberg's work gave it a shape and a name. And as reactions to and subsequent scholarship reveals, *the narratives concerning what happens over this time span do not aggregate.*[12] Finally, what the narrative explains cannot be explained in any other way. For narratives "create" what they simultaneously set out to explain, not because they "make things up," but precisely for the reason that narrativists such as Hayden White have for so long insisted: only by this means does a historian provide meaning and structure to a morass of details that otherwise has neither.

Recall that responding to the methodological objections would emerge in answering three questions: (1) What determines that an explanation has in some critical or essential respect a narrative form? (2) How does a narrative in such cases come to constitute a plausible explanation? and (3) How do the first two considerations yield a basis for evaluating an explanation offered as a narrative? The account provided so far constitutes my answers to (1) and (2), and so the charge of logical formlessness. How does this bear, in turn, on the charge of evaluative intractability?

With regard to justification, a key aspect of the irrealist position that I defend comes out most forcefully in my claim that essentially narrative explanations create the explanandum event. They do so by utilizing a narrative sentence. Historical events, on this view, exist only under a description. This description, in turn, makes it possible to formulate truths about that event. The analysis above focuses primarily on internal factors that bear on justifying narrative explanation, and particularly on why a sequencing of apparently descriptive statements unavoidably assumes the normative burden of justification in essentially narrative explanations. Elsewhere (particularly Roth 1998, 2004) I emphasize and explore the critically important comparative aspects regarding evaluating competing narrative explanations.[13] But although there will be factors both internal to a narrative explanation (assessing the sequencing) and external to it (comparison with competing narratives, if any), I suggest that evaluation in the end can only be on a case-by-case basis. The fact that narratives cannot be expected to aggregate will be a limiting factor; that the events explained have been standardized, at least to some extent, will abet comparative evaluation. In other words, nonaggregativity and nonstandardization force this result; no general test can be had.

The focus so far has been on a proposed category of essentially narrative explanation and has been developed and illustrated by reference to certain well-known historical texts. But does this category relate to narratives in the historical natural sciences like evolutionary biology and historical social sciences like cultural anthropology, and if so how? Inter alia and so unlike those rehearsed above, these other cases may appear to be somewhat standardized in a theoretical sense. For example, what is the relation of essentially narrative explanation in evolutionary biology to the usual explanatory structure found there, e.g., general principles of variation and natural selection, standardized taxonomic language of organisms, and standardized events like mutations and extinctions? These theoretically specified aspects of evolutionary biology would appear to work right along with and even be integrated into essentially narrative explanation. Do these considerations require modifying how essentially narrative explanations have been characterized?[14]

I cannot here address all these questions. The cultural anthropology case can, I suggest, be readily assimilated to those already discussed, but demonstrating that would require an attention to the details of specific ethnographies. I focus instead on a case from evolutionary biology, since that prima facie appears the hard case for essentially narrative explanations as developed to this point. But the difficulties turn out to be more apparent than real. In particular, another route to grounding the features claimed herein for narrative explanation can be found by examining a closely related position urged by John Beatty and Isabel Carrera (2011), who argue for narrative explanations from the perspective of evolutionary biology. After developing details of this case, I return to questions raised above regarding how it fits with essentially narrative explanations.

Beatty and Carrera, attending to remarks made by Stephen J. Gould, note a distinction between two very different senses of historical contingency. On one, the notion can be parsed in terms of a standard counterfactual rendering: if certain facts about the past had been different, then there would be differences going forward. But on a second sense of historical contingency that they find in Gould's writings, one fraught with significance for evolutionary biology, differences going forward might emerge even assuming an unaltered antecedent state. Following Gould, they call this "replaying life's tape" (Beatty and Carrera 2011, 472–73). In this thought experiment, Gould maintains that if one could erase "life's tape," going back to some particular point, and then "replay" it from that point (start over with the state description of that time t, so to speak), Gould doubted that from a biological/evolutionary standpoint the tape would "play out" exactly as before.

Beatty and Carrera (2011, 482) observe that Gould did not seem alert to these two very different senses of historical contingency that he invokes. They set out to explore whether the "replay" scenario can be made plausible, but with their own twist: "History matters . . . when the past that had to happen (in order to realize the future) was not bound to happen, but did. By switching our focus from the unpredictability of the outcome to the unpredictability of antecedent events, we have moved from a situation where one and the same past event is consistent with alternative possible future events . . . [i.e.,] to a situation where, of all the past events that might have been, the one that had to occur in order to bring about the future event of interest did in fact occur." But what does it mean to focus on "the unpredictability of antecedent events"? Here Beatty and Carrera, by way of illustrating the unpredictability of adaptive traits that emerge in orchids, cite an ingenious experiment that actually instantiates in some key respects Gould's "replay" of nature's tape *Gedankenexperiment*: "The basic (ongoing) experimental setup involves the investigation of twelve, initially identical (cloned) populations of the bacterium E. coli, as they evolve in identical (and identically altered) environments. The investigators have detected a number of differences in evolutionary outcomes among the twelve lines, differences that cannot be attributed to differential selection pressures (since the groups have faced identical selection pressures in their identical environments), but that seem instead to be causally dependent on chance differences in the variations (and order of variations) that have arisen in the different lineages" (488). After 31,500 generations, one lineage exhibited an extremely rare but highly adaptive mutation. The question addressed by the researchers in line with the "replay" scenario concerned whether or not this mutation would occur in the other populations as well, or "whether the population in question had by that time, though a series of contingencies, evolved to become uniquely capable of taking the final evolutionary steps in the direction of citrate metabolism" (488). Because the researchers preserved samples of each of the dozen initially identical E coli strains every five hundred generations, they could "rerun" the tape, so to speak, and replay the evolutionary cycle by taking a preserved sample from some point antecedent to when the mutation emerges and see if it emerged again. "And what they found was that the ability to metabolize citrate arose over and over again, suggesting that, by this point, the lineage in question had become uniquely capable of making the evolutionary breakthrough" (489). So although "life's tape" begins identically for all twelve of the lineages under study, only one manifests the mutation of interest. Upon a "replay" of nature's tape, no such mutation occurs in the other strains.

This suggests the conclusion that, starting from a genetically identical initial state and holding the environment constant, in some worlds (at least one, anyway) a specific mutation emerges, and in some (indeed, most) it does not. There will be, moreover, no predicting that this mutation might ultimately emerge because "in the beginning" all these "possible worlds" share a point of origin.

From this consideration of contingency/unpredictability (since none of the other eleven strains made this leap, and since they start as biologically identical), Beatty and Carrera suggest certain conclusions regarding the function of a narrative explanation. They follow W. B. Gallie in suggesting that (quoting here from Gallie) "the unpredictable developments of a story stand out, as worth making a story of, and as worth following" (Beatty and Carrera 2011, 490). As they gloss the moral here, "The outcome may seem improbable at the beginning of the story, but really should not seem improbable at the end" (490). But why ascribe as Gallie does primacy to unpredictability/contingency in structuring or identifying the specifically historical? For surely a reader of, e.g., Hilberg's work or Braudel's opus does not begin in ignorance of how matters turn out. As Mink (1987, 47–48) noted in criticism of Gallie's view, "What he [Gallie] has provided is a description of the naïve reader, that is, the reader who does not know how the story ends," and what this reveals is that "to know an event by retrospection is categorically, not incidentally, different from knowing it by prediction or anticipation." Granted, Beatty and Carrera do not insist that unpredictability represents a necessary feature of narrative explanation. But is unpredictability a feature that in fact creates a special place for narratives in the spectrum of scientific explanations?

In this regard, their own phrasing of the announced moral does not square with their chosen emphasis on unpredictability: "What narratives are especially good for—what makes them worth telling, and renders them non-superfluous—are situations where history matters: where a particular past had to happen in order to realize a particular future, and when the past that had to happen (in order to realize that future) was not bound to happen, but did" (Beatty and Carrera 2011, 491). But this characterization of why "history matters" emphasizes, I suggest, retrospective insight. Narratives certainly show their worth when history matters. But the mattering emerges, as they themselves put it, when one now knows what "was not bound to happen, but did." One only knows it was not bound to happen because retrospectively something now known to matter emerges, and knowledge so gained through hindsight can be used to fashion a narrative that then charts a developmental course from a beginning to an end. This may also have been unpredictable, in the sense scouted earlier. But unpredictability just serves to emphasize that this insight could be obtained only retrospectively.

Beatty and Carrera note that what narratives provide but that predictive accounts cannot involves explanations that offer, as they put it, a "stepwise" path from beginning to end. This point also underlines that they too have characterized what I term an essentially narrative explanation, i.e., one where there exists no explanation of how this came to be as we find them apart from a sequencing of events. Their quote cited immediately above continues as follows: "A representation or account of such a situation would need to proceed stepwise, because some stages—those marked by a fork in the road—require information not derivable from previous stages. We need to be told which paths were taken; the narrative supplies this information, as it is needed. The more forks in the road on the way to the actual outcome, the more points at which history matters" (Beatty and Carrera 2011, 491). As their own remarks here make clear, their actual emphasis falls on the importance of retrospective knowledge, on knowing where the noteworthy forks exist and what did happen at those points. This new information about the past, in short, becomes available only upon assuming a retrospective view. This hindsight allows one to identify truths about an earlier time not then knowable as true. One marks the end of this narrative—the admittedly unpredictable mutation that marks the terminus of their laboratory tale (for the moment), because once that mutation emerges, a story exists to tell. As Wallace Martin noted, knowing the end allows a beginning to be identified. What makes for a narrative, what makes for a tale to tell consists in having a full story in hand.[15]

The value that Beatty and Carrera find in narrative as a type of explanation thus can be transposed into an essentially narrative explanation, one emphasizing the role of narrative sentences. The experiment provides some insight or explanation into evolutionary possibilities because the explanandum event in such cases—e.g., a mutation that confers an adaptive advantage to an orchid—can be identified only in that way, as true of an earlier time but not knowable as such at that time. Retrospectively, one can know what proves adaptive and what does not. At the moment, the emergence cannot be predicted, and its relative advantage, if any, must await a test of time. But then one can later say truly of the earlier time that an adaptive advantage emerges then. Since time reveals what proves adaptive, adaptive mutations will be invisible even to an Ideal Chronicler at a given moment in time. But the importance of narrative resides in the fact that only through it can one express and explain such truths.

An evolutionary explanation as sketched by Beatty and Carrera manifests as well the other features that mark an explanation as having narrative form essentially. An explanation of the process that results in an adaptive mutation cannot be detached from the narrative of which it is a part. Only by contextualizing it—identifying retrospectively those steps "marked by a fork in the road"—does it get explained, and what explains must also be formed by contrast within that historical account.[16] The emphasis on unpredictability proves not to be fully misplaced, since it signals that the events of concern do not exist in some standardized form. An evolutionary narrative cannot be paraphrased into some other form and still capture what it aims to explain. Regarding connections between nonaggregativity as I discuss it and explanations in evolutionary biology, see the informative and illuminating discussion by Currie (2014).[17]

This leaves only the question of how this example fits with the final aspect of essentially narrative explanations, viz., that the event explained is nonstandardized. As noted at the outset of this section, events studied by evolutionary biology do appear to be standardized by virtue of belonging to a theory that assumes standardization for such cases, and so in contrast to other sorts of historical events that I discuss.[18] But even granting this, what counts as an adaptation remains contextually defined and retrospectively identified. To the extent that context remains ineliminable and so an adaptive mutation proves only retrospectively specifiable, then the explanandum event will in turn also be nonstandardized in the sense relevant to how essentially narrative explanations have been characterized. For under that description, the event has no nonnarrative explanation. Those other, more standardized aspects will enter into the sequencing, but they can neither displace nor replace a need to narrativize. Put another way, the relation of explanans and explanandum (whatever the content of statements in the explanans) remains essentially narrativized.

As responses to Hilberg's or Braudel's work earlier illustrated, the merits of such narrative explanations characteristically consist in how they focus and shape subsequent inquiry and debate. That is, historical texts in particular function to explain by providing the sole means to formulate and answer certain types of explanatory problems. And if an event can be explained only narratively, then (ceteris paribus) for that reason evaluating that explanation will have to be done comparatively, i.e., relative to a competing narrative.

To reject essentially narrative explanations would thus be to deny that at least some events expressible only as narrative sentences properly qualify for explanation, i.e., to declare a narrative sentence qua explanandum to be nonsense, as an inappropriate candidate to be evaluated for its truth or falsity. But this move surely lacks any plausibility. Conversely, if essentially narrative explanations do function to explain narrative sentences, this should begin to establish their naturalistic bona fides. Completing the argument for naturalizing narrative requires saying something more about how essentially narrative explanations intersect with and relate to other recognized forms of scientific explanation. I address that issue in the next three chapters.

5

The Silence of the Norms

> In history... expectations are far less precise, and there is correspondingly less agreement than in science about whether expectations "fit the facts" and about the sorts of data relevant to their evaluation.... The historian's problem is not simply that the facts do not speak for themselves but that, unlike the scientist's data, they speak exceedingly softly. Quiet is required if they are to be heard at all.
> —Thomas Kuhn, "The Halt and the Blind: Philosophy and History of Science"

Having developed an analysis of a category of narrative explanations, this chapter and the next offer an answer to a question that, as noted in earlier chapters, has dogged historiography since the nineteenth century: How does historical/narrative explanation relate to other forms of scientific explanation (on the assumption that history provides a form of empirical knowledge, and so counts as a science in some sense of the term)? My answer proceeds in two steps. The first (developed in this chapter and the next) examines Kuhn's impact on our understanding of what science is. Despite over a half-century of commentary on Kuhn's (1962/2012) *The Structure of Scientific Revolutions* (hereafter referred to as *SSR*), Kuhn's own historiographic method remains underexamined and its exact nature unappreciated. This chapter raises and sharpens the question of Kuhn's "missing historiography" (as I term it). The next chapter provides an account of Kuhn's historiographic method and its significance for understanding the relationship of history to other forms of scientific inquiry. In particular, I show that the structure of *SSR* exemplifies that of an essentially narrative explanation. The second step (chapter 7) uses the conclusion from the reading of *SSR* developed in chapters 5 and 6 to indicate how narrative explanations fit within a more general naturalist view of inquiry.

A philosophical mystery, one cloaked in a methodological irony, shrouds a key development in contemporary philosophy of science. The mystery? How to account for the logic of explanation that underwrites the influence and status of Kuhn's (1962/2012) widely celebrated and extensively studied *SSR*. What makes this a mystery? Consider the following irony: despite *SSR*'s status, there exists no generally accepted specification of those features that a historical explanation ought to possess.[1] In this key respect, fifty years of debate regarding the merits of *SSR* have proceeded virtually without mention of the philosophical void regarding the topic of historical explanation. Almost all readers of *SSR* have stared this mystery in the face for fifty years now without taking notice of or commenting on it.[2]

Indeed, the fact that the entire topic of historical explanation fell off the map of (analytical) philosophy decades ago compounds the mystery of how *SSR* could have been influential and the irony of its enduring impact. Just at a moment when philosophy of history arguably should have "taken off" as a core philosophical discipline, riding a wave of professional concern one might have expected Kuhn's work to generate, discussion instead effectively ceases and the topic disappears. And even those reporting "the naturalists' return" record no sightings or mentions of philosophy of history.

In this sense, the mystery runs deep. For it has managed (or so it seems) to elude detection even by those supposedly highly sensitized and trained to identify, analyze, and evaluate standards of explanation and argument. But why pursue this philosophical cold case—the unsolved and allegedly worrisome mystery of a philosophical topic gone missing? Why worry about the silence that surrounds questions regarding the norms of historical explanation? I suggest the following answer: breaking the silence should prove key to exposing still existing and important questions about the relation of history and philosophy, ones that presently go unasked and ignored in polite philosophical company. In order to reanimate interest in this mystery, I assemble reminders in this chapter of its connection to a basic task of philosophy: to clarify for ourselves the grounds for what we take to warrant belief. The next chapter breaks the silence.

Regarding the historical/philosophical context at the point when *SSR* first appears requires situating Kuhn's work relative to Hempel and to Quine. Reading Hempel's classic 1950 article, "Problems and Changes in the Empiricist Criterion of Meaning," alongside Quine's (1951) "Two Dogmas of Empiricism," a striking feature emerges. One finds in Hempel's article (see especially §5) not merely a recognition of the type of the holism that Quine so (in)famously promotes, but actually an embrace. Both acknowledge that holism radically broadens what counts as the unit of empirical significance with regard to explanation and testing in science as then philosophically conceived. Ironies abound here. On the one hand, Hempel betrays no anxiety that holism ultimately represents any principled problem for his favored analysis of the logic of science. On the other hand, Quine hypothesizes that holism makes it impossible to philosophically vindicate the verification criterion of meaning at the philosophical heart of positivism.

Kuhn (1962/2012, vi) for his part explicitly acknowledges Quine's critique in "Two Dogmas" as a key influence, particularly the holism it ushers into philosophical prominence (see also Zammito 2004). Kuhn's particular narrative of a history of science powerfully illustrates how this shift in a conceptualization of the unit of empirical significance effectively upends all prevailing accounts of what supposedly explains the rationality of theory change in science. And one might then imagine that precisely this turn of events—the emergence of a narrative of the history of science that profoundly alters and constrains any philosophical account of how rational evaluation of scientific reasoning could proceed—would galvanize philosophical concerns about and research into the nature of historical knowledge and historical explanation. Yet, as Danto (1995, 72–73) wryly notes, nothing of the sort happens:

> I can think of very little in the philosophy of history from the middle-1960s to the present. Somewhere someone sometime in the last decade must have written about explanation, even about historical explanation—but I cannot think of an example offhand. . . . It is not just that the topic is under extreme neglect. It is, rather, that there is hardly room in the present scene of philosophy for discussion of its issues. So to find someone actively working at them would be almost to encounter a historically displaced person, like someone doing abstract expressionist canvasses as if the whole subsequent history of art had not taken place.

The spell cast by positivism conjured analytical philosophy of history into existence. Those caught in the magic of that moment perceived a need to exorcise history of its possession by narrative form. But when the positivist spell breaks, such concerns vanish.

Danto (1995, 84–85), himself a key player in analytical philosophy of history in its prime, identifies Kuhn as the thinker who forces philosophers of science to rethink the philosophical role that they must accord to history:

> What makes Kuhn's work *historically* important is the fact that a good many thinkers, whose worlds very largely overlapped Hempel's . . . were

caused by Kuhn's work to turn into thinkers whose world overlapped Kuhn's world instead.... I can remember one of them saying with a cry of anguish that he wished Kuhn had never written that damned book.... [A sixteenth-century scholastic] said, in much the same spirit, that "The wretch Luther had emptied the lecture halls." For a long period there were questions with which scholastic thinkers dealt and with which everyone who shared their world regarded as of the greatest moment. And then, all at once, almost overnight, nobody cared any longer.... [Hempel's theory] just stopped being relevant, the way the whole philosophy of history it defined stopped being. It was replaced with a different set of questions, a world in effect, into which it no longer fit.

But Danto, his sophistication with regard to this topic notwithstanding, nonetheless never pauses to ask why philosophy of history fails to rise reborn from the ashes of positivism: "Kuhn advanced a view of history so powerful that history rather than being an applied science, as Hempel holds history to be, came to be the matrix for viewing *all* the sciences. It all at once became the philosophical fashion to view science historically rather than logically, as an evolving system rather than a timeless calculus, as something whose shifts over time are philosophically more central to its essence than the timeless edifice of theories" (72). But the de facto impact of Kuhn's historiographic practice proves false Hempel's attempt to legislate what the form of historical explanation needs to be. In short, Danto gives voice to the fact that Kuhn's work made passé all that prior to it had supposedly defined what a science of history had to be. Yet having commented on the surprising result of Kuhn's work—the complete and sudden overthrow of a powerful theory of scientific explanation by means of a work of history that supposedly does not have even prima facie status as a scientific explanation—and stared it in the face, Danto (like so many other philosophers) then simply turns away and makes no further comment.

Nonetheless, the old questions remain unanswered; the demise of positivist hegemony in philosophy of science only removes any felt pressure to answer them. In short, once positivist-inspired methodological debates cease to have any real point, interest in philosophy of history within analytical philosophy largely disappears.

Ironically, then, some time just subsequent to the publication of the first edition of *SSR*, i.e., as the history of science intrudes itself into a central role in philosophical debate regarding philosophy of science, philosophical discussion of historical explanation effectively ceases. And even as Kuhn's work, as has been widely noted and much discussed (see esp. Zammito 2004), gives impetus and life to a distinctive style of sociology of science and inspires the creation of a new discipline—science studies—questions of what makes for a proper historical explanation remain ignored.

But note the revolution wrought in philosophy at this moment. *SSR effectively reverses the received order of epistemic authority.* Prior to Kuhn a work of history, in order to count as providing a legitimate explanation, needed to conform to a certain standard determined by an ahistorical account of science. Post-Kuhn, philosophers fashion histories to account for which explanatory forms come to prevail and why.[3]

Moreover, Kuhn never receives attention as a historiographer or a philosopher of history, even before that philosophical tribe decamps and vanishes. Indeed, his own remarks on historical methodology prove sporadic and mostly unilluminating.[4] If analytical philosophy of history begins, for all intents and purposes, with Hempel's throwing down the gauntlet to historians and daring them to meet the challenge posed by standards of scientific explanation, it ironically ceases just at the point of a miraculous reversal of fortune. Despite decades of exile from the realm of scientific explanation, a work in the history of science overthrows extant accounts of the rationality of theory change in science. But how could this have happened given the absence of any accepted basis for taking a history as explanatory?

How, then, to account for this lack of interest in questions regarding historical explanation just at the moment when they should have been regarded as particularly relevant and pressing? One answer found in the literature can be considered but ultimately rejected, Giuseppina D'Oro's (2008) "The Ontological Backlash: Why Did Mainstream Analytic Philosophy Lose Interest in the Philosophy of History?" According to D'Oro, debate in philosophy of history concerns the status of reasons as causes. Unfortunately, D'Oro's narrative runs together and confuses two distinct strands, one emanating from a debate that chronologically predates logical positivism but foreshadows a number of key issues.

D'Oro's telling of the tale begins with the nineteenth-century dispute about the nature of explanation in the natural versus the human sciences, *Erklären* versus *Verstehen*. This earlier strand, as formulated by Dilthey and others, defends history as a science, but one characterized by its own special methods, methods that were tailored for the reconstruction of meaning structures specific to times and places. In this context, a principled distinction between the natural and the human sciences results from the different types of explanations that the natural as opposed to the human sciences seek to produce—the nomothetic as opposed to the idiographic. Nonreducibility of one science to the other here results from the fact that the human sciences seek the particularity of situations and so cannot generalize. The natural sciences, for their part, abstract from the particularities of time and place in order to identify invariant regularities at work. Explanations require causal laws; causal laws require invariant regularities. The friends of *Verstehen* denied that idiographic accounts yielded regularities of the requisite sort. History was held to reside firmly on the human sciences/*Verstehen* side of this divide. History could not be a science for this reason.

However, D'Oro attempts to weave this together with a second strand of debate, one where Davidson famously intervenes. This involves the dispute over "reasons as causes," a debate that emerges from a particular reading of the later Wittgenstein and *not* from any positivist strictures on explanation. Dilthey and those in this hermeneutic tradition defend history as a science, by which they mean a subject that produces truths by virtue of a special method. Those neo-Wittgensteinians who deny reasons as causes also deny as a matter of principle the possibility of a science of the social, history included. For the neo-Wittgensteinians, reason-giving represents a normative activity, and so cannot be characterized by mere descriptive inquiry. *But idiographic does not equate to normative.* In one case reason explanations prove compatible with history being a science, in the other case not. Ironically, D'Oro (2008, 405) mentions a key component of the actual debate but does not recognize it for what it is.

The problematic as configured by the *Verstehen/Erklären* debate does, to be sure, change with the appearance of logical positivism generally and Hempel's classic paper in particular.[5] The change is this: Hempel does *not* insist that, e.g., economics reduce to the laws of physics. What he does require concerns the *logical* form of scientific explanation. D'Oro overlooks and so misses the logical concerns of positivism and confuses them with the metaphysical views of those alleging the conceptual autonomy of reason explanations.

D'Oro's account thus ultimately mischaracterizes the issues at stake. For having set the narrative line that she does, once Davidson puts to rest doubts that reasons can be causes, the issues switch to metaphysical debates about mental causation: "My key claim is that the declining interest in the philosophy of history is linked to the return of a metaphysical conception of the task of philosophy" (D'Oro 2008, 404; see also 405). These questions were, in turn, appropriated by philosophy of mind. Questions of explanation within analytical philosophy of history, on her account, presuppose an account of mental causation. And those issues remain unsettled. But this confuses a metaphysical question about a type of causality and a logical question about the form of explanation. And the logical question alone bears on norms of explanation; the metaphysical question involves issues independent of those of logical form.

In sum, philosophy of history does not have its disappearance accounted for by arguing, *pace* D'Oro, that other areas preempted its core issues. That earlier debate, whatever its interest, does not call into question history's status as a legitimate science. It ties to later debates not via a metaphysics of causation but in virtue of norms of explanation specific to human sciences. What goes missing when philosophy of history disappears involves a basis for evaluating any imputed action explanation qua explanation, whatever the mechanism of action.[6]

Bojana Mladenovic (2007) offers a thoughtful account that addresses the question of what makes for actual explanation in Kuhn's history of science. Mladenovic examines some recent extended readings of *SSR* from the standpoint of how they treat Kuhn's historiography. While sympathetic to objections she raises to these specific works (e.g., book-length studies by Andersen, Bird, Sharrock and Read, as well as an article by Kindi), a particularly telling criticism she offers of Sharrock and Read bears noting.[7] On their account, the use of history in *SSR* has no explanatory but only a therapeutic intent. The desired outcome on their account would be quietist: "If philosophical therapy is successful [say Sharrock and Read], it will 'leave science as it is'; history of science, not philosophy of science, will then be the main source of understanding of scientific development" (Mladenovic 2007, 267). So, if Sharrock and Read are to be believed, the explanatory mystery goes away; indeed, it never existed in the first place.

Against this reading, Mladenovic (2007, 268) makes the following pointed response: "Philosophy cannot simply 'leave history as it is,' because history itself requires substantive philosophical assumptions which ground the individuation of historical phenomena and the selection of explanatory categories used in historical narratives. History, of course, can leave these assumptions unexamined, but that will not make them any less philosophical." In short, Sharrock and Read's interpretation confuses a symptom of the philosophical problem with its cause; continued denial does not represent a good therapeutic outcome (philosophical or otherwise).

Without a doubt, Kuhn engaged in a struggle against a received reading of the history of science, a reading that functioned very much as an unacknowledged prop for the nascent philosophy of science. This received reading—science as cumulative, and the history of science as one of progress—it should be noted, involves the same absence of a philosophical base. For the received historical account never receives any more scrutiny qua explanatory model than does its Kuhnian alternative. But this gets ahead of the story.

Mladenovic attributes (correctly, as I shall argue) a high degree of self-consciousness to Kuhn regarding the historiographic challenge he faced, whatever his lack of reflection on the mode of argument that history constitutes. His problem, as she notes, is that "one cannot *argue* against an image, or a metaphor. . . . Kuhn couldn't hope to be successful in erasing that image by producing specific arguments, however sound, against particular historiographical or philosophical claims and assumptions. Deeply entrenched images of this sort don't just fade away when deprived of evidence to support them, for the simple reason that images are not *supported* by evidence" (Mladenovic 2007, 268). On this basis, she labels Kuhn's endeavor metaphilosophical. This seems apt, since Kuhn's debate with the received view within the history of science (and, implicitly, within the philosophy of science as well) requires a recasting of the relationship between the history and philosophy of science (275).

Now Mladenovic (2007, 269) has her own account of how Kuhn proposes to "support" (her term) his model of scientific change, one she draws from Weber's theory of ideal types. But as she understands them, an ideal type functions for Weber only as "a methodological tool, and its use is strictly heuristic" (270). Think here of an actual Calvinist as embodying in the flesh Weber's ideal type of the Protestant ethic. But she then goes on to attribute to ideal types a role in explanation: "Kuhn's selection of ideal-type concepts is a reflection of his explanatory interest: he wanted to understand what and how science develops, and what the changes in that development imply from a philosophical point of view. . . . Nevertheless, 'revolution' is a useful ideal-type concept which accentuates incommensurability as the highly relevant feature for our understanding of scientific change; its presence explains rational disagreements among scientists" (273). But what explanatory work could her proposed types actually provide? What would be needed to fill out her story would be an account of revolutions analogous to how the Protestant ethic helps explain a link between actual Calvinists and a newly crafted theological license for achieving material success. Otherwise, the ideal type heuristic offers absolutely no explanatory purchase.

Part of the way in which Mladenovic's suggestions strain credibility here concerns the fact that Kuhnian revolutions simply do not "explain rational disagreements among scientists." Rather, they signal precisely the point at which "rational disagreement" ceases to be possible. In addition (and certainly not determinatively), Kuhn (e.g., 1962/2012, 92) himself gives no evidence that he takes the term to be more than a metaphor for the changes he hopes to characterize. More important, while the Weberian sense of ideal type provides explanatory insight (to the extent that it does) by approximation of actual cases to an analytic ideal, Kuhn simply has no ideal type of revolution on offer with respect to which actual cases can be illuminated. Rather, and not unlike those who unwittingly or not instigate such changes in theoretical views, he finds himself groping for a language which will allow others to see accepted facts in new ways. The novelty of *SSR*, in short, resides *not* in Kuhn's application of social science to the history of science but precisely in recasting relatively well-known historical data into a very different narrative structure.

Paul Hoyningen-Huene (1992, 490) voices a concern that more closely connects to themes central to this chapter when he states that he wants "only to show that and how the sociology and philosophy of science are dependent on the history of science. The upshot is: the history of science already determines, among other things, the realm of questions that can, in a sociological or philosophical perspective, be sensibly asked with respect to science." However, Hoyningen-Huene also records without comment a clear tension in Kuhn's account at precisely this point. For, as he characterizes Kuhn's discussion of the received historiography, Kuhn maintains that "we were possessed by a deceptive image of science" and that the challenge becomes one of understanding (again speaking for Kuhn) "how . . . [to] gain an undistorted image of past science" (489). But if the philosophy and sociology of science presuppose the history, then what marks a history of science as being of the requisite "undistorted" sort?

Just here Hoyningen-Huene's account fails to be on Kuhn's behalf sufficiently self-reflexive (just as Kuhn himself turns out to be). For Hoyningen-Huene notes that, with regard to the rationality of theory choice, the cognitive values in play themselves turn out to be artifacts of a scientist's historical situation. What else could they be? Hoyningen-Huene (1992, 497) suggests that just here Kuhn follows Hempel insofar as "Hempel and Kuhn agree on the possibility of a justification of cognitive values, and perhaps also on the fundamentals of the means of justification." But what could this means be? Certainly not by an abstraction of scientific method from the practice of science. Indeed, logical positivism just was a program predicated on this idea, and this in turn tied to accounts of logic that themselves did not prove out.[8] In short, no good reason exists for taking as free of historical determination those norms of science that philosophers hold near and dear.

Hoyningen-Huene (1992, 497) notes, in fact, just this concern, but only appears to hold science accountable to it: "What I find most fascinating about this approach is the prospect of a solution of a related problem in which sociological and philosophical aspects are also intertwined. It is the problem of the change of cognitive values in time, and of their difference in different scientific communities at the same time. Kuhn has described change and difference of cognitive values, but I think he has not answered the question how change and difference of cognitive values can be understood." Indeed, as Hoyningen-Huene explicitly recognizes, "the question arises how this change of values can be understood as a consequence of theory change, and whether such a change may count as justified. The latter question asks whether this sort of value change may be rational" (498). Ironically, he then goes on to suggest that the metaphilosophical issue—the rationality of value change, can be answered by examining the goal(s) of science! "Thus, how should theory change justify value change? The puzzle dissolves once one pays attention to the fact that cognitive values relate to the ultimate goal of science which was, in Hempel's words, 'an increasingly comprehensive, systematically organized, world view that is explanatory and predictive'" (498). But now his whole explanatory move has collapsed back on itself.

The problem began as one of the history of science predetermining what questions it made philosophical sense to ask. But when asked what to count as an "undistorted" view of the history of science, the answer on offer turns out to be one that a prior philosophical account of science tells the historian determines what counts as 'science.' This conflicts with a lesson from Kuhn that all accept, viz., that what to count as science has no historically stable boundaries. So Hoyningen-Huene's answer proves no answer at all. It simply restates the problem with which he began.

In accord with a previously noted point from Danto, Hoyningen-Huene also finds in Kuhn an ambivalence about embracing the role for history he so famously forges. Indeed, in his book that so closely examines the details of *SSR*, Hoyningen-Huene (1993, 20) characterizes Kuhn's procedure in *SSR* explicitly in terms of the construction of a narrative. He there also introduces two notions that underline the problematic character of the very nature of the history he goes on to so carefully explore, what he terms "narrative" and "pragmatic" relevance: "The moment of narrative relevance selects for material which must be taken into account if the resulting text is to be a proper narrative. . . . Finally, the moment of pragmatic relevance selects for material without which the pragmatic goal of a historical narrative cannot be realized. Thus the content of a historical narrative is determined in part by the audience to which it is addressed and in part by the effect it is meant to have on this audience" (14; see also Hoyningen-Huene 2012, 282–83). But this says nothing about the critical issues regarding what makes for a "proper narrative" and the notion of "audience" to whom to give the explanation.[9]

Kuhn himself also characterizes a history as a narrative. In one of the very few places he directly addresses this topic, he offers the following gloss on the notion of a narrative explanation:

> The final product of most historical research is a narrative, a story, about particulars of the past. In part it is a description of what

> occurred. ∴ . . . Its success, however, depends not only on accuracy but also on structure. The historical narrative must render plausible and comprehensible the events it describes. In a sense to which I shall later return, history is an explanatory enterprise, yet its explanatory functions are achieved with almost no recourse to explicit generalizations. (I may point out here, for later exploitation, that when philosophers discuss the role of covering laws in history, they characteristically draw their examples from the work of economists and sociologists, not of historians. In the writings of the latter, lawlike generalizations are extraordinarily hard to find.) (Kuhn 1977, 5)

This remark could hardly be more explicit in rejecting the then prevailing Hempelian account of explanation as descriptive of or prescriptive for historical work. Yet it also unabashedly endorses history as an "explanatory enterprise," one built on narrative structure. "But I do claim that, however much laws may add substance to an historical narrative, they are not essential to its explanatory force. That is carried . . . by the facts the historian presents and the manner in which he juxtaposes them" (Kuhn 1977, 16). But what marks some "manner" of juxtaposition as explanatory?

Kuhn (1977, xiv) states in his preface to *The Essential Tension* with regard to this essay that this "lecture itself can be read as an effort to deal in somewhat greater depth with the issues already introduced in the preface." Presumably this includes the point he makes in that very paragraph, viz., that the interest now shown by philosophers of science in history "has so far largely missed what I take to be the central philosophical point: the fundamental conceptual readjustment required of the historian to recapture the past or, conversely, of the past to develop toward the present" (xiv). And this in turn needs to be juxtaposed to his cryptic remark, a few pages prior to the one just quoted: "In history, more than in any other discipline I know, the finished product of research disguises the nature of the work that produced it" (x). Indeed, he clearly suggests that the finished product's disguise consists of the narrative form created by the historian, a form that itself does not reside "in" the world:

> I have elsewhere argued that the cognitive content of the physical sciences is in part dependent on the same primitive similarity relation between concrete examples, or paradigms, of successful scientific work. . . . Here I am suggesting that in history that obscure global relationship carries virtually the entire burden of connecting fact. If history is explanatory . . . it is because the reader who says, "Now I know what happened," is simultaneously saying, "Now it makes sense. . . . What

was for me previously a mere list of facts has fallen into a recognizable pattern." I urge that the experience he reports be taken seriously. (17–18)

At this point, it would be germane to note that the only reference found in Kuhn's oeuvre to a card-carrying philosopher of history occurs in this essay. Kuhn makes approving reference to a 1966 essay by Louis Mink, "The Autonomy of Historical Understanding" (reprinted in Mink 1987). And although he does not do more than mention the essay in passing, the points just made clearly bear Mink's stamp.[10]

This essay by Mink appears early in what became a series of very distinguished writings on this topic.[11] It would be a hermeneutic folly to read later Mink into early Kuhn. However, that said, it remains the case that Mink's (1966) remarks on the forms of "synoptic judgment" define for him (and by implication for Kuhn) what makes historical reasoning the sort of reasoning it is.

Importantly for purposes that will emerge forcefully in the next chapter, Mink's (1987, 79) notion of a synoptic judgment underwrites one of those features identified earlier as characterizing narrative explanations, viz., that historical conclusions are "nondetachable": "But despite the fact that an historian may 'summarize' conclusions in his final chapter, it seems clear that these are seldom or never detachable conclusions; not merely their validity but their meaning refers backward to the ordering of evidence in the total argument. The significant conclusions, one might say, . . . are represented by the narrative order itself. As ingredient conclusions they are exhibited rather than demonstrated." "Synoptic judgment" orders and structures the narrative, but the judgment cannot be supported or elucidated independently of the narrative that exhibits it. The narrative constitutes, in this specific sense, its own unique pattern of justificatory argument. This becomes, of course, the nondetachability characteristic already discussed.

Given the reference to Mink that precedes his discussion of this point, I suggest that Kuhn (1977, 19–20) can be read as endorsing this notion of nondetachability when he remarks, "Theories, as the historian knows them, cannot be decomposed into constituent elements for purposes of direct comparison either with nature or with each other. . . . For the historian, therefore, or at least for this one, theories are in certain essential respects holistic." Now, although talking about scientific theories, these remarks come at the conclusion of Kuhn's Minkian speculations about the nature of historical explanation and in what the autonomy of such historical explanation consists.

The familiar Kuhnian story about theory-ladenness, in short, not only applies to accounts of Aristotle's physics but characterizes as well the narrative structure historians deploy in trying to make this physics comprehensible to a later audience. In the penultimate paragraphs of his essay, Mink (1987, 88) puts his view this way:

> I have tried . . . to ask whether "history" differs from "science," not because it deals with different kinds of events and not because it uses models of explanation which differ from . . . the received model of explanation in the natural sciences, but because it cultivates the specialized habit of understanding which converts congeries of events into concatenations, and emphasizes and increases the scope of synoptic judgment in our reflection on experience.
>
> Now synoptic judgment is not a substitute for a methodology, any more than "empathy" is a substitute for evidence. . . . So far it is only an attempt to identify what distinguishes sophisticated historical thinking from both the everyday explanations of common sense and the theoretical explanations of natural science.

Nothing here, of course, functions to unpack what Mink indicates as the mark of "sophisticated historical thinking."

But in an essay published shortly after the one Kuhn cites, Mink (1987) adds a point of significance to understanding the respects in which a finished narrative disguises its explanatory intent. In a typical history, unlike a novel, the reader knows in advance (more or less) how the story turns out. The historian's craft consequently does not consist in surprising the reader with twists of plot or nuances of character development. Rather, it manifests what Mink comes to call a "configurational" mode of understanding, i.e., the significance of a historian's "emplotment" of the facts into narrative form. In this respect, Mink thus comes to argue, narratives "are in an important sense primary and irreducible. They are not imperfect substitutes for more sophisticated forms of explanation and understanding. . . . Stories are not lived but told. . . . There are hopes, plans, battles, and ideas, but only in retrospective stories are hopes unfulfilled, plans miscarried, battles decisive, and ideas seminal. . . . But it is from history and fiction that we learn how to tell and understand stories, and it is that stories answer questions" (60).[12] Alasdair MacIntyre, who shares Mink's appreciation of the primacy of narrative structure in matters related to historical understanding, finds in Mink's and Kuhn's accounts his own special set of worries. Interestingly, these bear comparison to Kuhn's own later concerns arising from the sociology of science that sprang from certain readings of *SSR*. For the stress on the primacy of narrative threatens, in MacIntyre's (1980, 73) pungent phrase, to condemn Kuhn to being "the Kafka of the history of science."[13]

But not everyone shares MacIntyre's worries here about the autonomy of narrative structure as a form of understanding. Norton Wise (2011, 351), himself a distinguished historian of science, claims that the "autonomy of written language [makes it] . . . a vehicle of critical reflection and creative imagination. This is as true in history and in science as it is in literature. . . . Their creative function reflects in part, I will argue, the capacity to support narrative of particular kinds about the objects of science. The narratives take on different forms in different areas and they change over time." Indeed, Wise goes on to complain that with respect to physics the "deductive structuring of the course of events has long defined what constituted an explanation in physics. The explanatory emphasis, however, has been on the deduction, to the exclusion of the attached narrative, and with that, the exclusion of anything like historicity in explanation" (355). He references in the course of this article Hempel's critique of historical explanation, but like Kuhn did decades ago, dismisses it because it "does little to illuminate how narratives are related to explanations in natural science that do not depend on general laws" (371). Moreover, although mentioning in a footnote what he terms Kuhn and Hanson's "historicizing 'revolution'" against the Hempelian model, he goes on to complain (unfairly, I would say) that this revolution "did not stress science as narrative, nor did it attack deduction as explanation" (371n16). Alas, Wise's own acquaintance with contemporary philosophy of history, at least as he records it in this piece, proves spotty at best and offers him no apparent resources to address what makes narratives explanatory even on the assumption (that I share) that they are.

My goal has been just to raise puzzles and questions that have oddly gone so long unasked and unexamined despite the massive influence narratives exert on how core issues in philosophy come to be understood. In this respect, the foregoing reflections only echo and elaborate frustrations voiced by John Zammito (2004, 100): "What seems to be lacking here is recognition that the problems of validity the philosophers stress in their theories about natural science apply with equal force to the utterly fallible, ineluctably empirical endeavor of history" (see also Novick 1988; Wise 1980). A willed blindness to this influence of history on philosophical thought also caught Stephen Toulmin's (1971, 63) attention more than four decades ago: "In both sociological theory and philosophy of science . . . questions about historical change were set aside at the turn of the century, in reaction against the historicism of the German idealist tradition and against the misconceived 'evolutionism' of Spencer and his successors. What we now have to do is to take up the discussion once again at the point where it broke off some 60 years ago." By Toulmin's calculation, analytical philosophy has passed the century mark in its refusal to reengage with these issues.

Yet like the return of the repressed, unacknowledged historiographic issues continue to manifest themselves, haunting and hampering efforts to evaluate what to count as rational because of an ongoing refusal on the part of philosophers to examine just how works of history exert their undeniable power and influence. Kuhn's example enduringly albeit ironically testifies to the hold that narratives exercise even on the philosophical imagination. Philosophical therapy (like other forms) can commence only by first admitting to and then attempting to comprehend the sources of this grip. Surely the time has also come to confront the detrimental effects of the discipline's strategy of denial with regard to the historiography of *SSR*.

6

Kuhn's Narrative Construction of Normal Science

Could there be a naturalistic justification of narrative explanations? Naturalism as understood here precludes assuming any a priori definition of 'science' and so demarcating science from nonscience in that way. (I develop this further in chapter 7.) Yet this question may also seem paradoxical because naturalism will sometimes be characterized by reference to "accepted" scientific practices. But assuming some such specification of science implicit in any account of naturalism suggests that attempted answers to the opening question would have to beg the question by virtue of presumptively including or excluding narrative explanations in the asking.

I propose in this chapter to forge an affirmative and yet non-question-begging answer to this question of "naturalizing narrative explanation" by taking an indirect approach, one that begins with and reflects on what Kuhn (1962/2012) terms "normal science," i.e., science provisionally understood and so labeled and practiced within a particular time. In chapter 7, a fuller account of methodological naturalism and empiricism is provided. My focus in this chapter is on a narrower question: how to account in a Kuhnian spirit for how what passes as normal science achieves that status?

Now Kuhn (1962/2012, 10) restricts a designation of "normal science" to those disciplines with accepted research practices, where by "research practices" he has in mind "examples which include law, theory, application, and instrumentation together," that in turn give rise to "coherent traditions of scientific research." What makes for normal science, of course, shifts with changes in paradigms on Kuhn's account. Now this specification has a whiff of circularity inasmuch as it defines normal science by reference to "scientific research," but that can be overlooked. Sufficient for my purpose will be to take as a 'science' whatever comes to pass as such. In this respect, given the century-old controversy noted in chapter 1 regarding history's status as a science, I propose focusing rather on the question of how whatever passes as "normal science" comes to achieve that status. As yet, this does not presumptively exclude narrative explanations, though it may seem to stack the deck against them since it is not at all obvious that a discipline such as history satisfies Kuhn's criteria for having a consensus-based tradition of research with regard to theory, etc.

My argument will be that any answer to a question about how normal science comes to be, i.e., one that develops a non–a priori causal/explanatory account, will have to utilize what has been identified as an "essentially narrative explanation." In other words, my account shows how in *SSR* Kuhn crafts a narrativized account of normal science. This will count as naturalistic in a minimalist sense inasmuch as it does not begin with any philosophical definition of what is or is not a science and utilizes in its explanation nothing more than facts about what happened to explain how what comes to be called science achieves that status.

In taking the problem that Kuhn sets regarding the status of normal science and relatedly scientific rationality both as live and requiring a historical reconstruction of the "route to normal science" as an answer, I am not alone (see Friedman 2001, esp. part 1, lecture 3 and part 2, Section 3; Daston 2016).[1] Since chapter 5 established that Kuhn already understands history as a narrative, and does so in terms equivalent to those identified in chapter 1 as characteristic of narrative explanations, my conclusion will be that what comes to be normal science requires an essentially narrative explanation. Thus, what science is cannot be separated from some narrative or other that explain its status.

Understanding Kuhn's work in this way helps naturalize narrative explanation through a form of mutual containment—since narrative helps constitute any explanation of what counts as normal science, narrative explanation cannot be divorced from what now counts as explanation in science. It would be highly ironic, that is, to reject an explanation form that in fact proves unavoidable for purposes of revealing why what passes as science at a particular time does so. Chapter 7 then more fully develops an account of naturalism that accommodates this result.

I take it that my claim that *SSR* offers an essentially narrative explanation of what constitutes normal science will need to surmount at least two challenges. The first concerns explanatory strategy, the "missing historiography" of *SSR* just discussed. What logic of explanation or justification does *SSR* in fact instantiate? The second challenge questions any proposal to read *SSR* as a narrative. That is, on what basis should *SSR* be read as offering a narrative explanation of anything at all? In what follows, I develop an answer to the second challenge that meets the first as well.

A sort of willed blindness persists with regard to construing Kuhn's naturalism specifically in terms of historiographic method. Kuhn certainly thought of himself as a historian, and of course *SSR* comes chockablock with historical examples. Yet the well-known opening sentence of

SSR calls for particular scrutiny in this regard: "History, if viewed as a repository for more than anecdote or chronology, could produce a decisive transformation in the image of science by which we are now possessed" (Kuhn 1962/2012, 1). This sentence poses an underappreciated puzzle. As noted in the previous chapter (see chapter 5, n2), Alexander Bird (2012, 865) does not even consider historiography in this context. Relatedly, Brendan Larvor (2003, 371) suggests that Kuhn simply confuses his roles as historian and as philosopher: "The claim of this paper is that Kuhn inadvertently allowed features of his procedure and experience as an historian to pass over into his general account of science." Even Zammito's (2004, 52) otherwise sophisticated account of Kuhn's influence negatively assesses Kuhn's work as a history: "This opening sentence offered a clarity of intent the whole work failed to sustain." But clearly Kuhn does not intend the historical cases in *SSR* just to function merely as counterexamples to then extant philosophical accounts of theory change in science. To assume he does makes it incomprehensible as to why he might have any reason to expect a "transformation in the image of science." For read only as a motley of counterexamples to verificationist or falsificationist models of theory change in science, no alternative notion of science follows. Yet from his very first sentence Kuhn cautions against reading *SSR* as an exercise in historical bricolage.

At the very least, then, any explanatory logic imputed to *SSR* must help make plausible how it proposes to effect such a "decisive transformation." By drawing upon the schematic features of narrative explanation rehearsed above, *SSR* can in fact be shown to be readily assimilable to that format. When read as I propose, there emerges a clear justification for Kuhn's claim that history—his history, anyway—should (and in fact of course did) produce the sort of transformation he maintains that historical considerations should motivate.

An early appreciative characterization of what role history plays in Kuhn's work appears in Gerd Buchdahl's 1965 review. As he observes, for Kuhn "we must regard the scientific enterprise as somehow fragmented into a number of relatively (temporarily and ideologically) isolated periods," from which "it must follow that the history of ideas, including philosophical ideas, will likewise appear as a series of 'Gestalt-views' in terms of which we shall tend to interpret more special enterprises like those of history in general, and history of science in particular" (Buchdahl 1965, 55). Buchdahl it seems is puzzled as to why one "must regard" the history of science as "fragmented" into "isolated periods." Yet as he also goes on to note, "there is no doubt that within their context, the main contentions of this book imply a refreshingly new approach to both science and its history" (56). Buchdahl, himself both a historian and a philosopher

CHAPTER 6

of science, exhibits a sensitivity to the fact that any distinction between describing and justifying becomes vanishingly small when doing history. "Reading this volume, one gets the suspicion that the author's facts are used to illustrate a preconceived notion of historiography, not to prove it. Nor is this necessarily a very damning criticism" (59). This, of course, acknowledges the point in chapter 5 that essentially narrative explanations effectively collapse any distinction between description and justification.

In striking contrast, another early review of Kuhn's book by Charles C. Gillispie (1962, 1251), a prominent historian of science, maintains that Kuhn "is not writing history of science proper. His essay is an argument about the nature of science, drawn in large part from its history." But this characterization fails to notice exactly what Kuhn takes to be a core issue: whether anything could (without distortion) count as a "history of science proper," or alternatively, what sense could be assigned to the phrase "science proper." Gillispie thus misses Kuhn's moral, or as I shall say, what he seeks to explain.[2] For as already noted, in essentially narrative explanations no functional distinction between proof and illustration—the normative and the descriptive—can be drawn. "But I think that after reading this book no historian and no philosopher of science will ever be quite the same again.... Of one thing one can be certain; that we have here a new historiographical paradigm which will surely leave its mark on future generations of historians of science" (Buchdahl 1965, 64). Buchdahl thus appreciates in a way a reader such as Gillispie did not that *SSR* instantiates qua history of science the very type of history and so philosophy of science for which Kuhn advocates.

Yet by the 1970s Kuhn's historicizing move came to be seen as his work's most enduring legacy.[3] This thought persists. In his introductory essay to the fiftieth-anniversary edition of *SSR*, Hacking (2012, x) explicitly asks, "But is the book history or philosophy?" Hacking never attempts to answer his question. I propose, then, to return to and focus further on Buchdahl's provocative and important suggestion that *SSR* offers "a new historiographical paradigm." Yet challenging a narrative explanation most typically requires constructing a competing narrative. And so Kuhn does. But how?

To begin, note that the features of an essentially narrative explanation readily emerge as characteristics both of *SSR* and Kuhn's own reflections on how he thinks of what historians do. Recall that Kuhn (1977, 13) explicitly glosses historical inquiry as having a narrative form, a "concern with development over time." He also harbors no doubts that "history is an explanatory enterprise," albeit one where "its explanatory functions are achieved with almost no recourse to explicit generalizations" (5). Rather, he explicitly characterizes the "final product" of historical research as a "narrative" or "story" (5). Kuhn situates *SSR* as a work in the history of science. As he remarks in the introduction, the bulk of the book develops "complementary notions of normal science and of scientific revolutions"; the net impact of this will be a "historical study" that he insists offers a "conceptual transformation" of the understanding of the nature of science (Kuhn 1962/2012, 8).

Kuhn (1977, 16, 17, 19, 20) also foreshadows how narratives collapse the description/justification distinction, a point I emphasized in chapter 4. With reference to what he regularly refers to as his "limited holism," his own characterization indicates that his conclusions will be nondetachable from the narrative that presents them. There exists only an "obscure global relationship."

SSR does not examine events that come in some standardized format, and it provides a narrative of the history of science that does not aggregate either with then current histories or as the history of a stable something called 'science.' Regarding standardization, the "revolutions" that Kuhn identifies possess a "structure" only in a figurative sense, inasmuch as much of his account goes to show that there can be neither any specifying of exactly when one paradigm will be overwhelmed by anomalies nor exactly what considerations induce scientists to shift from one theory to the next. The very contrast between "normal" and "revolutionary" science—"complementary notions" as Kuhn (1962/2012, 8) terms them—itself proves contingent and contextual. "Scientific fact and theory are not categorically separable, except perhaps within a single tradition of normal-scientific practice" (7). As Kuhn also notes, what counts as "revolutionary" change may be invisible to all but a limited group engaged in a highly specialized undertaking (180). *The events exist only as described retrospectively, for that alone reveals them as normal or revolutionary.*

As a narrative about science, the history that *SSR* presents aggregates neither internally—thus incommensurability—nor with standard "textbook" histories of science. Indeed, Kuhn emphatically sets his account in opposition to those histories that maintain that accounts of scientific change do aggregate. That the account of what comes to be called at any given time a "science" fails to aggregate is at one with the claim that the various revolutions show successor theories to be incommensurable with those they displace/replace. The infamous consequence that results concerns how this makes it notoriously difficult to cash out any claim regarding scientific progress. And while this constitutes no proof of incommensurability, it does establish that the depiction of science found in *SSR*, insofar as it presents a nonaggregative account, also leaves Kuhn without some continuing stable notion of science. Kuhn's science proves quite protean. Boundaries that contemporary observers find well delineated prove when viewed historically to be remarkably fluid and unsettled.

It becomes important to note in this regard that Kuhn very deliberately challenges the suggestion that a settled notion of science can be used to answer a question of the form "Who counts as a scientist?" "If science is the constellation of facts, theories, and methods collected in current texts, then scientists are the men who, successfully or not, have striven to contribute one or another element to that particular constellation" (Kuhn 1962/2012, 2). Against this, Kuhn famously protests, "a few historians of science [including Kuhn] have been finding it more and more difficult to fulfill the functions that the concept of development-by-accumulation assigns to them" (2). This creates the following problem for a historian of science who resists the development-by-accumulation view: "These same historians confront growing difficulties in distinguishing the 'scientific' component of past observation and belief from what their predecessors had readily labeled 'error' and 'superstition'" (2). Historians of science, insofar as "they attempt to display the historical integrity of that science in its own time" will, "by implication, at least, . . . suggest the possibility of a new image of science. *This essay aims to delineate that image by making explicit some of the new historiography's implications*" (3–4; emphasis mine). Kuhn then turns to an enumeration of some of these features.

A crucial feature of the "new historiography" turns out to be how to answer the question "Who counts as a scientist?" But why worry about who counts as scientists since this sounds like a sociological, not a philosophical, question? This fails to recognize a fundamental philosophical point Kuhn quite rightly takes to be at issue, as well as a basic rhetorical puzzle he needs to solve. Since his narrative stresses the *noncontinuity* of what counts as science, his sequencing must relocate what it needs to track in order to forge a narrative about its putative subject. Kuhn's rhetorical problem arises precisely because he sets himself in opposition to the development-by-accumulation view of science. *For by doing so he seemingly deprives himself of any resources for saying what science is.* That is, it cannot be codified or characterized by perduring rules, methods, or the like. (Galison 1997, esp. ch. 9, and Daston 2016 reinforce this point.)

So if there exists no "science" as a stable, continuing item for such a narrative to be about, what then constitutes the subject of Kuhn's tale of change? He replaces a guiding assumption of the "old historiography," that what constitutes science could be picked out before the fact, with what he identifies as the basic insight of the new historiography, viz., the "attempt to display the historical integrity of that science in its own time" (Kuhn 1962/2012, 3). Kuhn translates that into identifying the community of scientists at a given time:

> Each of them [scientific revolutions] necessitated the *community's* rejection of one time-honored scientific theory in favor of another incompatible with it. (6; emphasis mine)
>
> Competition between segments of the scientific *community* is the only historical process that ever actually results in the rejection of one previously accepted theory or in the adoption of another. (8; emphasis mine)
>
> Again, *many of my generalizations are about the sociology or social psychology of scientists*; yet at least a few of my conclusions belong traditionally to logic or epistemology. (8; emphasis mine)
>
> *Both normal science and revolutions are, however, community-based activities. To discover and analyze them, one must first unravel the changing community structure of the sciences over time.* A paradigm governs, in the first instance, not a subject matter but rather a group of practitioners. (179; emphasis mine)

In each of these quotes, the added emphasis falls on the fact that in the end Kuhn sees the locus of activity in terms of communities of practitioners, the bearers of a tradition.

It is important to note here that my discussion leaves entirely open the question of how to account for such communities. Kuhn himself emphatically rejects "externalist" or sociological accounts (see esp. discussion in Wise 2016, 37–40). In this respect, I would emphasize that the degree of alleged incommensurability does not have to be as radical as Kuhn claims in *SSR*. The view that Galison (1997, 2010) elaborates suffices for the account given here. As Galison (2010, 30) remarks, "We are getting nowhere if we start with the idea that there is a pure, stable, transcendental 'nature' of physics, chemistry, biomedicine, or mathematics." Galison's (1997, 782) proposal to "historiographically and philosophically" account for the disunity of science by an intercalated narrative suffices for purposes of requiring an essentially narrative explanation for what passes for normal science.

Kuhn's work thus shifts historiographic focus from the methodological proscriptions thought to underwrite the development-by-accumulation view to those community practices instrumental in forming and re-forming who counts as a scientist. His broadsides regarding scientific education represent just one part of his larger concern with the dynamics of what makes for a community of scientists.[4] "[The practitioners of this new historiography] insist upon studying the opinions of that group and other similar ones from the viewpoint . . . that gives those opinions the maximum internal coherence and the closest possible fit to nature. . . . By implication, at least, these historical studies suggest the possibility of a new image of science" (Kuhn 1962/2012, 3). Does this "reduce" the notion of community to some nonempirical will-o'-the-wisp? Hardly. The philosophically significant point is that nothing external to that community and its activities—no transhistorical account of science, no ahistorical demarcation of science from nonscience—can now be used to specify what makes for normal science. Precisely this shift of focus holds the promise for transforming the image of science.

This sets (or perhaps I should say resets) the problem. For narrating a history of science (or of reason) that is not also a history of Science (or of Reason) proves to be a tricky matter indeed. In particular, Kuhn's quicksilver view of science foists on him a severe rhetorical challenge. What remains for a history of science to be a history of? Kuhn's awareness of the rhetorical challenge—What does a history of science now take as its object?—pushes him to fashion a novel answer: how a certain type of community constitutes what counts as science.

As a result, the meaning of 'science' comes to depend on specifying a community of practitioners of a certain sort, but where the factors that constitute the community in its turn cannot trace to some historically prior or abstract definition or delimitation of what counts as science. Like histories of biological adaptations, what proves adaptive as a "scientific" strategy comes to be known only retrospectively. But quite unlike cases in evolutionary biology, that which adapts—the community of scientists—does not itself represent a clear analog to biological organisms or systems. Like the proverbial ship of Theseus, criteria of continuity prove distressingly elusive.

As already noted, *SSR* arguably manifests the suggested characteristics of a narrative given a minimalist and liberal sense of that term. Indeed, Kuhn's title, *The Structure of Scientific Revolutions*, can be read as adumbrating a narrative sentence. For scientific revolutions in Kuhn's sense can be identified only retrospectively, i.e., upon their successful completion. Otherwise it could not be said that a revolution took place. Thus, for example, to maintain that the discovery of oxygen presages the chemical revolution involves all of the familiar issues that arise with narrative sentences, since inter alia the term "oxygen" can be applied only retrospectively to whatever Scheele or Lavoisier or Priestley thought he had isolated. And as Kuhn (1962/2012, 54) maintains, "This pattern of discovery raises a question that can be asked about every novel phenomenon that has ever entered the consciousness of scientists." Working from a very different perspective, Friedman (2001, 101; emphasis mine) also identifies a retrospective stance as a critical element in understanding scientific change and development: "Now the relationship set up between succeeding conceptual frameworks by this type of inter-paradigm convergence is . . . a retrospective one. *It is only from the point of view of the new framework that the earlier framework can be seen as a special case.*" So there exists at least a prima facie basis for thinking that all discussions of normal science, revolutionary science, and related scientific discoveries state truths retrospectively revealed regarding earlier times. These require narrative sentences to express. And since the events named in these sentences come in no standardized format, any explanation of them must have narrative form essentially.

Reading *SSR* as providing an essentially narrative explanation requires identifying a narrative sentence as explanandum. A temptation looms large to formulate any proposed explanandum in terms of an abstract characterization, such as "the image of science." The temptation arises because of course Kuhn announces in his first sentence that history ought to exercise such a transformation on the then received understanding. But that result constitutes a lemma, so to speak, with respect to what I have identified as the book's main shift in historiographic focus, viz., that "each scientific revolution alters the historical perspective of the community that experiences it" (Kuhn 1962/2012, xliii). In other words, such revolutions alter who counts as conducting rational empirical inquiry. Kuhn certainly appreciates that what underwrites the development-by-accumulation view consists of a notion of a timeless (or nearly so) account of scientific method, and that this method in turn prescribes and proscribes what passes as rational inquiry. That fight over who does science and who does not in the end turns out to be a dispute about who acts rationally and who does not. "However obscurely presented, my own position has from the start been that the choice between theories (and also the identification of anomalies, a process which raises similar problems) has to be made by a very special sort of community; otherwise there would be no science. . . . Without such values the community's decisions would be different, and something other than science would be the result" (Kuhn 1970, 146). *SSR* thus narrates, as Alan Richardson (2002) so nicely puts it, a history of reason itself. But, one must add, Kuhn offers a decidedly non-Hegelian history of reason.

As I read him, Kuhn stresses the historical contingency of the meaning of "scientific" and its cognates, and that this will be why any history of such an "extended episode" of changes simply cannot be "additive." The conjunction of each true statement in narrative sentence form again will be inconsistent with the textbook view of science and the models of theory change that Kuhn opposes (see Kuhn 1962/2012, 53; see also 55–56).

CHAPTER 6

The textbook image has that community as constituted derivatively, by reference to some prior and historically independent standard. Scientists become scientists by virtue of instantiating that standard. But Kuhn detaches that which constitutes a community of science from any timeless standard. One can even ignore here claims that so-called paradigms serve as replacements for the explanatory work presumed done by rules, methods, and the like. All that matters for purposes of historicizing the notion of science involves the fact that identifying what science is for Kuhn cannot happen until and unless one identifies what counts as normal science at a given time. What will emerge as normal science cannot be predicted on the basis of what passed previously as such. Until the proverbial dust from a revolution settles, no clear view can be had regarding what counts as normal science.

Kuhn thus argues that historical study reveals that methods and much else alter with each "revolutionary" change of theory, and so who gets to count as a scientist must be explained in some other way (recall, e.g., Kuhn 1962/2012, 179). That other way can only be by historical reconstruction, for nothing else remains as a basis for assessing who does science at a particular time.

Returning to the question of the explanandum, the variant of "each scientific revolution alters the historical perspective of the community that experiences it" that expresses the appropriate narrative sentence commensurate with Kuhn's historiography would read:

> NS [=Narrative Sentence]: Each scientific revolution began with anomalies and a crisis that motivated a *community's* rejection of one time-honored theory in favor of another incompatible with it. (Compare: "Each of them [scientific revolutions] necessitated the community's rejection of one time-honored scientific theory in favor of another incompatible with it" [Kuhn 1962/2012, 6]).

So phrased, this adds a truth about a specific group to however many points in time historians retrospectively identify as experiencing such a change.[5] For the beginning of a revolution can be identified only when it has ended, an end marked by its successful replacement of the previous standard for normal science. NS references what a later time reveals (a successful revolution) in order to be able to specify truths about an earlier time (e.g., the point at which the successor-to-be was introduced). NS requires a narrative explanation, i.e., a sequencing of events that details a dynamic that begins with challenges to community beliefs, recounts those scientific disputes that result, and concludes by showing how a community resolves those disputes by coalescing around an alternative theory.

It might be objected that the model explanandum sentence is analytic as stated, and so hardly in need of explanation. The term "revolution" means, that complaint would go, that which leads to a community's rejection of one theory in favor of an incompatible alternative. But this misses the critical point that what counts as a scientific revolution must also identify what counts as science before and after. As has already been argued in chapter 4, forging a narrative for an "event" that proves to be widely dispersed both geographically and temporally and includes a multitude of human as well as nonhuman "actors" (e.g., technological or other material innovations) poses no principled obstacle. Thus, the meaning of "scientific" in the sentence will depend on the details peculiar to each case.

Kuhn's interest in community building here thus functions in the service, as he notes, of answering questions that "belong traditionally to logic or epistemology." In this regard, he cuts the rhetorical knot that seemingly tied his narrative to a nonexistent subject by boldly making "science" (or, perhaps, "natural science") synonymous with whatever counts as normal science, but with the proviso that normal science must always be indexed to a time and a set of like-minded practitioners. For now what makes for "science," and so "scientists" and so a "community of rational inquiry" cannot be identified except relative to whatever passes for normal science. Nothing "in the abstract" answers to the term otherwise, and so nothing in the abstract answers ahistorically to any query about what science is. What makes for normal science cannot be separated from the relevant community. Nothing else exists to anchor any putative history of science.

Kuhn's "historiographic revolution" has nothing to do with finding something new in the archives. A type of cognitive dissonance led prior historians to impose a continuity that Kuhn claims is absent. He understands this quite well. This is why the narrative of *SSR* pivots on key instances of theory choice. Kuhn (1962/2012, 8) registers an acute awareness of the fact that he will be charged with ignoring accepted distinctions between, on the one hand, descriptive accounts and, on the other hand, interpretive and normative statements. And in fact he clearly self-consciously problematizes the descriptive/normative distinction. For only by relentlessly redescribing through his narrative how what passes for science changes and develops does he succeed in historicizing that notion. As he puts the matter, "By shifting emphasis from the cognitive to the normative functions of paradigms, the preceding examples enlarge our understanding of the ways in which paradigms give form to the scientific life. . . . In learning a paradigm the scientist acquires theory, methods, and standards together, usually in an inextricable mixture"

(108–9). Kuhn constructs a new mosaic from pieces already familiar to historians before he came on the scene.

An exchange that Kuhn has with Hempel proves particularly illustrative of Kuhn's awareness of his need to elide any descriptive/normative distinction. Kuhn (2000, 208–9) registers Hempel's "apparent concern with which I switch from descriptive to normative generalizations, and he has repeatedly wondered whether I quite see the difference between explaining behavior, on the one hand, and justifying it, on the other." Hempel puzzles as to why a descriptive statement regarding the desiderata for determining a good theory—those that promote "an increasingly comprehensive, systematically organized, world view that is explanatory and predictive" (Kuhn 2000, 210, quoting Hempel)—should be taken as justifying a theory in other than a "near trivial" way (Hempel's phrase). However, Kuhn then remarks, "Hempel is less satisfied than I with this approach to the problem of the rationality of theory choice. He refers to it as 'near trivial' . . . apparently because it rests on something very like a tautology, and he finds it correspondingly lacking in the philosophical bite one expects from a satisfactory justification of the norms for rational theory choice" (210). Yet inasmuch as it is those models of theory choice that offer ahistorical standards that Kuhn criticizes, Hempel's complaint misses the very point Kuhn takes to be at issue.[6]

Kuhn thus turns to directly challenging the suggestion that describing the relevant criteria of theory choice will be "near trivial." Indeed, identifying and "describing" those criteria turn out to be the central historiographic issue: "If norms are to be derived from a description of the essential aspects of science . . . then the choice of the description that serves as premise for the near-trivial approach itself requires justification which neither of us appears to provide" (Kuhn 2000, 210–11). In short, in order to answer any question of which norms to endorse, one first has to answer the question of how properly to describe what counts as science, or scientific activity. But this of course assumes precisely what Kuhn challenges, viz., some stable notion of what science is, and so nonhistorical access to identifying so-called norms of science.[7]

Against Hempel's suggestion that Kuhn's view is "near trivial," Kuhn (2000, 211; emphasis mine) has no choice but to (re)assert his counter-narrative: "I shall sketch an argument suggesting that *a particular sort of descriptive premise requires no further justification and that the near-trivial approach itself is therefore deeper and more fundamental than Hempel supposes.*" What "particular sort" of descriptive premise does Kuhn have in mind here? "If I am right, the descriptive premise of the near-trivial approach exhibits, within the language used to describe human actions, two closely related characteristics that I have previously insisted are essential features also of the language used to describe natural phenomena" (211). The first feature concerns the sort of linguistic holism that Kuhn takes from Quine and Wittgenstein: "The first characteristic is one I have recently been calling 'local holism.' Many of the referring terms of at least scientific languages cannot be acquired or defined one at a time but must instead be learned in clusters" (211). From this he notes that a second characteristic follows. Within those terms so acquired, some will be more central to the web and others will lie at the periphery. All, that is, are revisable, but some cannot be changed without in effect sacrificing many or most of the others. Kuhn illustrates this using Newton's second law (212). Going back to Kuhn's remark about the language used to describe human actions, describing actions as scientific or not will depend on learning how to master such center-periphery distinctions.

Friedman (2001, 53) likewise emphasizes that responding to "the issue of conceptual relativism arising in the wake of Kuhn's own historiographical work" as primary among the problems that Kuhn's work raises and that remain to be resolved: "What is controversial, rather, is the further idea that the scientific enterprise thereby counts as a privileged model or exemplar of rational knowledge of—rational inquiry into—nature." Hacking (2012, xvi–xvii) also points to Kuhn's description of normal science as a perduring element of Kuhn's account: "A lot of scientific readers were a bit shocked [by Kuhn's characterization of normal science], but then had to admit that is how it is in much of their daily work. . . . Nowadays even scientists skeptical of Kuhn's thought about revolutions have great respect for his account of normal science." Disputes about the nature of scientific rationality, in other words, cannot be disentangled from the question of how normal science comes to be normal science.

Thus a basic philosophical reason for tracking what such a community does will be that "scientific behavior, taken as a whole, is the best example we have of rationality" (Kuhn 1970, 144). "Behavior" is the operative term here. Kuhn (2000, 212) explicitly makes this point: "Return now to the near-trivial justification of the norms or desiderata for theory choice, and begin by asking about the people who embody those norms. What is it to be a scientist? What does the term 'scientist' mean?" In line with the points just made, Kuhn maintains that what it means to be a scientist or to do science can be ascertained only by learning how those terms for communities of users contrast to other terms in its near linguistic vicinity, e.g., humanist or artist: "One recognizes a group's activity as scientific (or artistic, or medical) in part by its resemblance to other fields in the same cluster and in part by its difference from the activities belonging to other disciplinary clusters. . . . The name of disciplines thus label taxonomic categories, several of which must, like the terms 'mass' and 'force,' be learned together" (213). In short, who counts as a scientist, and what counts as doing science, presuppose a particular taxonomy. "Though a given sample of activity can be referred to under many descriptions, only those cast in this vocabulary of disciplinary characteristics permit its identification as, say, science; for that vocabulary alone can locate the activity close to other scientific disciplines and at a distance from disciplines other than science" (214). And, of course, how this taxonomy applies itself depends on social factors: "One can no more decide for oneself what 'science' means than what science is" (214). That is, what one describes extends well beyond a mere characterization of linguistic conventions.

As Kuhn (2000, 214) puts it, "Rather, what is being set aside is the empirically derived taxonomy of disciplines, one that is embodied in the vocabulary of disciplines and applied by virtue of the associated field of disciplinary characteristics." Revolutionary science and normal science thus come to constitute, as Kuhn tells us, complementary notions precisely because the only way to identify each turns out to be by contrasting one with the other. This contrast turns on changes in community practices over a period of time, viz., the transition period that represents the revolution. Both exist only as historical descriptions and not as standardized elements in some larger theoretical frame.

Kuhn's use of taxonomy here goes proxy for deeply embedded intellectual assumptions that demarcate disciplines, and so implicitly science and nonscience. In this sense, what Hempel takes to be a "near trivial" view represents for Kuhn a vast web of cultural assumptions, ones that give sense to a group's form of life.

Kuhn faced an apparent dilemma. The old historiography fashioned a false continuity by crafting a narrative line based on a notion of science as constituted by development-by-accumulation or philosophical fictions regarding scientific method. The new historiography left Kuhn without this as his narrative anchor. *SSR* replaces a notion of science in the abstract with that of concrete communities, but then owes some account of what "binds" this group as a community. Kuhn attempts several different answers—problem-solving, paradigms, gestalts—but each replaces the clear rationale of the old historiography with mechanisms that prove much more difficult to specify. Thus Kuhn reluctantly concludes that he can offer only an "obscure global relationship" to underwrite his narrative. But of course given the narrative sentence that represents his explanandum, a descriptive sequencing is all that can be offered.

As his exchange with Hempel shows, Kuhn appreciates this as well. So while Kuhn the scientist looks for "something more," Kuhn the historian realizes there is nothing more. Thus, his imagined dilemma arises. But the dilemma proves false because given what he sets out to explain, no other strategy but redescription exists. It seems near trivial because it offers no new facts; it yields a deeply nontrivial account because it rearranges the mosaic and presents a startlingly different picture. Science as a historically stable object disappears.[8]

The foregoing thus provides the core of the missing historiography of *SSR* and so the logic of explanation that it instantiates. Each revolution does not constitute some theoretically specified type predictable by laws. As a consequence, any explanation of so-called scientific change, and so of what counts as rational by way of empirical inquiry, will depend essentially on a narrative presentation of the transitional process, i.e., a descriptive sequencing. The narrative sentence that constitutes its explanandum cannot be rephrased into nonnarrative form since what turns out to be a science and to be a revolution emerges only in retrospect. Until the end of that process—one theoretical view replacing another—one cannot know even approximately when it began. There may be strong intuitions that things will change (e.g., Lavoisier's letter), but a revolution names a completed process. The sequencing of events cannot be given a nonnarrative format, and since each revolution is a unique kind of event—e.g., impacts what passes for science in a particular community at a particular time—the event explained will be nondetachable from that narrative.

Earlier I noted that Buchdahl suggests that *SSR* instantiates the historiography it advocates. Buchdahl has this right, but his account lacks any specification of what that historiography happens to be. My analysis has shown how to fill in that lacuna. In order to oppose a narrative one needs a counternarrative, and of course Kuhn supplies just that. He can effectively criticize and so hope to transform the image of science only in that way, since each account has narrative form essentially.

Kuhn provides, then, a highly naturalistic account of what comes to be called at any particular time normal science. It qualifies as naturalistic because it invokes no prior definitions of science and no explanatory factors driving change not subject to empirical check. *SSR offers an essentially narrative explanation because that turns out to be the only form that can accommodate what needs to be explained—how what was not science came to be science.*

Ironically, Kuhn's alternative narrative creates for Kuhn the historian a tremendous rhetorical challenge: How does he write a history of a subject that in effect he argues does not exist as historically continuous? My account shows how he in fact handles this challenge, and in this context why the notion of paradigm plays a notoriously vexed but historiographically inconsequential role. For whether or not "paradigms" offer a solution to the riddle of community building and rebuilding does not matter for Kuhn's transformative claim to be justified, or so I have argued. That strategy requires only a narrative of discontinuities, one in which community practices and membership shift in certain key ways during the transition periods of interest.

By showing how Kuhn's actual narrative cleverly provides a surrogate for the presumed topic of such histories—uses scientists to locate what science is, rather than the other way around—*SSR* qua narrative explanation answers an interesting and important question of why science comes to be as we find it. In crafting this, Kuhn innovatively and simultaneously (as he must) develops (dare I say it) a paradigm for doing histories of science. And as the old saw has it, the rest is history.

7

Methodological Naturalism and Its Consequences

As noted in chapter 1, disputes emanating from the nineteenth century regarding the status of historical explanation turn on a presumed contrast between idiographic as opposed to "legitimate" forms of scientific explanation. Some time around the middle of the twentieth century, the idiographic comes to be recast as narrative, with all the scientific shortcomings imputed to the former being retained by the latter in this terminological change. The preceding chapter shows this supposed contrast to be doubly mistaken. First, at present there exists no generic logical form of scientific explanation from which historical explanation—or, at least, essentially narrative explanations—critically deviates. Second, and more important on my view, those disciplines accorded the status of a science at any particular time require an essentially narrative historical explanation to account for this. Chapter 6 concludes that these two considerations provide compelling reasons for including essentially narrative explanations within any catalog of acceptable explanatory forms formulated by a naturalist. For a naturalist relies on some notion of science in order to characterize or explicate what passes as naturalism in philosophy. And inasmuch as a narrative explanation will be required to help identify what now counts as a science, these will be a part of any such naturalist account.

But perhaps the conclusion to be reached in view of this epistemic situation would be so much the worse for naturalism. For the charge might be that this connection to narrative explanations simply further muddies and obscures a position, i.e., philosophical naturalism, which has no clear or canonical formulation to begin with.

In light of this worry, this chapter addresses what for purposes of my account I take a viable philosophical naturalism to be and how that provides a cogent and unified perspective for the positions taken in this book. The structure of discussion that follows in this chapter will be to begin in part I by providing a general characterization of naturalism as I prefer to understand it (see also Roth 1999a, 1999b, 2006, 2008a). This account, I acknowledge (and typically for Quinean accounts such as my own), confronts three interrelated criticisms. Part I continues by showing how the account of naturalism sketched readily resists two of these challenges—concerns arising from whether naturalism fails because it cannot derive normative recommendations from the descriptive practices of science or founders because the term proves on examination vacuous. I devote part II to rebutting a third criticism, that naturalism proves viciously circular because it uses the sciences to develop an account of scientific norms.

Having argued in parts I and II for an understanding of naturalism that includes narrative explanations as a part and in addition proves immune to some standard criticisms of a naturalist position, part III then addresses the following question: From within this broadened naturalist perspective, one that maintains that there exists no timeless demarcation of what makes for scientific goodness and yet in light of those features of narrative explanation previously identified—nonstandardization, nondetachability, nonaggregativity—how can one proceed in evaluating narrative explanations? The challenge proves especially sharp in light of a much discussed problem within historical theory that I term *the disappearance of the empirical*. This returns to an upshot already noted in earlier chapters, viz., that evaluation of essentially narrative explanation will, ceteris paribus, have to be comparative and done on a case-by-case basis.

I. Why Naturalism Can Be Normative

A concern to understand why the natural sciences succeed where they do and as well as they do has typically prompted their philosophical study. What makes (or was thought to make) the study of the presumed secrets of scientific success philosophical involved a level of generality and the utilization of techniques not themselves part of any particular science. Philosophical naturalists, in contrast, study what passes as science not because they imagine that contemporary science embodies timeless methodological insights that other erstwhile claimants to knowledge do not. Rather, naturalists hypothesize, no techniques of inquiry apart from those that current sciences employ hold any serious promise for offering successful guides to acquiring any empirical knowledge worthy of the name. Philosophers become naturalists once convinced that any explanation of scientific success does not involve factors which themselves cannot be accessed, studied, and explained by a study of these very sciences (see Roth 1999a). The acknowledged contingency of what passes for science at any given moment makes naturalism a dynamic practice, i.e., one that recognizes that what promotes success in inquiry changes and evolves.

Naturalism in epistemology can be characterized negatively by its eschewal of any notions of analytic or a priori truths. Positively, naturalism asserts a normative and methodological continuity between epistemological and scientific inquiry. The techniques endemic to the former are only a subset of the historically received and contingently held norms and methods of the latter.[1]

Naturalists such as Quine are committed to what might be termed *methodological monism*.[2] What marks questions as epistemological for Quine is that they are questions about the processes sustaining and generating scientific beliefs. But he views such questions neither as receiving some distinctively philosophical answer nor as pursued by some special philosophical method. But how, then, critics ask, can a Quinean approach provide epistemological (typically normative) prescriptions?

Since the standards of science themselves fall within the purview of what the sciences examine, philosophical naturalism, as I prefer to think of it, locates all putatively distinctive philosophical (e.g., normative) issues as continuous with and part of what the sciences study. The sciences in turn have no further justification for their ways of proceeding other than what account they provide of their sources and methods.[3] Such is the import of Quine's (1969, 83) "mutual containment" of epistemology within empirical psychology and empirical psychology within epistemology. Insofar as the sciences self-applied can provide an account of how they came to be, the sciences collectively and broadly understood function as a framework for doing epistemology. Insofar as epistemology invokes no standards or procedures alien to scientific inquiry, it resides within science.

Moreover, naturalism bases this refusal to honor any appeals to extrascientific justification for the sciences on studies of the history and philosophy of science, as the previous chapter argues it must. That what goes by the title of "science" shifts need not trouble a naturalist just so long as what the title includes proves an asset in efforts to provide a systematic and integrated account of experience.[4]

Philosophy as a naturalist conceives of it shares with more conventional philosophical approaches a concern to conduct a type of meta-level examination of particular sciences.[5] That is, a philosopher qua naturalist examines, systematizes, and generally seeks to make explicit the rules by which the first-order endeavor proceeds, including those circumstances under which the rules of inquiry themselves might be modified. But a key difference between naturalism so understood and some other philosophical positions in formulating and articulating such matters arises from naturalism's view that in doing this, philosophy has access to no special methods or resources other than those which belong to the disciplines collectively examined. Normative recommendations (including what passes as logical or rational) can only draw from studies of scientific practice broadly conceived and contingently accepted. Moreover, there exists no final resting place, no *summa scientia*.

The demise of positivism as a philosophy of science, and so by extension as a philosophy of social science, did not preordain the rise of naturalism to philosophical prominence in its stead. For naturalists often stand accused of ignoring just those aspects of the social which undid the positivists' efforts to provide general templates for explanation and demarcation. Brian Fay (1984, 542) put the issue succinctly some time back: "Many philosophers of the social sciences who have rejected naturalism have not done so because they saw the natural sciences through positivist lenses. (Think of Schutz, Winch, Taylor, von Wright, Gadamer, Habermas, MacIntyre, Harre and Secord, Levi-Strauss, and Putnam, to name just a few anti-naturalists: none of them are positivists.) Instead, they have rejected naturalism because there is not enough in the natural sciences that is helpful in dealing with the essentially historical, culturally defined, meaningful, mental, and rational character of human phenomena." However, Fay's characterization presumes that "science" must mean all and only "natural science," i.e., inquiry which excludes study of the "meaningful" as he sketches it. But unless history and related disciplines have been denied membership in the club of science for some now unspecified reason, no a priori argument excludes the investigation of meaningful behavior from the realm of what can count as science. As the arguments of the previous chapters suggest, naturalism need make no distinction between sciences hard and soft, or even attempt to demarcate timelessly what science is. History and sociology, inter alia, must be utilized to determine what science was and is.

The term "nature" connotes only the world as our sciences collectively picture it. Naturalism so imagined situates the study of humans, in all their aspects, as of a piece with those methods and theories used to investigate other objects in nature so conceived. This naturalizing approach, as Fay observes above, was considered less plausible when what counted as science seemed inadequate to the task of fully accounting for creatures like us, enculturated beings capable of creating both systems of meaning as well as complex theories of the world. The understanding/explanation divide receives its basic motivation from the thought that explanation requires laws—causal or at least correlational regularities—while social life is marked by localities of reasoning and meaning which do not generalize cross-culturally over time in the requisite ways for a "genuine" scientific explanation. But by freeing itself to embrace a wider range of explanatory forms, as has been argued for in previous chapters, naturalism need not maintain that human beings qua knowledge-producing creatures constitute a sui generis phenomenon, one to be studied only by methods uniquely suited to and tailored for conceptualizing creatures.

In this respect, naturalism can now best be delineated by contrasting it with what it presently *excludes* for purposes of explanation, e.g., supernaturalism—views that the natural world requires for its explanation something not found among its objects and the processes governing their interaction. Naturalism rejects "unexplained explainers," such as certainties about the nature of ordinary experience, not explicable in turn by the sciences themselves. These exclusions prove to be a strength, not a weakness of the position. For it relieves a naturalist of the historically futile attempts to specify what must be, must remain, or cannot become a science. Any demand for such a prior specification of normative frameworks comes to no more than a denial that one be both a philosopher and a naturalist. But why accept that?

Despite the trumpeted "naturalists' return,"[6] the very pervasiveness of the term on the current philosophical scene gives rise to fears that the term has become too polyvocal to be useful or a suspicion that the term has become vacuous. Worries about vacuity tie in part, I suspect, to an absence of a canonical account of philosophical naturalism. Historically, the term connotes more a loose school than to a specific doctrine.[7] This helps fuel concerns that any characterization of naturalism will prove unilluminating for one of two reasons. First, naturalism presumes to derive an "ought" from an "is"—science is descriptive, not prescriptive. Hence, descriptive studies of scientific practices cannot as such justify the evaluative canons embedded in those practices. A second charge, not unrelated to the first, concerns the circularity of using methods of science to justify those methods. This complaint claims that in order to consider science as a *normative* standard, a justification of the norms of science must have an extrascientific rationale. Otherwise, any "proof" of normativity relies on the very methods needed for that proof, i.e., the methods of received science, and so would be patently circular. In this section, I examine the first of these complaints, addressing along the way the charge that the notion of science has been rendered too vague or vacuous to do any interesting philosophical work. The next section examines the circularity charge and disarms it.

How should one say what science is, and so begin to determine whether or not adjudicating normative issues falls within its purview? A dividing line between what naturalists embrace and what they exclude seemed clearer when thinkers had confidence that the "real" sciences and their related methods could be formally demarcated from the proposals of pretenders. In this regard, some attention must be paid to how the notion of science has itself evolved postpositivism in order to appreciate what one endorses if one declares for naturalism.

This question also underlines the concern that naturalism fails to mark out any special ontological or methodological realm because no philosophically principled lines can be drawn between scientific approaches and others, and so no ontological line between the objects of science and others. Erstwhile naturalists might well fear that their doctrine proves empty because the social has so expanded as to include "the realm of science" within its ambit of explanation, and not vice versa. If the sciences form only a motley, so much the worse for any doctrine which seemingly relies by definition on some delineation of science which current accounts fail to provide.

Ironically, this very lack of a philosophically principled demarcation of science from other forms of inquiry does not mark the passing of or threaten vacuity to naturalism but rather has made possible its resurgence and reestablished its relevance. For wresting free what counts as science from formalist shackles to which it had become tied through much of the twentieth century allows for a notion that ranges over the variety of ways humans systematically explore and account for the world as they find it—from physics to history. Better to acknowledge that this notion appears fated to remain contested than to pretend to more determinate knowledge than, in fact, we do or can expect to possess.

It would be a mistake to construe the cut between naturalism and its philosophical Other as rooted in a metaphysics of objects or primary processes. For that would be to make an assumption a naturalist does not, viz., that one can in principle draw some line between what counts and does not as science. Naturalists need not (and, on my view, ought not) be in the business of prescribing in advance what can or cannot be part of the ontology or causal order. In this regard, to claim that there exists, e.g., a normative realm (in logic, in ethics, or wherever) over and above the world science examines simply fails to add to our knowledge, unless one has some special notion of knowledge on offer. Were there to be had some nonstipulative knowledge of these other supposed realms of being, then all would be well. But absent some "physics of the normative," no one knows what one knows and how one knows it for these other realms.

Naturalism in this respect is *not* a philosophical theory of knowledge. Some, to be sure, have tried to make it so. For Quine, as for American naturalists historically, the methods of science include the full panoply of procedures employed in fact-driven research programs in any area of inquiry. As John Herman Randall Jr. (1944, 361) puts it, "The 'new' or 'contemporary' naturalism . . . stands in fundamental opposition not only to all forms of supernaturalism, but also to all types of reductionist thinking which up to this generation often arrogated to itself the adjective 'naturalistic.' . . . [Naturalists agree] that the richness and variety of natural phenomena and human experience cannot be explained away and 'reduced' to something else. The world is not really 'nothing but' something other than it appears to be; it is what it is, in all its manifold variety, with all its distinctive kinds of activity." Quinean naturalism, in particular, demands no strict demarcation criteria of what to count as science or scientific (see Roth 1999a). Nor are there any philosophical-cum-ontological requirements regarding the necessary building blocks of knowledge. Science and logic are conceived from the outset as systems that stand in a dynamic relation to their rules, rules which are in turn chosen for and adjusted to achieve certain ends. Reflexive adjustment of means and ends is just part of what it is to have and maintain such a system.

Over fifty years ago, Abraham Edel mounted a defense of naturalism in ethics germane to this discussion of naturalism as a legitimate source of *normative* insight for the sciences. Edel nicely articulates naturalism's reflexivity regarding its normative commitments. In the quote that follows, imaginatively replace each use of "ethics," "morality," or cognate terms with the appropriate form of the term "science":

> The whole articulation of a morality within a society under given conditions, the problems of change and adjustment within it, require constant valuational activity. We find our commitments as what we are committed to in the specific lines of choice and directions of striving in which we are engaged. Even the major permanent ends we may thus elicit on analysis . . . do not become the objects of isolated independent selection. Their evaluation rests on the whole network of choices and the kind and quality of life to which they commit us.
>
> . . . Mr. [Arthur E.] Murphy seems to me to pose the question almost as if an ethical theory must somehow equip a hypothetical man who holds no values to choose between conflicting values. If he means to eliminate all reference to an existent value-pattern of the self as already settling the moral problem, then he poses an impossible task. The question "What values should I choose if I had no values?" is meaningful only if it asks what others who had values would recommend for a person in my position. All justification is in a matrix of existent values. Scientific method is applicable to values in so far as it provides a way of identifying one's existent values, testing them, and refining or revising them in choice. (Edel 1946, 146–47; see also 144; reference is to Murphy 1945)

Humans have ends important to them, and so have systems, which, hopefully, will abet achieving those ends. If the ends seem to require rules found overly restrictive, one can alter or drop the goal; if a rule does not function well relative to the end in view, one can change the rule. This is as true for science as for ethics.

Questions of what ends one ought to choose, in abstraction from lived experience and human history, are meaningless. For such questions cannot apply to us, or anyone known to us. Barring a satisfactory account of just how norms of justification are somehow summoned from realms beyond time and history, there is then no good reason to believe that a naturalistic perspective impedes epistemology's normative aims (see Turner 2010; Roth 2003, 2016b). Put another way, a naturalist view of science allows science to be normatively reflexive, and so unhindered by a charge that science cannot be both the source of descriptive claims and the source of the modes of evaluation as well—the norms employed in evaluating the claims. Consideration of the methods of science includes, I thus assume, those standards with which scientists now work. Limiting examination to the announced results—the products, not the processes—represents an arbitrary limit not backed by any sound argument. Yet only by such an arbitrary limit do the norms of science themselves not count as a product of scientific inquiry and so open to systematic explanation and scrutiny.

So-called naturalist positions that promise more by way of normative edification than does Quine (Philip Kitcher or Alvin Goldman come to mind here) invariably fail to justify such normative claims naturalistically (or at all). As Miriam Solomon (1995, 207) quite properly notes with regard to Kitcher's pseudo-naturalism—a position she dubs "legend naturalism"—his "naturalism does no work—no data or theories from psychology or sociology shape the epistemic account—the naturalism is just window-dressing for a previously and independently developed account of scientific rationality."[8] Much the same is true, I have elsewhere argued, regarding Goldman (Roth 1999b).

In short, if any examination of what counts as a science includes accounts of its methodological rationales and not just productive results (descriptions), then the supposed is/ought issue for a naturalist goes away. One now becomes free to ask why a science adopts those norms it does, and for what purposes and under what pressures those standards have evolved. The only reason for not including methods of science as part of a description of that science (and so exclude consideration of norms internal to a science from consideration for further adoption or adaptation) would be because of a lingering assumption that questions about methods were to be answered by discerning what counts as a "scientific method" in some *other* philosophical way. This would have made such sciences already a result of a *prior* methodological sorting. But what one has represents only a disciplinary motley from the start, a result of historically contingent factors.

I propose in this light to examine another common criticism of naturalism, viz., that the characterization of naturalism proves too vague to be of any use.[9] Bas van Fraassen (1996, 172), for example, remarks, "To identify what naturalism is . . . I have found nigh-impossible." But just how vague is the notion of naturalism? No more vague, I suggest, than our ability to catalog the methods of science. Naturalism, moreover, does not yoke what counts as science to some philosophical characterization. It is ironic, then, to find philosophers such as van Fraassen making continued references to "science" as if they knew exactly what that means, and yet complaining all the while about the vagueness of naturalism. It proves perfectly consistent with and appropriate to a naturalist approach to accept as a science what counts in the moment as such and then to adapt and alter one's naturalism as disciplinary statuses evolve.

In sum, then, naturalism is not a *philosophical* theory; it is empirical through and through, from its conception of logic to its conception of methods to what even to count as science. Naturalism so conceived is untainted by prior philosophical commitments to reduction or to a hierarchy of sciences. As argued in previous chapters and above, naturalism will evolve in tandem with changing conceptions of what to count as science. No area of belief stands aloof from alteration or emendation. Even the preference for naturalism itself is result-driven. Should some approaches other than those that now pass as sciences prove more efficacious in furthering our goals, the commitment to naturalism itself would then be jettisoned. There is no more vagueness to the notion of what naturalism is than there is to collectively cataloging what the methods of the sciences themselves are. There is no more an obstacle to examining, emending, or excluding norms within a naturalistic approach than there is in any self-critical scientific approach. Which is to say, there is none at all.

II. Naturalism, Empiricism, and Circularity

Few epistemological doctrines seem to fit the sciences more readily than does empiricism, taken as a philosophical doctrine about evidence, and naturalism, understood as developed in part I. Empiricism explains how scientific theories connect to the world; naturalism proposes how to determine optimal procedures for learning about the world. But a fundamental problem appears to attach to these doctrines. For the very type of knowledge these philosophical doctrines purport to support and clarify turns out to be implicated in supporting and clarifying empiricism and naturalism themselves. Examining this threat of circularity and its consequences leads, I suggest, to reconceptualizing the status and role of philosophical inquiry vis-à-vis scientific inquiry and empirical knowledge.

Because Quine's writings have decisively influenced two lines of debate within epistemology generally and the relation between epistemology and science in particular—holism and naturalism, respectively—his account provides a convenient basis for determining in what respects empiricism remains epistemologically fundamental as an account of scientific knowledge naturalistically conceived.

In what follows, I examine lines of argument drawn from Quine's (1969) "Epistemology Naturalized," arguments that systematically strip away attempts to justify science independently of science. In developing this reading, I provide an answer to the circularity charge broached at the beginning of this chapter. But this line of response engenders in turn key problems with regard to specifying what to count as empirical, and so as evidence for and against individual scientific claims. Assessing some consequences of this, and so consideration favoring a comparative account of explanation evaluation urged in earlier chapters, will be examined in part III.

By way of approaching the charge that a naturalistic justification of scientific norms must be unacceptably circular, consider in this regard the reference to "the whole of natural science" from "Epistemology Naturalized" (written circa 1968) in light of the context of an earlier use of that phrase in "Two Dogmas of Empiricism" (Quine 1951; written circa 1950–51). In the latter case, Quine urges a vast enlargement of the unit assessed as having (or lacking) empirical significance. In the former, he declares for naturalism, i.e., treating epistemological questions as questions within science, and so using science to account for how humans manage to acquire such knowledge. By implication, the notion of empirical significance must itself be subject to naturalistic scrutiny along with all other aspects of scientific method and theorizing. Unpacking just why Quine makes use of so vague a phrase reveals just how radically his critique of empiricism forces a reconception of the relation between epistemology and the philosophy of science. In particular, I suggest, terms such as "empiricism" no longer hold promise of epistemological insight regarding the basis for scientific knowledge. Rather, a naturalist gives epistemic priority to empiricism because one first chooses to accept science as the best systematized account of knowledge. From this perspective one then limits or specifies what can count as evidence. Notions of science and of evidence, in other words, evolve and develop together. *Empiricism simply ceases to have standing as an epistemological doctrine apart from science as currently conceived. It becomes, rather, a consequence of naturalism (and pragmatism), a thesis about the nature of scientific evidence maintained on the basis of scientific investigation.*

Toward the end of "Two Dogmas," Quine offers as his "countersuggestion" to the analytic-synthetic distinction that the measure of epistemic goodness be taken as the "whole of science." But how is this to be understood? For in his phrase "the unit of empirical significance," the term "empirical significance" should be understood as "meaningful in terms of experience." Note that the problematic terms here—the questions raised by the phrase—involve the terms "unit" and "empirical." For a unit to be a unit, it must be bounded. So, the first question to be answered would be: What bounds or determines the unit tested for empirical significance? The second question concerns the epistemic work to be done by an appeal to a notion of the empirical. Traditionally, the job of the empirical was to filter out the supposed core of an evidential basis for the assessment of knowledge claims. For it seems as if there must be a way of avoiding situations where the unit under test also certifies as appropriate the elements used to test it. *For 'empirical significance' to be of epistemic moment, a notion of experience independent of the unit being assessed must be carved off.* Otherwise the unit under test certifies as appropriate the elements used to test it. And if the unit of empirical significance turns out to be strongly implicated in determining that which supposedly tests it, the empirical forfeits any claim to epistemic advantage.[10]

The allusion to the "whole of science" suggests that any attempted epistemic assessment of a single belief implicates all those beliefs comprising that theory to which a sentence belongs. For how what go by the label "beliefs" (sentences held true) and how what goes by the label "experience" (perception) fit together can be logically accommodated in any number of ways. Attempts to differentiate structurally among types of linguistic items and to identify a logical and evidentiary fit between the linguistic and the nonlinguistic ultimately reveal that there exists no such logically neat interrelationship between how the world works on us and what we think about it. In this regard, attempts to distinguish between, e.g., some type of limited holism and a more global form presuppose an ability to mark off one type of theory (e.g., those in physics) from other types (those in economics). But our beliefs do not come so neatly packaged, and their areas of possible interdependence or independence so clearly marked.

Reflections on the logic of science, the history of science, and the sociology of science all confirm this point, each in its own way. (Let me be clear here that what I take to be called into question involves a notion of the empirical or experience that can be made sense of as epistemically basic independently of appeal to science.) But why then believe that there exists any epistemic leverage in appeals to the empirical?

The two questions—the unit of empirical significance and the content of the notion of the empirical—moreover, prove deeply interrelated. For a variety of scientific theories (broadly construed, so as to include the social sciences) serves to determine just which experiences count and under what conditions they count as relevant for assessment purposes. Science ultimately delimits, e.g., how many senses there are, how they function, and so what even the senses properly so-called could provide qua evidence. Both questions give rise to worries about how diffuse the notion of the empirical becomes once it cannot be restricted to terms or simple statements.

One of the most philosophically unsettling consequences of epistemic assessments so conceived involves the many ways of accommodating experience to theory. If notions of sense and sensing themselves require scientific investigation in order to articulate the respects in which they support science, then the very empirical base to which science appeals becomes one best understood through science. Thus, in charting how the "unit question" and the corresponding "experience question" evolved to something like their present forms, an understanding emerges regarding how these notions in turn affect what the terms "epistemology" and "science" connote. Unlike empiricists of old, Quine does not look to the notion of experience to clarify those of thought or belief: all three, he maintains, stand in need of clarification. Quine (1981, 184) links the notions of meaning, thought, belief, and experience as kindred concepts in the sense that "they are in equal measure very ill suited for use as instruments of philosophical and scientific clarification and analysis. If someone accepts these notions outright for such use, I am at a loss to imagine what he can have deemed more in need of clarification and analysis than the things he has thus accepted." In particular, by conceiving of the notion of empirical knowledge as of a piece with the articulated theorizing of experience that sciences provide, the suggestion regarding the unit of empirical significance made in "Two Dogmas" turns out to imply the "reciprocal containment" of science and epistemology proposed in "Epistemology Naturalized."

Ironically, this relocation of empiricism as a position maintained from *within* science breaks down whatever divides may be thought to remain between philosophy of science and science studies. Philosophy of science and science studies were distinguished primarily by the elements that were cited in the explanans for a given explanandum event (e.g., theory change, theoretical commitment, confirmation). Typically, philosophers downplay and science studies researchers emphasize how the practice of science involves extrascientific customs and mores (see Zammito 2004; Novick 1988).

I suggest that those problems that led, in the first place, to the expansion of the unit of empirical significance and the theorizing of the empirical makes moot those disputes. What counts as experiences and how to assess their effects (e.g., social psychology vs. neurology) will depend in part on the science at issue. For while socially mediated experiences cannot, in principle, be excluded from epistemological consideration, attempts to map those experiences to individual beliefs remain subject to all the usual indeterminacies. In this respect, basic problems inherent in the epistemological project on the philosophical side—bounding the unit of experience and theorizing the empirical—emerge, like the return of the repressed, in efforts to provide a "social epistemology."

Consider, for example, how accounts offered by Galison (1987) differ from what one finds in Pickering (1984). Both of these accounts, moreover, appear to be relatively internal histories—they do not look much beyond the scientific communities. But Galison emphasizes how debate in a scientific community becomes settled by citing the reasons which prevailed, while Pickering emphasizes unacknowledged concerns—for instance, the need to be able to recycle expertise and yet have a more viable theory—as leading scientists to favor one view over another. These approaches can be contrasted in turn with, for example, Schaffer and Shapin (1985), who take a yet wider view of the factors determining one's theoretical preferences. Background beliefs regarding social status or religious affiliation might influence which individual beliefs count or how they count. In addition, which beliefs might be open to revision will be determined by perceptions regarding how those beliefs connect to religious or political views deemed important. Consideration such as these makes the "unit of empirical significance" culture-size.

In saying this, I acknowledge some discomfort in moving from theories conceived as linguistic entities to cultures so conceived. As I indicate in what follows, the question of the relevant "unit" being assessed has become increasingly diffuse and problematic. I find no general answer to the question of how to bound or otherwise specify the unit in which to embed the epistemic evaluation of a specific knowledge claim.

Thus, I take there to be a type of affinity between, on the one hand, the alleged independence of epistemology and a bottom–up strategy, as opposed to, on the other hand, conceiving of epistemology as pursued from within a scientific account of the world. Epistemology-within-science proceeds top-down, that is, by asking how, given an explanatory

CHAPTER 7

theory and its justificatory norms provisionally accepted, to encompass within it an account of beliefs their acquisition and their legitimation. Naturalizing epistemology by making it part of science exemplifies this top-down strategy. Bottom-up strategies take an ultimately dogmatic stance (knowledge begins here), while top-down strategies allow for a pragmatic approach to judging a theory's merit. From the standpoint of examining the relationship between philosophy of science and epistemology, those strategies yield very different results. Viewed bottom-up, justification consists only of inferential links. Traditional puzzles here concern justifying generalizations—typically, laws; related epistemic problems involve articulating the logic that connects evidence to experimental tests, experimental tests to theories, and the logical connections that exist among those statements comprising a scientific theory. Epistemic evaluation involves justified inference and nothing else.

Quine (1995, 15) takes science to be about trying to construct a "systematization of our sensory intake." The initial systematization comes with learning the language one first learns to speak, and of the objects and events about which we communicate with others. The "reciprocal containment" of epistemology and natural science takes epistemology to be a part of an attempt to systematize experience. But, though only an aspect of the scientific enterprise, epistemology so conceived contains the scientific enterprise, since all of it results in the end from shared stimulations. Quine's reconceptualization of knowledge still takes knowledge to be the best systematic account for beliefs held, but takes science to constitute this.

Quine's very liberal view of what to count as science can be adopted here without epistemological loss. For by taking science to be just the extensional equivalent of those empirically oriented disciplines and their collective methods, one does not assume the burden of discerning deep relations between, for example, physics and history, on the one hand, while, on the other hand, one can criticize freely those forms of inquiry, for instance, astrology, that might assume some of the techniques of science (measurement, prediction) but without the desired results. The appeal to the empirical remains one that the sciences themselves endorse, but it may be jettisoned if results warrant that conclusion. Should a Ouija board prove a better predictor than physics, it would be rational to abandon physics and go with the Ouija board.

Quine's conceptualization of the relation of epistemology and science proves deeply ironic. Empiricism requires science to explicate that notion—experience—on which, in turn, to base confidence in science. A further irony involves the fact that the proposed unit of empirical significance—"the whole of science"—cannot itself be tested qua unit. So confidence in the whole of science cannot be licensed in this way—the way in which science supposedly issues such license.

Empiricism disappears as a supposed foundation for scientific theory. It retains unquestioned importance with regard to theories that accept more or less congruent accounts of what passes as a matter of fact. Reflecting back on specifically historical accounts in this regard, and given characteristics of essentially narrative explanations previously detailed, assessing the goodness of such accounts will typically not be settled by appeal to agreed upon facts. This point has been evident throughout discussions in this book, but especially in light of chapters 3 and 4. To speak of the disappearance of the empirical, then, acknowledges how the notion of what counts as a fact has become incorporated into a more general account of theory (see Zammito 2004).

III. The Disappearance of the Empirical and Its Methodological Consequences

I conclude this chapter by reflecting on how those explanations I have identified as distinctive of historical explanation—essentially narrative explanations—and the naturalistic view of knowledge sketched in the first two parts effectively force a comparative standard on the evaluation of historical explanation. This section does this by examining how the notion of experience as evidence functions in one important line of debate in historiography/philosophy of history. The focus shall be on the presumably crucial role some notion of the empirical plays in the *assessment* of knowledge claims. For, in a way in which I hope the discussion below makes vivid and compelling, no appeal to "facts" will in all likelihood be able to settle such debates.

Problems arise primarily because, for reasons developed in parts I and II, theories become implicated in constituting the very facts then marshaled as evidence on behalf of the way it portrays the world to be. Construing theories as discursive formations replaces construing them as sources of testable hypotheses or even as narratives liable to certain canons of evidence. The significance of 'the empirical' disappears on the assumption that theories either determine what counts as experience or explain away any apparently discordant evidence. What comes to be termed 'empirical' can readily become instead an artifact of theorizing. The empirical so understood then ceases to have a determinate function in the assessment of theories under consideration.[11]

One consequence of this, developing from the so-called linguistic

CHAPTER 7

turn that arose in historiography, has been the suggestion—more assumed than made explicit—that the analysis of meaning somehow replaces or supplants that played by evidence qua fact (see Spiegel 2013). The phrase "analysis of meaning" as used in this context and throughout my discussion primarily concerns how perception comes to be categorized, and so connects to discussions of (primarily Goodmanian) issues of categorization and category formation in earlier chapters. Somewhat ironically, as discussion of Scott's work below indicates, those who wish to so theorize the empirical nonetheless write as if some stable, determinate notion of meaning emerges unscathed from the rubble of the positivist edifice. But, as I argue, as goes any philosophically defensible notion of verificationism, so goes any determinate conception of meaning. In philosophy as elsewhere, one confronts Santayana's insight that those who cannot remember the past are condemned to repeat it. In this regard, celebrations of the demise of positivism evince a sad failure to comprehend the simultaneous demise as well of assumptions about determinacy of meaning some theorists employ and hold dear.

Throughout this book I have been concerned to examine how debates about historical explanation spin off, directly or indirectly, from concerns dating from nineteenth-century disputes with regard to how historians establish connections in the absence of regularities or laws that license them (see esp. Patton 2015). Narrativist models of explanation, I have maintained, share with other accounts of explanation a concern with identifying coherence-making strategies.

So here in a nutshell one has the apparent Scylla and Charybdis of historiography. Coherence results, it appears, either from implicit adverting to law-like regularities which historians have never actually possessed, or by assimilating historical writing to a form of fictionalizing—events connect as a result of the "tropic of discourse" a historian, wittingly or not, chooses to employ. Debates between narrativists and philosophers concerned with explanation, as noted in chapter 1 and throughout, have tended to focus on whether or not narratives provide a licit type of connectedness, a rationally evaluable form for the licensing of inferential/causal connections. As Novick (1988) suggests, working historians react to this epistemological unpleasantness largely by ignoring it.

Ironically, even as the grip of the positivist model fell away from the notion of explanation, debates over the character of narrative explanation within historical theory intensified rather than waned. As debate about narrative explanation evolved since the late 1970s, it became an in-house fight between proponents of differing conceptions of narrative. The new critique underscored instead history as a creative endeavor, a writing of fiction rather than a recording of what is (see Spiegel 2013). The coherence given events, the categories used to structure events, and the significance assigned those categories were now taken as impositions—self-conscious or not—of the writer of history. History as literary artifact characterized not simply the text but what the text was about. Because of the emphasis given to narrative devices, those debating these issues talked more of "meaning" than of logic, but, as noted, debates about meaning can best be understood as contested accounts regarding how to categorize experience.

From the 1980s forward, key articles surveying "history of meaning" as it develops within historiography (Spiegel 1990, Toews 1987, Zammito 1993, 2000 are among the most influential) chronicle challenges to received notions of evidence and experience similar to those which arose earlier within philosophy. In this context, John Toews (1987, 885) proposes to understand what taking the "linguistic turn" in historiography implies as a question of which theory of meaning to choose: "The question of whether or not intellectual history should take a linguistic turn involves the preliminary question of which among a variety of linguistic theories of meaning a historian should choose." And the varieties here, as a footnote makes clear, involve distinctly German variants (Gadamer vs. Habermas), with, as always, the French lurking in the wings. The core of this view, however named or renamed, Toews articulates as follows: "Such a commitment would seem to imply that language not only shapes experienced reality but constitutes it, that different languages create different, discontinuous, and incommensurable worlds, that the creation of meaning is impersonal, operating 'behind the backs' of language users whose linguistic actions can merely exemplify the rules and procedures of languages they inhabit but do not control, that all specialized language usages in the culture (scientific, poetic, philosophical, historical) are similarly determined by and constitutive of their putative objects" (882). What passed as experience—e.g., of one's sexual identity, the normal and the abnormal—was itself something to be analyzed, itself a product of time and place.

However, Toews (1987, 882) refuses to embrace an "apocalyptic fear" of the collapse of the edifice of history into the semiological sea. He avers "that, in spite of the relative autonomy of cultural meanings, human subjects still make and remake the worlds of meaning in which they are suspended and to insist that these worlds are not creations ex nihilo but responses to, and shapings of, changing worlds of experience ultimately irreducible to the linguistic forms in which they appear." Put another way, he denies that historical texts become mere literary artifacts by maintaining the autonomy of experiences which can "speak against" texts. This retains, Toews believes, a viable conception of history as a product of a "dialectical unity of and difference between meaning and experience (as all historians must) in the wake of the linguistic turn" (882). He reaffirms the autonomy of history, in this regard, by asserting the independence of experience from the texts discussing it.

Significantly, Toews's sweeping overview of books about the "linguistic turn" includes not only the usual German and French suspects but also debates chronicled by David Hollinger emanating from the historicizing of the philosophy of science often attributed to Thomas Kuhn.[12] It is in his discussions of this more "analytic" account of "post-metaphysical knowledge" that Toews (1987, 904) puts his finger on a core issue: "The notion of general cultural critique is not an adequate basis for public discourse. Because community, discourse, and effective social action are intimately related, the question raised by Hollinger is actually whether consensual communities able to engage in public discourse and direct action can exist or whether consensus on the validity of knowledge and substance of value is always imposed, hegemonic, or repressive." Given the challenges posed to standing accounts of knowledge, Toews asks, on what basis can theories be assessed? If experience becomes the product of theories and not the evidence for them, then scholarly debate seemingly has no fixed point by which to adjudicate disagreements.

The contrast could hardly be starker. Either build your politics on shared knowledge or view knowledge as built on shared politics. The winners not only write history, but also determine what counts as knowledge. But while much hangs in the balance, Toews in 1987 is not quite convinced by his own insistence that a "dialectical unity" can persevere.

Can one provide an account of experience which sees it both as shaped by and shaping beliefs? The philosophical issue finds expression in Kant's apothegm that experience without concepts is blind. For something to even be recognizable by us, it must come in a form which can inhabit what Wilfrid Sellars later calls the space of reasons, i.e., as belonging to a discursive category. So what I shall call a Kantian truism underlies what Toews (1987, 906) rightly worries will be the "new reductionism," viz. "the reduction of experience to the meanings that shape it. [For] along with this possibility, a new form of intellectual hubris has emerged, the hubris of wordmakers who claim to be makers of reality." Before an experience can even enter into the realm of the public—into discourse, as some might say—it has already been conceptualized. But then any proposed separation of evidence/experience and theorizing becomes impossible—one cannot recover whatever was the experiential grist for the conceptual mill.

Whatever the latest theoretical fashion might be, the basic philosophical landscape remained unchanged. The thesis of the inseparability of experience and meaning remains firmly in place. Yet what becomes incorporated quite uncritically turns out to be a view of meaning as constituting a *system*, a set of codes with a structure. For example, surveying the poststructuralist scene just three years after the publication of Toews's work, Gabrielle Spiegel (1990, 68) quizzically inquires, "What, then, is the 'real'?" The answer, she finds, is that "what is real are the semiotic codes that govern the representation of life both in writing and in incorporated social structures." In other words, determinate structure attaches not to an unvarnished notion of sensory information, but to whatever structures structure perception—the "semiotic codes."

At this point, even while providing a lucid exposition of positions she opposes, Spiegel joins with Toews to complain about the reduction of reality to categories—meaning.

> What cultural history achieves by this equation of the imaginary and the real within the structures of discourse is a radical foregrounding and reconceptualization of the problem of text and context. If . . . there are no epistemological grounds for distinguishing between them, then it is impossible to create an explanatory hierarchy that establishes a causal relationship between history and literature, life and thought, matter and meaning. The context in which a text is situated is itself composed of constituted meanings . . . and the connections between them are essentially intertextual. It becomes impossible, on this basis, to identify aspects of social, political, or economic life which somehow stand apart from or make up a "reality" independent of the cultural construction which historically conditioned discourses generate; text and context are collapsed into one broad vein of discursive production. . . . To put it at its starkest: it is as if, for cultural history, there are no acts other than speech acts, no forms of being which are not assimilated to textuality and thus made accessible to the workings of the text analogy. (Spiegel 1990, 68–69; see also Spiegel 2013)

It might help to recall here one line of philosophical opposition to Kuhn's *Structure of Scientific Revolutions*. A chief philosophical dogma Kuhn challenged in that work concerned the ability of experiences to falsify a hypothesis and so defeat some favored theory. Critics complained that this deprived accounts of scientific change of a rational basis—e.g., cases where experience spoke against the hypothesis and made it instead into a type of "mob psychology" (Lakatos 1970, 178).[13] It thus appears to be politics all the way down.

The parallels between debates in cultural history in the wake of the various "posts" and in philosophy of science and science studies has not escaped the notice of others. In particular, John Zammito's characterization of the situation within contemporary philosophy of science and its contests with science studies practitioners echoes his own earlier writings on disputes within historiography. Specifically, Zammito in 1993 enters the following complaint against the then "New Historicism": "The notion that texts and agents are determined by structure is one of the unsettling elements in New Historicism that it shares with some older approaches to history. While the old language of determinism [Marxism] . . . has been debunked . . . it is not clear that *cultural system* or *episteme* is being wielded with less cavalier determinism or that either can be more epistemologically accessible than text or agent" (793). Zammito expresses at this juncture an understandable ambivalence regarding just what historians may hope to take away by way of positive advice or guidance from philosophers. With regard to contributions of theories drawn from literature, however, he offers a less generous appraisal:

> The "revenge of literature"—of "theory"—has about it a tincture of megalomania that richly deserves a bit of the irony it lavishes on its own targets.
> History should not be reduced to literature by an absolutist, pantextualist "theoretical" move. Veridicality and coherence are indispensable to the practice of history, but the standards of appraisal are disciplinary, not absolute. (812)

Yet the "absolutist, pantextualist" move against which Zammito protests requires that experience and theory be separated, at least insofar as to allow for an account of how the latter influences the former.

But about a decade later he comes to appreciate that one cannot look to philosophy of science to clarify this key point. For as Zammito himself chronicles, debates here turn out to be caught in a fundamentally similar and unresolved philosophical quandary. He concludes his 2004 survey of the post-Quinean (the "post" here being dated from about 1950 onward) situation in philosophy of science/science studies with a set of complaints about philosophy of science which bear a striking resemblance to his earlier complaints about historiographic theory. Zammito remarks that "some 'theorists' have drawn upon post-positivism to initiate an attack upon the *practice of empirical inquiry itself*" (1; see also Ankersmit 2001). He elaborates this complaint by charging that philosophy of science has become ensnared in "a philosophy of language so 'holistic' as to deny determinate purchase on the world of which we speak. History and sociology of science has become so 'reflexive' that it has plunged . . . [into] an almost absolute skepticism. . . . Hyperbolic 'theory' threatens especially the prospects of learning anything from others that we did not already presume" (Zammito 2004, 274). Clearly, Zammito views the situation as having worsened.

Zammito has something quite right, and something quite wrong, in his complaint here. The wrong point, widely missed, is that there is no unscrambling of how theory and experience mix. But Zammito has just right a related and important insight. Foundational projects should be rejected as philosophical nonstarters. Here it becomes crucial to recall the two defining features widely attributed to positivism, both of which have ceased to have any philosophical standing. One concerns what Quine calls the dogma of reductionism, i.e., the view that each individual belief about the world stands before the tribunal of experience alone. But the other dogma, one that remains alive and well, concerns a belief that conceptual schemes exist as logically determinate structures shaping perceptions. This dogma lives no longer within positivism but within the very view that claims to have overcome the failures of insight to which positivism was prone. Having rejected some notion of experience as determinate or fixed, some self-styled postpositivist thinkers still cling to a notion of theory as providing what experience supposedly cannot, i.e., a fixed or determinate scheme of evaluation. But, or so I shall argue, one has no more entitlement to a determinate notion of theory than to that of experience.

On my account, how philosophical history repeats itself can be brought into focus by looking at the discussion of experience as analyzed in Joan Wallach Scott's (1996) essay, "The Evidence of Experience." Scott's essay remains a key theoretical statement by a historian for historians on the "constructedness" of experience, and so presumably is deeply antifoundational at least in this respect. Since I raise no challenges to the Kantian truism—any information about the world, to count as information, must already be conceptualized—where, then, does someone like Scott go wrong?

To see the problem, consider a running example in Scott's essay concerning gender identity, and in particular identities as a homosexual or a heterosexual. She worries, rightly I would say, about these identities being taken as ahistorical givens. Interestingly, but more problematically, she sketches how the concepts link in a codependent fashion. Why problematically? Well, what determines exactly how two such "identities" (for lack of a better term) precisely relate? Or that there exist just two? By what criteria does one distinguish an 'identity' as a countable unit? The approach to experience Scott takes ultimately deprives her (and those who follow her) even potentially of resources to answer these questions. For note that Scott maintains that historians fail to do justice to their own best practices if such categories qua categories of living in or experiencing the world become taken for granted. Life experiences so understood demand interrogation, not uncritical appropriation.

> To the extent that *this system* constructs desiring subjects . . . it simultaneously establishes them and itself as given and outside of time, as the way things work, the way they inevitably *are*.
>
> The project of making experience visible precludes analysis of the working of this system and of its historicity. Instead, it reproduces its terms. . . . What we do not have is a way of placing those alternatives within the framework of (historically contingent) dominant patterns of sexuality and ideology that supports them. We know they exist but not how they have been constructed. . . . We know that difference exists, but we do not understand it as *relationally constituted*. For that, we need to attend to the historical processes that, through discourse, position subjects and produce their experiences. It is not individuals who have experience but subjects who are constituted through experience. Experience in this definition then becomes not the origin of our explanation, not the authoritative (because seen or felt) evidence that grounds what is known but rather that which we seek to explain, that about which knowledge is produced. . . . This kind of historicizing represents a reply to the many contemporary historians who have argued that an unproblematicized "experience" is the foundation of their practice. It is a historicizing that implies critical scrutiny of all explanatory categories usually taken for granted, including the category of "experience." (Scott 1996, 384–85, 381; emphasis mine)

But then, she goes on to wonder, what would a history which so problematizes the notion of lived experience look like? If an individual's experience should be treated not as something fact-like, and so as evidence for how things really are, but only as itself a product of a complex theoretical process at work behind the proverbial backs of individuals, where should investigation begin to analyze, in turn, why experience has the shape it does?

Notice how Scott's problem about experience assumes what I shall call a Cartesian form. For while we may experience the world in a certain way, she posits the equivalent of a Cartesian evil demon—a person's experience of the world cannot be taken as a reliable guide to knowledge of how the world actually is. For Scott, as for Descartes, experience must be viewed as a source of systematic deception. Descartes's solution—that God is not a deceiver—I assume would not appeal to Scott. But then the problem facing Scott can be understood as an analog to the "Cartesian circle"—how to recover in a non-question-begging way a guide to reliability despite a threat of systematic deception.

Scott does not appreciate the logical box into which she has placed herself. To see this, note the complaint she enters near the start of her essay against what she terms the "conventional historical understanding of evidence." On her account, the conventional view takes the challenge of diversity to require only by way of an answer the collection of yet more points of view, an "enlargement of the picture, a corrective to oversights resulting from inaccurate or incomplete vision" (Scott 1996, 382–83). But she insists that the problem goes well beyond any such nod to inclusiveness. The "evidence as enlargement" view (the sort promulgated, e.g., by television news broadcasts that imagine that simply by soliciting a range of extreme views, somehow balance has been achieved) actually hinders the process of obtaining a critical perspective on the experiences so recorded. For it takes "meaning as transparent, reproduces rather than contests given ideological systems—those that assume that the facts of history speak for themselves" (382–83). The "let every group have its say" view of experience thus only "masks the necessarily discursive character of these experiences" (392), i.e., elides the Kantian truism.

Here Scott enters a criticism, specifically citing Toews, or those (such as Spiegel or Zammito) who would try to prise apart and seek to keep as independent notions both that of experience and its theorization or meaning. But this proclivity on their part, she complains, obscures more than it offers to illuminate. For it leads historians to imagine that they do not actively produce representations:

> This has an effect (among others) of removing historians from critical scrutiny as active producers of knowledge. . . . Inclusiveness is achieved by denying that exclusion is inevitable, that difference is established through exclusion, and that the fundamental differences that accompany inequalities of power and position cannot be overcome by persuasion. . . . It establishes a realm of reality outside of discourse, and it authorizes the historian who has access to it. . . . And yet it is precisely the questions precluded—questions about discourse, difference, and subjectivity as well as about what counts as experience and who gets to make that determination—that would enable us to historicize experience and to reflect critically on the history we write about it rather than to premise our history on it. (Scott 1996, 393–94)

Yet Scott also denies that her account indulges in "a new form of linguistic determinism," just the sort of specter raised by Zammito and others.

But what, then, serves as the analog to experience as a counterpoise to received categories? How, in Harold Garfinkel's great phrase, does one avoid treating people as "cultural dopes," mindlessly inhabiting and acting out the norms of those discursive formations bequeathed them by accident of birth? Scott's apparent answer insists that there exists "conflicts of interpretations" (my phrasing, not hers) which open the way out from cultural dopism.

Treating the emergence of a new identity as a discursive event is not to introduce a new form of linguistic determinism nor to deprive subjects of agency. "*It is to refuse a separation between 'experience' and language and to insist instead on the productive quality of discourse.* Subjects are constituted discursively, but there are conflicts among discursive systems, contradictions within any one of them, multiple meanings possible for the concepts they deploy. . . . Subjects are constituted discursively and experience is a linguistic event (it does not happen outside established meanings), but neither is it confined to a fixed order of meaning" (Scott 1996, 396; emphasis mine). Here, I confess, I find the theoretical tides running fast and high. On the one hand, Scott emphatically maintains the Kantian truism, couched in the language of discursive formations. But, she insists, cultural dopism does not result because these "discursive events" themselves have no determinate structure, indeed, they coexist with other structures.

But now in what space do these discursive structures exist? They have a life independent of any specific individual, but must also reside, to recur to my Cartesian imagery, in the understanding of individuals. Scott appears to echo just this point: "Because discourse is by definition shared, experience is collective as well as individual." Yet she maintains that discourse shapes the individual's understanding. "Experience is a subject's history. . . . Language is the site of history's enactment. Historical explanation cannot, therefore, separate the two." Sitting between the sentences just quoted are the following: "Experience can both confirm what is already known (we see what we have learned to see) and upset what has been taken for granted (when different meanings are in conflict we readjust our vision to take account of the conflict or to resolve it—that is meant by 'learning from experience,' though not everyone learns the same lesson or learns it at the same time or in the same way)" (Scott 1996, 396–97). But this cannot be. Based on what Scott has said, experience comes prefigured. So how can it but fail to confirm and conform? And if it fails to confirm and conform, then what can it mean to say it comes prefigured?

This, by the way, is a standing problem in Kant's account: Just how do experiences get categorized in the way that they do, and what makes it the case that experiences get linked in particular ways? Indeed, a great deal of very interesting social psychological research on concept formation, cognitive dissonance, and the like simply underscores rather than resolves these standing problems regarding how conceptualization proceeds. "Discursiveness" in Scott's sense here names a problem, not a solution.

I do not fault Scott for failing to solve problems Kant bequeathed us. Rather, my purpose is to question, in the spirit in which I began, just where the linguistic moves leave us. Unlike Toews or Zammito, I do not want to affirm the "really real" by thumping on the lectern or praising the standards practitioners embrace. Rather, granting as I would a full measure of credibility to the philosophical critiques of empiricism, positivism, etc., the question remains whether the friends of discursiveness in the end have any more satisfactory notions to put in its stead. Note what Scott (1996, 397) herself says: "The kind of reading I have in mind would not assume a direct correspondence between words and things, confine itself to single meanings, or aim for the resolution of contradiction. It would neither render process as linear nor rest explanation on simple correlations or single variables. Rather, it would grant to 'the literary' an integral, even irreducible, status of its own. To grant such status is not to make 'the literary' foundational but to open new possibilities for analyzing discursive productions of social and political reality as complex, contradictory processes." She repeats this point a page later, toward the close of her essay: "The question of representation . . . is a question of social categories, personal understanding, and language, all of which are connected and none of which are or can be [a] direct reflection of the others. . . . [The] social and the personal are imbricated in one another and . . . both are historically variable. The meanings of the categories of identity change and with them the possibilities for thinking the self. . . . [The categories] are discursive productions of knowledge of the self, not reflections either of external or internal truth" (398). But what now can be made of talk of "production" or even "analysis"? What produces; what exists to analyze? The relation of linguistic items to one another and to what about the world (dare I say experience?) they make available to humans through discourse no longer can be given any clear sense. Concepts do not operate algorithmically on what happens at our nerve endings to synthesize these into discursive events; concepts do not link regularly or tightly to determine how one infers meanings from one to the other.

I have offered two different characterizations of how to think philosophically about how approaches that emphasize the analysis of meaning embrace a key failing they hoped to transcend. But as goes foundationalism, so goes the analysis of meaning. As Quine taught us a half-century ago, the two dogmas are at root identical. If one could, in fact, determine just how concepts interrelate by some form of abstract analysis—analysis of meaning—one would then know what experience contributes to the account. It would be that which mere logic did not. But without a way to identify what experience specifically adds to understanding, no lines of analysis of meaning exist either.

We have words, and the words get used, but how the system works cannot be ascertained by abstraction. In this regard, the "linguistic turn" in cultural history recapitulates positivism, albeit as "positivism of the mental," or, alternatively, an account where notions such as "semiotic code" supposedly do the work to have been done by translating scientific theories into the formalism of predicate logic. Yet appeal to codes and such here function as a *façon de parler* rather than being a determinant of inferential structure. In this important respect, the structuralist/poststructuralist idea of a semiotic code falls foul of the core Quinean objections to positivism. Poststructuralists took over certain untenable philosophical assumptions from aspects of positivism. Appreciating this hopefully points toward a more pragmatic view of language, meaning, narrative, etc., one more likely to be fruitful for the human sciences.[14]

This chapter began by sketching a defensible form of naturalism, one that can be normative and embrace the full panoply of human endeavors. Thus it readily accommodates essentially narrative explanations. But naturalism as outlined does not provide or posit any foundational notions of evidence. Combined with the irrealism defended in earlier chapters, this has implications for understanding debates in history. Part III explored one such case, but others have been noted throughout. What I have termed "the disappearance of the empirical" arouses in some worries about a type of postmodern epistemic anarchy. But the account offered of essentially narrative explanations and discussion throughout should forestall this "Chicken Little" response. When one examines how historical disputes (and not just historical, I believe, though I have not defended this view here) actually play out, the sort of comparative method of assessment outlined in previous chapters proves to be quite common.[15] Given the parallels stressed with Kuhn, this should come as no surprise. Moreover, and quite unlike the natural sciences, the low cost of developing a competing paradigm in history and other human sciences leads unsurprisingly to multiple accounts simultaneously being in play. This book has attempted to say why this result should not surprise us, and in fact should be expected. The thought that there must be a determinate order of things manifests, I suspect, only an unrequited religious impulse, mourning that no sense any longer exists to postulating a world seen sub specie aeternitatis. But this loss does not translate into a defensible epistemology. In this key respect, naturalism, irrealism, and narrativism humanize and do not abandon a basic philosophical aspiration to articulate how things hang together.

Conclusion

> To catch mind in its connexion with the entrance of the novel into the course of the world is to be on the road to see that intelligence is itself the most promising of all novelties, the revelation of the meaning of that transformation of past into future which is the reality of every present.
> —John Dewey, "The Need for a Recovery of Philosophy"

To identify the form of narrative explanation and the character of the historical is not to assert that philosophers know something that, for example, working historians do not. Rather (and without suggesting that the achievements compare), an analogy to what has been argued here would be Russell's Theory of Descriptions. No competent speaker needs Russell's theory to appreciate that both "The present king of France is bald" and its negation are false. The puzzle is logical and philosophical because it is far from obvious how to provide an analysis of logical form that accounts for this judgment. Russell's celebrated theory provides a technique to exhibit a semantic and logical structure that answers a peculiarly philosophical question regarding how to represent a logic that accords with what in key respects is already known.

In this regard, one way to read the course of debate about historical explanation since the nineteenth century is to see it as instantiating an aporia between a sanctioned practice and a logically obscure explanatory form. This book has offered an account of what makes that form obscure and so why the dispute has persisted. Additionally and most importantly, it reveals a logic of narrative explanation that opens it to rational evaluation and demonstrates why a fully naturalized understanding of science itself requires such an explanation. Establishing this connection to naturalism completes the *philosophical* solution to problems supposedly attending narrative explanations. And so insofar as anything has been achieved by this, it is to have provided a philosophical solution to something practitioners and readers already knew, that is, that narratives explain.

CONCLUSION

In sum, then, the solution articulated herein to the problem of how narratives explain does *not* contribute to any theory of narrative as a literary form. Rather, the argument has been to establish that narrative has a place as well within epistemology (as primarily developed in chapters 2, 3, and 7) and the theory of explanation (as argued in chapters 1, 4, 5, and 6). Narrative explanations from a variety of works have been used as illustration, including Braudel's (1976) *The Mediterranean and the Mediterranean World in the Age of Philip II*, Friedman's (2000) *A Parting of the Ways*, Hilberg's (1985) *The Destruction of the European Jews*, and Kuhn's (1962/2012) *The Structure of Scientific Revolution*. The arguments throughout have been to motivate changes in or rejection of ill-considered metaphysical and epistemic preconceptions about structural features of human history and explanatory strategies.

Up to this point, these works have been used to illustrate characteristics of an essentially narrative explanation. My frequent use of Hilberg in particular has been deliberate both because of the role that debates about the Holocaust have played in discussions of constructivist positions in historiography and because of the literally paradigmatic status of Hilberg's history. However, even granting that the works discussed have the form attributed to them, nothing said so far may yet appear to address, much less substantiate, my initial suggestion that the solution to the charge of logical formlessness provided in chapter 4 functions to answer as well complaints about evaluative intractability noted at the beginning of chapter 2.[1]

What should be expected of a "philosophical" account of evaluative criteria? Clearly *not* something on the model of the verification theory of meaning or a Carnapian *Wissenschaftlogik*. Logical positivism is often understood as the last great philosophical effort to articulate a fully general theory of scientific rationality and rational evaluation. Yet this view presupposed a type of unity of reasoning or method that even positivists came to deny. Discussions going forward regarding what makes for science and rationality need to learn from that failure, not to insistently repeat it.

The allusion above to Russell's classic analysis, however, already hints at what answer I take to be feasible with respect to the charge of evaluative intractability. Once the form has been articulated, the problem of evaluative intractability has been given as much of a solution as *philosophically* possible. This is *not* to claim that analyses of the form allows of one solution only. Rather, evaluative intractability was taken to be an immediate consequence of lacking a logical form. So, absent some further argument, specifying what logical structure the form permits solves by dissolving a seeming obstacle to reasoned evaluation. It cannot be an ob-

CONCLUSION

jection that practitioners will almost certainly continue to differ on how to frame or analyze particular issues or events, and so identifying a form ipso facto fails to settle questions of which form is best. History proves no different from any other science insofar as arguments persist regarding the "proper" form to provide for specific issues or topics.

And certainly here there will be a philosophical parting of the ways with others who write on these topics, one presaged by the account of naturalism offered in chapter 7.[2] Kuukkanen (2018, 88) for one urges a continued search for more philosophical standards regarding rational acceptability in historiography: "I agree with Roth that justification is a theme of central importance. I take it that no one wishes to accept that just any interpretation or view is equally good. . . . There must be something that limits acceptability but at the moment we are left in the dark as to what this may be." Indeed (and alas) Kuukkanen puts me in a league with Rorty's cooperative freshman. For my naturalism holds that there exists "no *a priori* domain of normativity or *a priori* method to decide what normativity and justification are" (88). This position, he goes on to allege, carries "substantial" risks, including no less than that of losing "the entire aspect of normativity and capacity to evaluate rival views epistemologically. It would be the situation of anything goes more familiar to postmodernist theorizing" (89).[3] But he nowhere details why my naturalism precipitates so drastic a slide. In short, it is hard to comprehend based on what Kuukkanen actually writes which *evaluative* standards of historians supposedly cry out for a *philosophical* solution. Empirical knowledge claims, based as they must be on inductive practices, will be fallible. Practices will vary from theory to theory and discipline to discipline. As Quine (1969, 72) famously quipped, "The Humean predicament is the human predicament." But theories (including statistical) exist to help structure and guide inductive practices.[4]

Returning anew, then, to questions of the relation of form and evaluation, recall that in chapter 4 it was argued that the following narrative sentences can be used to state one important conclusion for which Hilberg (1985, 1044) argues: "The destruction of the Jews was thus no accident. When in the early days of 1933 the first [German] civil servant wrote the first definition of 'non-Aryan' into a civil service ordinance, the fate of European Jewry was sealed." Or, reworded as a narrative sentence: The Holocaust began in 1933. The sequencing of events that Hilberg details, memo by memo, meeting by meeting, country by country, collectively constitute the explanatory details justifying this claim. Equally clearly, it is just philosophical foolishness, a combination of bad semantics and bad epistemology, to imagine that historiographic terms such as this receive clarifications from some philosophical theory of reference.

CONCLUSION

Terms such as "Holocaust" do not denote but connote a widely dispersed series of events and actions. Whether Hilberg's claim is correct depends, at least in part, on what one takes to link the events as part of a common account in the way that Hilberg does.

How, then, to rationally evaluate or challenge a history such as Hilberg's? With this question, and a very vague ceteris paribus clause, one confronts the issue on which Hayden White has long insisted, viz., that any decision on how to write history will represent a moral choice on the part of the historian. As Charles S. Maier (1997, ix) perceptively noted on the controversy regarding Holocaust history known as the *Historikerstreit*, "The debate revealed that German intellectuals were divided over how centrally their country's acknowledging past aggression and genocide should underlie political consciousness." But, he then adds, "All historical understanding must ultimately rest on comparison. . . . As a historian, I wanted to probe that fundamental tension of our discipline" (x). And lest this characterization be mistaken as a peculiarly American take on a German debate, principals in that debate such as Jürgen Habermas (1997, 234) share Maier's assessment: "After Auschwitz our national self-consciousness can be derived only from the better traditions in our history, a history that is not unexamined but instead appropriated critically. The context of our national life . . . can be continued and further developed only in the light of the traditions that stand up to the scrutiny of a gaze educated by the moral catastrophe, a gaze that is, in a word, suspicious." Debate over Holocaust historiography of the kind that triggered the *Historikerstreit* turned in key respects on whether or not to situate Hitler as a great anti-Communist crusader. Habermas responds by emphasizing the moral perversity embedded in this apologetic for the Nazis. The issue, in other words, turns on the moral consequences of the framing, not any dispute about some matter of fact.[5]

More recently and from a very different perspective, Timothy Snyder (2010, 380; emphasis mine) has maintained that Hilberg's account needs to be "corrected" *not* because of some factual misstep but because it neglects to situate the facts within the proper historical frame: "To describe their course [the policies of Hitler and Stalin] has been to introduce to European history its *central event*. Without an account of all the major killing policies in their common European setting, comparisons between Nazi Germany and the Soviet Union must be inadequate." Snyder, in opposition to many of the current "schools" of historical interpretation, bluntly declares that "Europe's epoch of mass killing is overtheorized and misunderstood" (383). "Overtheorized" because the emphasis on death camps misses the fact that most killings were not carried out in the death factories erected by the Nazis. It is misunderstood even today,

CONCLUSION

Snyder maintains, because of a failure to confront the extent to which these policies were "not a step in a logical plan so much as an element in an aesthetic vision" (389). By use of the phrase "aesthetic vision," Snyder means to imply that the killings must be understood as choices on the part of those participating: "No matter which technology was used, the killing was personal" (xv). And until this fact can be appreciated and assimilated both into histories of the period and into self-understanding, the key lessons will remain unlearned. Where Ernst Nolte wanted to use postwar political developments to reframe an understanding of Hitler's actions in a way that made his treatment of the Jews a reaction to and so a consequence of Stalinist policies, Snyder reframes the issues to look at the killing of the Jews in a perspective fashioned by temporally and geographically related mass murders. Both in different ways would change the significance Hilberg attributes to the destruction of Europe's Jews.

This snapshot cannot begin to provide a general overview of the problems that incite debates with regard to Holocaust historiography. My point, rather, is that one does not have to look far to find such cases. (But with specific reference to Holocaust historiography, see esp. Stone [2017]. For a sample of disputes regarding the American Civil War, see Towers [2011]. Wise [1980] and Novick [1988] also remain well worth reading in this regard.) In short, there exists no good reason to imagine that there might exist special yet undiscovered philosophical canons of justification or relevance that will resolve such disputes. Assessment will, ceteris paribus, turn on appeal to factors other than "the facts."[6] As argued in other chapters (especially chapters 4, 5, and 6), if an event can be explained only narratively, then evaluating that explanation will typically have to be done comparatively, i.e., relative to a competing narrative. Narrative as a form of explanation has been vindicated by making that form explicit, accounting for why it is unique, and establishing why it is both an unavoidable and a legitimate strategy. It is neither here nor there that historical disputes cannot be given some final verdict about their rational acceptability. This feature does not distinguish or mar disagreements about historical explanations from those found in any other field of inquiry. Form serves as a propaedeutic to evaluation, but there cannot be a general answer to evaluative questions.[7]

Yet, I also insist, by attending to the form of narrative explanation and the factors characteristic of this form, possibilities for rational debate and evaluation have been clarified and advanced. Since the narrative offers a developmental sequence not underwritten by laws, inductive standards must be applied. By way of suggesting a possible avenue for further development, and with the important caveat that the explanandum will be characterized retrospectively by a narrative sentence and discussed

CONCLUSION

more below, note that essentially narrative explanations bear an interesting and important prima facie relation to the explanatory strategy of "inference to best explanation" (IBE).[8] It signals yet another link between narrativizing strategies and those already recognized in other sciences insofar as the logic of the explanation resides in the use of the explanandum to bring order and significance to previously known facts.

In his classic study of this topic, Peter Lipton (1993, 1) characterizes IBE thus: "Beginning with the evidence available to us, we infer what would, if true, provide the best explanation of that evidence." Lipton does not have historical explanation or practice in mind when discussing explanatory considerations, but the relation between IBE and narrative explanations deserves consideration. As Lipton acknowledges, as a model of inference this has the logically distinctive feature of having the consequence (the imputed explanation) license the inference from the premises (the explanans). As Lipton puts it, "Explanatory considerations are our guide to inference" (22; see also 1). Thus quite unlike the Hempelian model, explanation in this case is *not* a consequence of mimicking a certain inferential form. Rather, it could be said, the explanandum determines what to count as explanans by virtue of providing an explanation for those factors. In this important respect, IBEs share the key feature of nondetachability characteristic of essentially narrative explanations.

Lipton (1993, 35) goes on to acknowledge, "The causes that explain depend on our interests." And although he has concerns and issues to which this book has its own answers—e.g., the issue of scientific realism or of the notion of a "true" explanation—what he says in favor of IBE as a form of contrastive explanation is germane to the view defended in regard to narratives. In particular, as he notes, his "contrastive analysis of explanation shows how what counts as a good explanation can be genuinely interest relative without thereby being subjective in a sense that would make explanatory considerations unsuitable guides to inference" (187). Lipton also echoes Quine and Neurath: "Because our system of beliefs evolves like a complex organ, we build new inferences on old explanations" (132). The evaluation of inductive practices does not disappear due to interest relativity.

In addition and of particular relevance to earlier discussion, Lipton suggests how to incorporate IBE within a Kuhnian perspective. What Lipton's discussion highlights, and what bears further consideration, is how elements such as interests and prior theoretical commitments prove closely interrelated in the process of inferring to the "best explanation." The important point is that interest-relativity does not make the inferential practices subjective in the sense that Kuukkanen seems to fear. Rather, providing a structure to the inferential sequencing *opens* the pro-

CONCLUSION

cess to rational scrutiny. Lipton's account of IBE also fits nicely with the retrospective structure that defines essentially narrative explanations.[9]

An obvious difference between IBEs as Lipton discusses them and an essentially narrative explanation is that the former unifies evidence in terms of hypothesized cause, while the unity in the latter case results from using a later event to forge a developmental sequencing. With IBE, one infers from the observed phenomena to an unseen but hypothesized cause (from witnessing language acquisition and use to the inference of algorithms that provide an innate grammatical competence, for example). But this is less of a difference than it might first seem. The point to be considered concerns how IBE functions in the historiographic cases just as narrative sentences do, or what Kuukkanen discusses with regard to colligatory concepts.

As Kuukkanen (2015, 98) phrases it, what connects Danto's narrative sentences, Mink's configurational mode, and Hayden White's tropes "is that they integrate units of information to form something new and to thus create novel historiographical information which cannot be thought to have existed before this act of creation." 'The Renaissance' and 'the Holocaust' colligate, but they do so by functioning as explanations, indeed, as IBEs. That is, from an explanatory perspective, what licenses the inference to positing them as events is their explanatory merit. From the standpoint defended in chapter 3, one does not assume an ontology of preexisting "events." Historical events are not natural kinds. *Most important, their epistemic justification derives from their utility for purposes of explanation and not from the fact that they answer to some philosophical theory of reference.* The unifying principles reflect their organizational utility for us, not their capacity to function as a mirror of the world.

As objections to narrative explanations, the allegations of logical formlessness and evaluative intractability stand or fall together. In addition, insofar as the analysis provided of narratives demonstrates how historical events function epistemically in the service of explanation, objections arising from traditional forms of philosophical semantics prove to be beside the point. Wedding oneself to traditional semantic idioms does little more than ensure that pointless quarrels endure. Chapters 3 and 7 establish that those semantic views can and should be discarded (see also Roth 2013b). As noted at the outset of this conclusion, the moral is to avoid such philosophical excesses, not to keep compulsively indulging in them.

History is a science. The primary explanatory form it utilizes—narrative explanation—is not, as once was thought, sui generis. Other sciences use this form as well. But it predominates in histories for reasons detailed in chapters 3 and 4. Having argued throughout that objections

CONCLUSION

thought to preclude including histories as explanatory and as providing knowledge no longer can be credited, this book ends where it began, i.e., by situating itself relative to the work of Danto, Mink, and White. In particular, notice should be taken of how White in a late essay appropriates Danto's notion of a narrative sentence. Discussing the work of Erich Auerbach, White (1999, 89) provides a characterization of what makes a work "historical" that eerily echoes Danto:

> A given historical event can be viewed as the fulfillment of an earlier and apparently utterly unconnected event when the agents responsible for the occurrence of the later event link it "genealogically" to the earlier one. The linkage between historical events of this kind is neither causal nor genetic. . . . The relationships between earlier and the later phenomena are purely retrospective, consisting of the decisions on the parts of a number of historical agents. . . . The linkage is established from the point in time experienced as a present to a past, not, as in genetic relationships, from the past to the present.

In saying that the relationship is not causal, I take White to be correctly observing that no laws or any law-like connections link these events through time. More important, and in keeping with the key feature of a narrative sentence, the genealogy can be apprehended only retrospectively. Only from a standpoint afforded by a later time does the significance of the earlier moment become known. In denying that the relationship is genetic, again White is insisting properly that nothing in the earlier moment fated that the development take place. "Replaying life's tape" would not, as discussed in chapter 4, ensure the same outcome. Equally important, White insists that there is nonetheless a sequencing of events that does allow a retrospective linking of events. In the terms used since chapter 4, this marks the sequencing as essentially narrative.

In his characteristic emphasis on the role of agency in history, White's remarks anticipate Snyder's emphasis on "aesthetic vision" and the role of choices. White concludes his essay on Auerbach by enumerating, again in characteristic fashion, Auerbach's list of the "distinguishing stylistic characteristics" of literary modernism, features that White (1999, 100) himself has long argued historians should apply to their writings. But precisely this aspect of White's thought—the drive to assimilate historical writing more self-consciously to literature—invariably excites worries about casting histories adrift, of failing to anchor the works to reality by utilization of the requisite senses of "truth" and "reference." Mink (1987, 203) expresses this common concern as follows: "Narrative

CONCLUSION

history and narrative fiction move closer together than common sense could well accept. Yet the common-sense belief that history is true in a sense in which fiction is not is by no means abrogated, even though what that sense is must be revised. It would be disastrous, I believe, if common sense were to be routed from its last stronghold on this point." Mink's worry here has a point only if one expects to find a *formal* method that demarcates between kinds of works, e.g., history and fiction.

The search for a demarcation criterion is one more residue of the positivist project of attempting to specify a formal criterion for separating science and nonscience. The problem resides not in the absence of this criterion but in the belief that one is even needed. For as even classical positivists came to concede (see esp. Hempel 1950), once the "unit of empirical evaluation" becomes the whole of science, a formal demarcation criterion becomes a *logical* nonstarter. Hempel and Carnap recognized this by the 1950s. *Mink's worry thus has no point from within a fully naturalized philosophical perspective.* Sophisticated and informed historical practice already does what no purely logical criterion could do, i.e., do the best we can to separate fact from fiction. To infer the absence of standards for doing this from their contingency is, as noted above, a non sequitur.

Danto (1965 16) writes at the conclusion of chapter 1 of his classic work on this subject, "I shall maintain that our knowledge of the past is significantly limited by our ignorance of the future. The identification of limits is the general business of philosophy, and the identification of this limit is the special business of analytical philosophy of history as I understand it." Yet post-Kuhn, Danto seemingly lost all hope that anything philosophically could be said about the limits of historical explanation. But on that point he was mistaken, or so I have maintained. White and Mink understood well that narrative form functions as a cognitive instrument. White saw no reason to expect that a philosophical focus on the natural sciences held any prospect for illumination of narrative form. Mink shared this skepticism, but held out for the prospect that more could be said than White would allow about the specifically cognitive or epistemic functions of narrative. White's skepticism about philosophy of science as he knew it was well-founded, as was Mink's belief that there was still more to say. But White paid no real heed to how post-Kuhnian philosophy of science developed, and Mink died before the postpositivist revolution in philosophy took real shape.

This book has argued for the legitimacy of narrative (retrospective) historical explanation as a form of scientific knowledge. It has examined as well as the epistemic and metaphysical factors that account for how it is alike and different from other forms of scientific knowledge. It has

CONCLUSION

explored the factors that make historical explanations open to rational evaluation. More generally, the book has also worked to establish the importance and philosophical relevance of historical explanation. One reason for this stands out. The link between past and present is dynamic, not static. As a consequence, in order to understand to what extent we author our fate, we need to examine how we write our histories.

Notes

Preface

1. Hayden once joked to me that narrative theory could tell one everything about a narrative except what made it good.

2. Since I suppose I will be expected to say something somewhere about "relativism," let me say it here. At a first pass, my response to the charge of relativism echoes Richard Rorty's (1980, 727): "Except for the occasional cooperative freshman, one cannot find anybody who says that two incompatible opinions on an important topic are equally good. The philosophers who get called 'relativists' are those who say that the grounds for choosing between such opinions are less algorithmic than had been thought." If someone actually establishes that my position has that implication attributed to the "occasional cooperative freshman," that would certainly be good reason to rethink it. But if, as Rorty also observes, relativism just means failing to provide an algorithm as to how beliefs map to an imagined Reality, a world supposedly seen sub specie aeternitatis, then I am guilty as charged. But I deny committing some sin against philosophy. Following views developed in Roth (1999a, 2003, 2006, 2016a), my heresy abjures at least one particular article of certain philosophical faiths, viz., that an account of empirical knowledge must entail that legitimate knowledge claims have immunity from error. On my view, relativism so construed is *not* a fall from epistemic grace requiring philosophical redemption. The yearning for a guarantee that Truth is One is, rather, a symptom of a particular philosophical disease. For a proposed cure, see chapter 7.

Chapter 1

An earlier version of this chapter was published as "Reviving Philosophy of History," in *Towards a Revival of Analytical Philosophy of History*, edited by Krzysztof Brzechczyn (Boston: Brill, 2018), 9–27.

1. This adumbrated story further simplifies the picture by excluding Popper's (1957) influential intervention, *The Poverty of Historicism*. But Popper certainly never promoted history as a science.

2. Richard Vann, who served as executive editor of *History and Theory* for many years, uses as the epigraph for "Turning Linguistic" (Vann 1995) the following statement by noted literary critic Frank Kermode: "It seems . . . that phi-

losophy of history is the business of those who teach novels." Vann then observes, "Kermode's view would have been considered bizarre indeed in 1950 [the heyday of positivist debate]. In 1968 it was still avant-garde; by 1975 the problems that such a comment raises had moved to the forefront of debate in the philosophy of history in the English-speaking world. I shall try to show how, and in what institutional settings, this happened" (40).

3. Note a concurrent observation by Vann (1987, 2) regarding Mink, a philosopher tied to *History and Theory* from its inception: "As he [Mink] wrote in 1974, 'It could be said without exaggeration that until almost 1965 the critical philosophy of history was the controversy over the covering law model.'"

4. The context suggests it to be Danto's own coinage. Close anticipations of Danto's term can be found in Gallie (1968, 113–24, but esp. 124) and Popper (1957, 143–44). One might well read Collingwood as suggesting this as well. I thank Hayden White for these references.

5. My remarks should not be taken to slight the importance of Hayden White's work to the development and discussion of the philosophical issues that attached to historical explanation. I have elsewhere elaborated on the significance of White's work in this regard. However, since one moral of my chapter will be that, qua philosophers, one should attend *less* to issues of narrative form, White does not figure in my discussion here.

6. For criticisms of Carroll's views that press points not discussed here, see Stueber (2015).

7. The example is "Aristarchus hypothesized the heliocentric theory thereby anticipating Copernicus' discovery by many centuries" (Carroll 2001, 125). Carroll uses this example because Danto (1965, 156) employs it to illustrate his (Danto's) notions of a "narrative sentence." Since I am insisting on a need to return to issues in a form first raised by Danto and then Mink, this lack of recognition on Velleman's part proves critical. See Carroll (2007) for his response to Velleman.

8. Turner (2018) provides a discussion of how the notion of narrative compares to Weber's notion of adequacy at the level of meaning.

9. For an important exception, see particularly Stueber (2015). Stueber's intuition, in line with the view that I develop below, stresses the contextual aspect of narratives qua explanations. Yet Stueber complains in that essay that neither Mink nor I "sufficiently distinguish between the explanatory power of theories and narratives" (394n1). My account later in this book of essentially narrative explanation means to rebut that charge.

10. Hacking (1995b, ch. 17) in effect rediscovers these points of Danto's and Mink's and exploits them in his work. For a discussion of Hacking in this connection, see Roth (2002) and chapter 5, n1.

11. Mink articulates in a paper presented in 1972 what would now be termed a Foucauldian point. However, I have no reason to think that the view to which Mink gives voice here is anything other than his own: "To adapt the title of Peter Laslett's book, one can now think of history as the discovery of the world we have lost rather than as the rediscovery of the world which survives in our culture. . . . And that change just may be, as I have suggested, the recognition of

the past as more discontinuous with the present than we have thought, and the perception of the past as the Last Frontier, whose exploration can disclose a range of human possibilities more complex and more different from our own conceptions than has ever been thought before" (Mink 1987, 101–4).

12. Stueber too takes it that both Mink and I somehow create a contrast between the narrative and the causal. For example, he charges us both with "insufficiently articulating how it is that the various events are causally woven together" (Stueber 2015, 408). But if "insufficiently" here means that lack of provision of necessary and sufficient conditions for an explication of causality, then I am uncertain that any theory meets the bar. If he insists that one cannot understand what "cause" means absent the use of a generalization, then he renders quite mysterious why he takes historicists to have offered any example worth following, although apparently he does (395). But, more to the theoretical point, he gives no reason whatsoever for believing that histories as written do any more than mystery-monger, which they must if one gives credibility to his account of what causal explanation requires.

13. In Roth (1998) I argue that the way in which history comes to be understood can significantly impact how people imagine their options going forward. In this sense at least, writing or rewriting history can causally influence us.

14. Consider the following remark by Tom Ricketts (2004, 182), whose work I much admire: "On the story I tell, the central strand of the analytic tradition in philosophy decisively shaped by our three figures [Frege, Carnap, and Quine] has, I think it is fair to say, no salient continuation among those who name themselves the heirs of that tradition."

Chapter 2

An earlier version of this chapter was published as "Narrative Explanation: The Case of History," *History & Theory* 27 (1988):1–13.

1. The roots of this debate extend back to at least the late nineteenth century and center on questions of how contextual information provided by narratives answer demands for causal connections.

2. See discussion of these issues in Kuukkanen (2015) and my review (Roth 2016a).

3. Nagel (1961, 547–48) traces this terminology to Windelband..

Chapter 3

Portions of this chapter were published in earlier versions in "Ways of Pastmaking," *History of the Human Sciences* 15 (2002):125–43; and "The Pasts," *History and Theory* 51 (2012): 313–39.

1. "Induction requires taking some classes to the exclusion of others as relevant kinds.

... The uniformity of nature we marvel at or the unreliability we protest belongs to a world of our own making" (Goodman 1978, 10). See also Goodman (1979, 96–97).

2. "A broad mind is no substitute for hard work" (Goodman 1979, 21).

3. Hacking offers a general account of "styles of reasoning" in Galison and Stump's (1996) *The Disunity of Science*. He explores some specific attributes of different styles in a number of essays, including Hacking (1992a, 1992b, 1993).

4. Chapter 5 in Hacking (1999) is a lightly revised version of his essay "World-Making by Kind-Making: Child Abuse for Example" (1992c). The number in brackets provides the citation for the earlier version.

5. "I . . . suggest that there is a case (of sorts) for saying that the very objects of physical science are not merely recategorized and rearranged, as Kuhn says, but brought into being by human ingenuity. My 'experimental realism' no more invites nominalism than Brecht's materialism. I think that the physical phenomena that are created by human beings are rather resilient to theoretical change" (Hacking 1985, 118). And again, "Like Kuhn's revolutionary nominalism, Foucault's dynamic nominalism is an historicized nominalism. But there is something fundamentally different. History plays an essential role in the constitution of the objects, where the objects are the people and ways in which they behave. Despite my radical doctrine about the experimental creation of phenomena, I hold the common-sense view that the photo-electric effect is timeless at least to this extent: if one does do certain things, certain phenomena will appear. They never did appear until our century. We made them. But what happens is constrained by 'the world.' The categories created by what Foucault calls anatomopolitics and biopolitics, and the 'intermediary cluster of relations' between the two politics, are constituted in an essentially historical setting. Yet it is these very categories in terms of which the human sciences venture to describe us. Moreover, they bring into being new categories which, in part, bring into being new kinds of people. We remake the world, but we make up people" (124).

6. See especially Hacking (1999, 103–6). For a fuller development of Hacking on this point, see Murphy (2001).

7. "Of course part of the difference between tame beasts and people is that the latter understand how they are described, and act or rethink themselves accordingly. The possibilities open to them—their possible futures—change. That is a dramatic making literal of Goodman's talk about world-making" (Hacking 1992c, 190–91). Hacking (1995a) more fully discusses these issues in "The Looping Effects of Human Kinds."

8. For Hacking (1986b, 233), this point is perfectly general: "Thus the idea of making up people is enriched; it applies not to the unfortunate elect but to all of us. It is not just the making up of people of a kind that did not exist before; not only are the split and the waiter made up, but each of us is made up. We are not only what we are but what we might have been, and the possibilities for what we might have been are transformed." The generality extends, as this quote makes plain, backward in time.

9. Hacking (1995b, 294n3) writes with regard to precisely this Wittgensteinian point linking a way of speaking about ourselves to the presence of a determinate and shared mental something, "I shall write like an Anscombian hard-liner." For related reflections, see Hacking (1982).

10. "Philosophical analysis is the analysis of concepts. Concepts are words in their sites. Sites include sentences, uttered or transcribed, always in a larger site of neighborhood, institution, authority, language. If one took seriously the project of philosophical analysis, one would require a history of the words in their sites, in order to comprehend what the concept was.... To invoke the history of a concept is not to uncover its elements but to investigate the principles that cause it to be useful—or problematic" (Hacking 1995c, 313). The allusion here to Foucault provides an important key, for Hacking (rightly, in my view) finds a suggestive link between Anscombe's Wittgensteinian doctrine and Foucault's move from talk of concepts to talk of how certain ways of words become entrenched in a community. He explicitly draws this link as follows: "I subscribe to G. E. M. Anscombe's view in *Intention*, that by and large intentional action is action under a description. So there have to be descriptions. If we can show that descriptions change, some dropping in, some dropping out, then there simply is a change in what we can (as a matter of logic) do or not do. One can reread many of Foucault's books as in part stories about the connection between certain kinds of description coming into being or going out of existence, and certain kinds of people coming into being or going out of existence" (Hacking 1985, 122).

11. I should note here that Hacking himself regularly cautions his readers that his own analytic scheme for approaching these matters is itself provisional. It is less a theory than an invitation to pay attention to the historical details of the concepts that interest us. "But just because it [his account of 'dynamic nominalism'] invites us to examine the intricacies of real life, it has little chance of being a general philosophical theory. Although we may find it useful to arrange influences according to Foucault's poles and my vectors, such metaphors are mere suggestions of what to look for next" (Hacking 1986b, 236). Hacking in this regard as well proves very Wittgensteinian, i.e., more intent upon assembling reminders for particular purposes than offering a detailed theory of this or that.

12. This identifies contexts that effectively blur the usual ways of trying to distinguish between the notion of explanation and understanding. I elaborate this in the next chapter.

13. It is with regard to the kinds of things—the entities—of which human narrative history is made that I part company with Adrian Haddock's (2002) sympathetic reconstruction of Hacking's argument for the indeterminacy of the past. On my view, Haddock does not appreciate how radical Hacking's view is regarding kinds, and so wishes to "save" what he takes to be Hacking's argument by an account of changes operating "only at the level of the predicates that apply to entities and not at the level of the properties of the entities themselves" (19). Regarding actions, no such distinction can be drawn. As I noted earlier, Hacking in effect "rediscovers" Danto's narrative sentences.

14. Hacking struggles throughout with very deep and interesting issues he terms "memoro-politics." His fascinating Foucauldian speculations on how the soul becomes an object of science, how in this regard memories become objects of possible knowledge used to define the self, is an account which I find suggestive and fascinating. I regret that this is not the place to follow out Hacking's concerns on this point. Particularly noteworthy in this regard is his observation on how memoro-politics alters one's understanding of the injunction to "know thyself"

NOTE TO PAGE 45

(see Hacking 1995b, 260). At its core, a scientized account of self-knowledge is being foisted on us, one that Hacking worries will, if not shut off deeper springs of a self, at least yoke whatever autonomy we possess to a false yet constraining set of ways for expressing and understanding who we are. He worries "that the end product is a thoroughly crafted person, but not a person who serves the ends for which we are persons" (266). Although he does not cite John Stuart Mill, I find the concerns here resonate with those of Mill in *On Liberty*, linked, that is, to the worry of respecting an adult's fundamental right to make her own choices. As Hacking himself stresses, these psychological concepts come morally freighted.

A related issue much worth an examination is how the accepting of certain taxonomic classifications also allows for the creation of a corresponding expertise. Hacking (1992c, 193) fears that the creation of a psychological disease category, its status as an object of knowledge, and experts in that kind of knowledge and its treatment comprise an underappreciated problem: "Child abuse was first presented and is still intended to be a 'scientific' concept. There are demarcation disputes for sure. . . . Whatever the standpoint, there are plenty of experts firmly convinced that there are important truths about child abuse. Research and experiment should reveal them. We hope that cause and effect are relevant, that we can find predictors of future abuse, that we can explain it, that we can prevent it, that we can determine its consequences and counteract them. Yet there hovers in the background a criticism that is hard to formulate. Maybe we fail to help children because all our endeavours assume that we are dealing with a scientific kind? This worry has been expressed in terms of the 'medicalization' of child abuse, but thus far it complains only about the type of expert, not about the very possibility of expertise." One danger is that we miss what we aim to prevent—the physical abuse of children—by constituting a pseudo-kind: child abusers. It may be the case, inter alia, that those who abuse make up no serviceable sort of kind.

15. I take Hacking's "historicogenetic" style to be of a piece with what he elsewhere refers to as his "local" historicism.

> "Moral" inquiries not far removed from what I have in mind have been undertaken in all sorts of piecemeal and goal-directed ways. No one commonly recognizes them as either philosophy or history. . . . It is interested in, among other things, how the invention of a classification for people, and its application, does several things. It affects how we think of, treat, and try to control people so classified. It affects how they see themselves. It has strongly to do with evaluation, with the creating of values, and, in some cases considered (homosexuality, juvenile delinquency), with manufacturing a social problem about the kind of person, who must then be subjected to reform, isolation, or discipline. . . . Often, I believe, public or social problems are closely linked with what are called problems of philosophy. Gusfield and Garfinkel provided quasi-historical studies of kinds of behavior—not natural kinds but social kinds and I would say moral kinds. For a mature adult to drive under the influence of drink is immoral. . . . Everyone here knows that, but not, perhaps, how it became immoral. That leads to a question both historicist and philosophical: How do the conditions of formation of this conception determine

its logical relations and moral connotations? We here arrive at philosophical analysis, conducted in terms of the origins of the concept. (Hacking 1995c, 312)

And again:

My contrast with the social sciences is as follows. In natural science our invention of categories does not "really" change the way the world works. Even though we create new phenomena which did not exist before our scientific endeavours, we do so only with a licence from the world (or so we think). But in social phenomena we may generate kinds of people and kinds of action as we devise new classifications and categories. My claim is that we "make up people" in a stronger sense than we "make up" the world. The difference is, as I say, connected with the ancient question of nominalism. It is also connected with history, because the objects of the social sciences—people and groups of people—are constituted by an historical process, while the objects of the natural sciences, particular experimental apparatus, are created in time, but, in some sense, they are not constituted historically. (Hacking 1985, 115)

16. This account further blurs the lines in what Donald Spence (1982) refers to as the distinction between "narrative truth" and "historical truth." I have argued that the distinction is not a tenable one. Spence agrees. See Roth (1991b) and Spence's (1991) reply. As noted above, Hacking worries most about memoro-politics as a source of a particularly poisonous, anti-Millian "false consciousness." But, as he recognizes in other moods, the ability to reclassify and reconfigure the past may also be a source of help and solace. In this regard, the psychoanalytic theory of Roy Schafer makes a virtue out of the necessity of our narrativized creation of a past. See Roth (1998).

17. "We might have been content with the thought of replacing our 'forms of hegemony' by others so long as we had the Romantic illusion of true humankind, a true me, or even a true madness. But whatever Foucault means by detaching truth from forms of hegemony, he does not want the comfort of the Romantic illusions.... Foucault said that the concept Man is a fraud, not that you and I are as nothing. Likewise the concept Hope is all wrong. The hopes attributed to Marx or Rousseau are perhaps part of that very concept Man, and they are a sorry basis for optimism. Optimism, pessimism, nihilism, and the like are all concepts that make sense only within the idea of a transcendental or enduring subject. Foucault is not in the least incoherent about all this. If we're not satisfied, it should not be because he is pessimistic. It is because he has given no surrogate for whatever it is that springs eternal in the human breast" (Hacking 1986a, 39–40).

18. Wright (1993, 7) takes as an implication of the realist view the claim that the objectivity of truth and the objectivity of judgment about history cannot come apart. As cases where the two do come apart Wright suggests Hume on causation and, more generally, inferences from facts to states of affairs that have a clear normative component, as in moral and aesthetic judgments. Hence, one fundamental philosophical question that lurks here concerns where or whether

a line gets drawn between the factual/descriptive and the normative, that is, what makes for the supposed difference in types of judgments about the past.

19. I characterize this view of historical realism as the "woolly mammoth" view of the past. This stems from an article that I once read concerning how explorers in some Arctic region found an entire woolly mammoth frozen, embedded in the ice. Realists view past events on analogy with such a discovery. As past, events stand forever locked into some fixed configuration, awaiting a historian to come along and chip away the excrescences of time so that "the past" can stand revealed in all of its original glory.

Danto (1962, 151/148) too uses such imagery to attack the conception of the past as static: "But anyway, 'there,' in the Past, are situated all the events which ever have happened, like frozen *tableaux*" (see generally 146–51/143–48. 161/159; example at 155/152). Danto (1962) appears, with very slight stylistic changes only as chapter 8 of his *Analytical Philosophy of History* (1965). That book in turn has been reprinted as part of Danto (1985). The reprint preserves the pagination of the original book. Page references are to the original article, followed by the corresponding book page(s). Analogously, see White (2010, 136) and Vann (1987, esp. 12–13).

20. Michael Williams terms the epistemological position that I find shared by realism and antirealism alike "epistemological realism." A characteristic of epistemological realism involves a view of a type of natural ordering of justification between basic and nonbasic beliefs. Williams rejects epistemological realism and its associated metaphysics; he has advanced his views in a number of books and papers. For a representative statement of the position, see Williams (2001, 170–72).

21. "The past as it actually was is not open to our observation, and there is no reason to think that any remains we now have of it constitute in themselves what might be termed unvarnished transcripts of past reality. Historical conclusions must accord with the evidence; but evidence, too, is not something that is fixed, finished, and uncontroversial in its meaning and implications. Evidence has to be authenticated, and again evidence has to be assessed" (Walsh 1977, 54). Likewise, Danto (1962, 167/167) remarks, "Not to have a criterion for picking out some happenings as relevant and others as irrelevant is simply not to be in a position to write history at all."

22. Indeed, an alternative to an ahistorical notion of observation can in fact be gleaned from Dummett's writings. For Dummett (1978, 147) notes that nominalism, while usually contrasted with realism, does not entail the specific form of antirealism he considers: a "nominalist does not seem to be committed to being an anti-realist in this sense." The context of Dummett's discussion here proves important. He notes that nominalism normally would be understood as the philosophical antithesis of realism. But although antithetical to realism as usually understood, nominalism does not equate to antirealism as Dummett discusses it. Dummett has a clear antipathy for Goodman's form of nominalism discussed below, but the reasons for that need not detain us.

23. Richard Rorty once remarked to me in conversation that he saw no difference between past and present on this point. I agree, but the arguments in this

chapter concern just those about the reality of the past. Although Danto's text might sometimes seem to suggest otherwise, he intends no antirealist or irrealist conclusions. See references provided to correspondence with Danto in Weberman (1997, 759n21; see also 751n6).

24. Danto himself was, I believe, committed to a type of realism about historical knowledge. Be that as it may, his account of narrative sentences does not depend on any such metaphysical assumption.

25. For a defense of a similar position, see Mead (2002, esp. 35–59) Danto (1985, 340–43) also hints at this.

Two other accounts bearing apparent similarities to the one I defend are Weberman (1997) and Bunzl (1996). But both tie their accounts to problematic aspects of particular theories of action. Weberman invokes the notion of a "skeletal event," a sort of minimalist notion of an event that can be descriptively "thickened" over time. Yet, he concedes, "to make this distinction precise would require criteria stipulating just what counts as physicalistic and just how thin a description must be to qualify an event as part of the skeletal past. It is doubtful that such criteria can be found.... We might think of the skeletal past as a sort of artificial or unrealizable limit" (Weberman 1997, 754). Bunzl (1996, 192) attempts to underwrite his account by distinguishing between "events" and "facts": "One of the aims of this paper has been to make sense of Danto's claim that the past changes while staying true to the intuition that (in some sense) the past is unchanging. The paradox is solved by distinguishing between events and facts." I find the distinction as Bunzl draws it highly problematic: "Let a historical fact be statable by a proposition that is true only at a particular location or set of locations in spacetime.... The need for the notion of an event drops out of consideration, and we can still have historical subjects (the Second World War), now understood as sets of facts which hold at different times and places" (192). In any case Bunzl's notion of a "fact" presumes a realist semantics I reject.

26. Goldstein's work has received little critical attention. For an appreciative exception, see O'Sullivan (2006). An obstacle to engaging with Goldstein's work arises from his allegiance to philosophically problematic doctrines. These obscure the general interest of some of his arguments. For example, he invokes a distinction between knowledge by acquaintance and other forms of knowledge acquisition in order to distinguish historical knowledge from other forms. Yet once relieved of such quasi-Russellian views of knowledge (perceptual or scientific), Goldstein's account of the constitution of the historical past emerges in a very different and philosophically more illuminating light.

27. For if the past were not fixed, realism would collapse into the position Dummett identifies as a limited antirealism about the past. Sentences would be true or false relative to a possible model of the past, and not true or false absolutely, as realism presumably requires (see Dummett 1978, 367). In a set of articles published subsequent to his book, Goldstein directly confronts a version of the sort of realism he disavows. For P. H. Nowell-Smith (1977, 7) maintains that a plausible realism "is committed only to the thesis that if a historian states truly that such and such happened, it happened whether or not anyone later found out that it happened or proved by constructionist methods that it must

have happened.... The less extreme realist thesis is not limited to events of the observable kind. If Schneider really showed that the urban oligarchy of Metz was transformed into a landowning aristocracy in the period from 1219 to 1324, then this transformation is something that actually happened, a slice of the real past, even though it was not, when it occurred, something which anyone could have 'observed' or with which anyone could have been 'acquainted.' ... The less extreme realist holds that the historian constructs an account of the real past—the only past there was—and that the real past plays the important role of being that to which historical statements, when true, refer." This "less extreme" realist view coincides with Nowell-Smith's own. See replies to Nowell-Smith by Walsh (1977) and by Goldstein (1977).

28. "But the comparison between untold stories and unknown knowledge seems to me misleading.... A better parallel would be between untold stories and unstated facts or undiscovered explanations.... It might be preferable, therefore, although in most contexts it would be an unnecessarily technical way of putting it, to speak of there being unknown narrativizable configurations—'tellables'—already there for the discovering. That, at any rate, is all that need be meant, and all that would generally be meant, by the claim that there are untold stories in the past" (Dray 1989, 162). For other examples and informed discussions of realism and antirealism in the philosophy of history, see, in particular, Norman (1998) and Lorenz (1998). See also Roth (2000).

29. "But there is no gain-saying the fact that we have no access to the historical past except through its constitution in historical research. Realists may seem to have some arguments against the claim that the objects of the external world are constituted by consciousness; it is by no means unintelligible that there are objects independent of consciousness which provide the touchstones to which our conceptions of things must conform. But no past of history exists in that realistic sense" (Goldstein 1976, xxi; see also Goldstein 1996, 161). For reasons that will be obvious as the discussion proceeds, Goldstein's doctrine should not be identified with views that receive the label "social constructionist" or "constructivist." I argue below that what holds for history so conceived holds, a fortiori, for ordinary understanding of the past (or the present).

30. The relevant sense of "best" here concerns whatever the desiderata happen to be for a scientific explanation. In retrospect, early (and neglected) works by Murphey (1973) as well as those by Goldstein mark attempts to view philosophy of history through the lens of an emerging holistic (but still analytical) philosophy of science. Murphey's book develops a view of history as a type of theory about the past in which people and events have the status of posits used for purposes of organizing experience. But Goldstein's work in particular stands out as advocating the position that historians constitute out of whole cloth the events of historical interest. However, these contributions were largely overlooked. Analytical philosophy of science, identified as it then was with Hempel, simply comes to be written off as irrelevant to historical practice. In addition, the near simultaneous publication of Hayden White's (1973) theoretical masterwork and the emergence of the Foucauldian paradigm for (re)doing history effectively swamped any influence that analytical philosophy of science might have hoped to exercise. For an elegiac assessment of the fate of analytical philosophy of history, see Danto (1995).

The view of historical constitution, in Goldstein's sense, as abductive inference finds confirmation in many remarks by Goldstein. See, in particular, Goldstein (1996, 216, 221, 225, 334–35). Goldstein distinguishes between explanations of evidence (explaining-what) and explanations of events (explaining-why). I return to the topic of abductive inference—inference to the best explanation—in the conclusion.

31. As Danto (1985, xii) puts this point, "Narrative structures penetrate our consciousness of events in ways parallel to those in which, in Hanson's view, theories penetrate observations in science." The key point here bears primarily on what might be termed the theoretical structure of the past and the model that results. The point emphasized above involves the past as a theoretical construction. The theory accounts, among other things, for who we take ourselves to be and why. Any discussion of the reality of the past constituting human history must then appreciate that the narrative determines the significance to assign observations as well as (often enough) what was in fact observed (under what description to characterize an action). See also Danto (1965, 122). The general point to keep in mind involves the fact that scientific reasoning begins as parasitic on "common sense," that is, whatever passes as received knowledge for a time and place. Science certainly refines such views and may in time transcend and transform "common sense." But reasoning begins from within some set of received views—Quine's "web of belief." See chapter 7 for a defense of methodological naturalism.

32. Goldstein throughout his writings presumes that historical knowledge cannot claim the perceptual base that scientific knowledge can. But his particular inference from a lack of knowledge by acquaintance of historical events to the lack of relevance of perceptual knowledge (since he takes the two notions to be equivalent) simply does not hold. "What we come to believe about the human past can never be confirmed by observation—can never be known by acquaintance—and so can never be put to the test of observation, the method of confirmation which is virtually the only one explicitly recognized by science and philosophy" (Goldstein 1976, xii).

33. "The historical way of knowing in no way involves seeing or any other of the senses. . . . He does not have sensory experiences of the events he attempts to construct. The very point of history is to provide knowledge of past events that cannot be had in the sensory way" (Goldstein 1976, 11).

34. "I have tried to emphasize that while historical knowledge is relative to the discipline of history, in the same way that any sort of knowledge is relative to the disciplined way in which it is produced, it is not relative to the subjectivity of historians" (Goldstein 1996, 161).

35. "According to the realist view, one would expect that the evidence would be grouped together according to what it was evidence for. All evidence concerning the essences, for example, would be placed in one intellectual pile. . . . To say that the evidence is to be grouped according to what it is evidence of is to make that which it is evidence of the criterion for the grouping. But in point of the actual practice of history, this is not the case at all. The criteria for the grouping are drawn entirely from those intellectual operations which are the practice of history itself" (Goldstein 1976, 132; see also 131).

36. "Like any intellectual enterprise, history is carried on collectively and self-correctively. . . . [Historians may find] new ways of dealing with a further enriched body of evidence and, arriving at what one may expect will be increasingly agreed to, historical truth" (Goldstein 1976, 90). Dummett (1978, 367) privileges statement meaning over that of meaning-relative-to-a-model, and so does not take limited antirealism as a serious candidate for a theory of understanding.

37. "In effect, so far as the future is open, the past is so as well; and insofar as we cannot tell what events will someday be seen as connected with the past, the past is always going to be differently described" (Danto 1985, 340; see also 196). This echoes remarks already found in "Narrative Sentences," for example, "The Past doesn't change, perhaps, but our manner of organizing it does" (Danto 1962, 167/166-67). See also the final paragraph of that piece.

38. "Their [sentences] being true is not a further bit of description, in virtue of which the reality described has a special property in addition to those it is described as having. And so, when something satisfies the truth-conditions of a sentence, there is not some further thing it needs to do to make the sentence true: being true is not a further truth-condition of the true sentence" (Danto 1985, 318). More generally, Danto fails to notice how uneasily his own account of narrative sentences fits with this "investigation-free" notion of truth. For a more extended critique of Danto's notion of evidence and truth along these lines, see discussion by Mink (1987, 139–41).

39. Dummett (2004, 44–46) takes an analysis of tensed statements to be the litmus test for determining whether an account can function successfully for purposes of a theory of understanding.

40. Again, Danto (1965, 163/162) anticipates this point: "In one sense, if we knew all of a man's behaviour during a certain interval, we would know everything he was doing. In another sense, however, we should have only the raw materials for knowing what he was doing. In the one sense, the I.C. tells us everything we want to know, in another sense it doesn't. Not to have the use of project verbs is to lack the linguistic wherewithal for organizing the various statements of the I.C., but more importantly, for the I.C. to lack the use of project words is to render it incapable of describing what men are doing—and so disqualifies it from setting down whatever happens, as it happens, the way it happens." I take Goldstein to be making essentially the same point. What happens to be perceptually available does not suffice to inform by "direct perception," absent some classificatory work, what actions occur or items exist.

41. Hacking makes the intriguing observation that application need not require a long history of use. Indeed, scientific revolutions appear to be precisely cases where new habits rapidly trump and replace entrenched predicates. But a community of users does prove indispensable to the process of having a working scheme of things. "If Kuhn is right, a scientific revolution can introduce a projectible term with no entrenchment. Revolutions override entrenchment. Projectibility does not need a record of past usage. But it needs something precious close to that. It needs communal usage, which is brought about by a revolution" (Hacking 1993, 305).

42. Danto (1965, 167/166–67) can be seen again to anticipate these points:

"Just which happenings there and then are to be counted part of the temporal structure denoted by 'The French Revolution' depends very much on our criteria of relevance. Doubtless there are shared criteria so that no disagreement exists over certain events. But insofar as there is disagreement over criteria, the disputants will collect different events and chart the temporal structure differently, and obviously our criteria will be modified in the light of new sociological and psychological insights. The Past does not change, perhaps, but our manner of organizing it does. To return to our map making metaphor: there is a sense in which the territories (read: temporal structures) which historians endeavour to map do change. They change as our criteria change, and at best our criteria are apt to be flexible."

A similar account of the indeterminacy of action can be found in the work of Roy Schafer (1978: 21): "Logically, the idea of multiple and new definitions of individual actions implies multiple and changeable life histories and multiple and changeable present subjective worlds for one and the same person. To entertain this consequence is no more complex an intellectual job than it is to entertain, as psychoanalysts customarily do, multiple and changeable determinants and multiple and changeable self- and object representations." Or again, "Put in historical perspective, there is far more to an action than could have entered into its creation at the moment of its execution. It is the same as the effect of a new and significant literary work or critical approach on all previous literature: inevitably, fresh possibilities of understanding and creation alter the literary past" (21). Schafer appreciates that from his conception it follows that each person can have multiple life histories. See, for example, Schafer (1978, 10, 19–20). On Schafer's debt to Goodman, see Schafer (1983, esp. 205, 206, 249, 276).

43. "For Goodman, the fact that the worldly extensions of our concepts are not entirely up to us is an effect of pragmatic constraints on worldmaking. Worldmaking is constrained by coherence, consistency, fit with intuitive judgement and intelligible purpose. Conceptual work aims at 'rightness' and the rightness of a version of things is not up to us" (Cox 2003, 42–43). For a related argument in support of Goodman here, see Schwartz (1986).

44. "But let me confront the contextualist counterargument on its own ground by showing how it is possible for someone to have an idea even though he or she has no linguistic means to express it. I take this challenge to be equivalent to showing just when it is justified to ascribe a concept to a person who lacks the linguistic means to express it. . . . In effect, one 'has' a concept when others are justified in ascribing it to one as a way of interpreting one's inferences, and when one engages in such inference-making in a way that is licensed only by such a concept" (Prudovsky 1997, 29; see also 18).

45. Prudovsky (1997, 20, 27–28) indulges in an unfortunate account of "reifying ideas." But this implausible move becomes unnecessary if one goes Goodman's way. What then determines the application of a concept requires only community practice.

46. I discuss this problem further in chapter 7, especially part III.

47. This points to the important parallel between the insistence of Goldstein and Mink that historians constitute the events they seek to study and what

Davidson refers to as "anomalous monism." There exists no a priori reason to expect that the events and regularities that interest historians should map onto any categories that happen to be those employed by other scientific theories.

Chapter 4

An earlier version of this chapter was published as "Essentially Narrative Explanations," *Studies in History and Philosophy of Science* 62 (2017): 42–50.

1. See, e.g., Velleman (2003) and the discussion of Velleman in chapter 1.

2. At least of the form that I defend in chapter 7.

3. In this regard, the attention that literary theorists devote to the analysis of narrative form typically focuses on those structural elements or rhetorical features that can be deployed to variously emplot narratives. However, while modes of emplotment impact explanatory accounts, their specific characteristics do not provide an explication of or connection to a logic of explanation or otherwise contribute to making explicit norms that might bear on logically evaluating claims to explain. These considerations indicate why those insights that literary theory offers regarding narratives invariably prove orthogonal to philosophical concerns about explanation. See Roth (1992).

4. This account, if correct, turns out to have interesting implications for understanding what science is, and thus provides an additional rationale for embracing narrative explanations (see chapter 6). Understanding Kuhn's work as a narrative naturalizes narrative explanation through a form of mutual containment—since narrative helps constitute what counts as normal science, narrative cannot be separated from an understanding of what science is.

5. I trust it is clear from the context that my uses of "essential" and "inessential" do not come metaphysically freighted. Rather, the terms mark off explanations that cannot be stripped of their narrative form and still provide an explanation from those that can.

6. I assume for the sake of argument that Reagan's acting career in part helps explain his later success in politics. All explanations of course will be defeasible.

7. For a thoughtful discussion of such cases, see Hawthorn (1991).

8. Words quoted from Braudel's 1972 preface to the English edition (Braudel 1976).

9. Megill (1989, 645) argues in this piece that *The Mediterranean and the Mediterranean World* should be viewed as a narrative history:

> It is simply tradition, when it is not uniformed prejudice, that insists on identifying narrative history with actions and happenings, for characters and setting can also in principle serve as foci.
>
> Accordingly, the crucial question to ask, in deciding whether a given work is best seen as an instance of narrative history, is not, "Is this text organized in a chronologically sequential order?" It is rather, "How prominent in the text are the elements of narrative?" [action by an agent and happenings to

that agent plus character and setting].... Succinctly put, *The Mediterranean and the Mediterranean World* is a work of narrative history that (except in Part Three) focuses not on events but on existents. Braudel turned the historical setting and the division and subdivisions of that setting into a vast collection of characters. These characters make up the single, all-embracing character that is "the Mediterranean and the Mediterranean world" itself.

10. I thank Professor Browning for generously providing me with a copy of his remarks. He reiterates the "founding father" characterization in Browning (2007b, 102). See also Browning (2008). For a detailed account of the impact of Hilberg's work as well as the trials and tribulations surrounding its publication, see Bush (2010).

11. As is now well known, Hilberg was discouraged from this research topic and had great difficulty finding a publisher. Over fifty years on from the initial publication of his book, it can be too easily overlooked that despite the book's appearance over a decade and a half after the official end of the Second World War, Hilberg created for all intents and purposes the Holocaust as a field of study. For example, when I ran a Google Ngram in late 2017 on the terms "Holocaust" and "Shoah," it registered no occurrences of these terms until the mid-1960s. It would be difficult to dispute Browning's characterization of Hilberg as "the 'founding father' of Holocaust Studies in North American scholarship."

12. For a detailed case study of the nonaggregativity of scholarship in this area, see Roth (2004). For a startling and important reframing of the debate, discussion of which would be beyond the scope of this chapter, see Snyder (2010). The literature on the Holocaust has become overwhelming, and in fact has spawned its own subgenre devoted just to historiographic issues relating to Holocaust studies. But precisely because this involves a timeframe that can still be viewed as relatively historically near and extremely well-documented and researched, a history of the emergence of the event and interpretive disputes connected to it prove to be philosophically of particular interest.

13. Although differing in some key respects from the analysis I develop, accounts that also emphasize the centrality of comparative evaluation of explanation can be found in Raymond Martin (1989, esp. ch. 3) and Kuukkanen (2015, esp. ch. 9). As Martin (1989, 6) puts the point, "The alternative that I favor is to . . . look instead at actual historical interpretations, with an eye to uncovering the evidential conventions in terms of which we construct them. To be realistic . . . this looking at historical interpretations must be done from a *comparative* perspective that takes seriously the limitations within which historians actually work; that is it must be done from the perspective of trying to determine how historians try to show that their favored interpretations are *better* than competing interpretations." I have in a number of articles developed arguments for why the notion of truth does not prove relevant to narratives, and how assessing narratives comparatively and as proto-theories or paradigms should proceed. See in particular Roth (1988, 2004). Currie (2014) deploys this strategy, explicitly using a comparative approach to assessing narrative explanations.

14. I owe an appreciation of a need to make explicit this connection, as

well as the two sentences preceding this one, to comments by Mary Morgan and Norton Wise.

15. I take this point to be confirmed by a recent account of this material: "Historically contingent traits require particular non-guaranteed antecedent states, which is to say a particular history, to evolve. Their origins are therefore complex, and require multiple mutational steps. Some of these steps may be neutral, not uniquely beneficial, or possibly even mildly detrimental. Because the required steps are not uniquely favored, cumulative selection cannot predictably and rapidly facilitate their accumulation. Instead, the accumulation of the necessary mutations must be an accident of an organism's history. As a consequence, historically contingent traits should typically display two characteristics. First, they will rarely evolve multiple times independently simply because the necessary historical sequences are unlikely to recur. Second, because natural selection cannot construct them directly, contingent traits will tend to arise long after the ecological opportunity or environmental challenge to which they provide adaptation appears" (Blount 2016, 5; see also remarks at 7). Or again: "Potentiation has so far proven to be very difficult to unravel even now that we know what mutations occurred during the population's history. *(This is akin to a historian knowing what events occurred, but not knowing their impact or relationships)*" (8; emphasis mine). The parenthetical phrase clearly invokes the sort of retrospective knowledge that a narrative sentence expresses and only a narrative can explain. For related and supporting reflections, see also Sepkoski (2016, 4–6). I thank Allan Megill for bringing these articles to my attention.

16. Beatty (2016, 5) emphasizes precisely this point in recent work: "But turning points, or eventful events (or kernels) are what make narratives worth telling. *Indeed, turning points make narratives essential.*" But of course what to count as a "kernel" in the relevant sense will be revealed only retrospectively.

17. Currie's far-ranging discussion intersects with many of the points raised here, although his way of drawing some of the distinctions that I rehearse utilizes his own terminology, e.g., his distinction between "simple" and "complex" narratives. Also as he notes, "The distinction I will draw between narratives is in terms of explanatory texts. Historical scientists apply different explanatory strategies in their attempts to describe the causal processes they target. . . . I am referring to the explanations historical scientists furnish, rather than the explanatory events in the world" (Currie 2014, 1168). On Currie's account, complex narratives shoulder their "explanatory load" (1169) by "drawing together a plethora of diffuse, contingent explanans and telling a well-supported, coherent story about sauropod lineage. There is no single unifying regularity which can be appealed to" (1169). Or, again: "A *complex* narrative requires specific details unique to the case at hand and is not subsumed under a particular model" (1170; see also 1171). For reasons why complex explanations in paleobiology need not aggregate, see his discussion of "explanatory monism" (1170–73, 1180–81).

18. Do I overstate this claim? No one denies that more and more information about particular periods sometimes becomes available. The opening (to some extent) of archives in former Soviet states illustrates this for my own running example of the Holocaust. But does this lead to standardization in some

theoretically relevant sense? This is an empirical claim, and so far as I can determine the additional information does not lend support to any theoretically substantive notion of standardization. I continue to use the Holocaust as an example because of, on the one hand, the wealth of information and scholarly attention it attracts and, on the other hand, its simultaneous resistance to standardization. Hayden White famously uses histories of the French Revolution to illustrate this point in his own way. For the case of the American Civil War, see Towers (2011).

Chapter 5

An earlier version of this chapter was published as "Silence of the Norms: The Missing Historiography of *The Structure of Scientific Revolutions*," *Studies in History and Philosophy of Science* 44 (2013): 545–52.

    1. The University of Chicago Press now has a fiftieth-anniversary edition of *The Structure of Scientific Revolutions*, featuring an introduction by Hacking, who himself has been justly celebrated for his historical studies. Yet Hacking nowhere mentions issues of historical explanation in his generally laudatory discussion of Kuhn's work and influence and despite his explicit acknowledgment of *SSR* as a work of history (see, e.g., Hacking 2012, x). A hint of why Hacking (1985, 119) displays no interest in questions of specifically historical explanation emerges in the following remark: "Thus I claim that Kuhn leads us into a 'revolutionary nominalism' which makes nominalism less mysterious by describing the historical processes whereby new categories come in to being. But I assert that a seemingly more radical step, literal belief in the creation of phenomena, shows why the objects of the sciences, although brought into being at moments of time, are not historically constituted. They are phenomena thereafter, regardless of what happens." Hacking's focus on styles of scientific reasoning and processes of categorization suggests (and here I speculate) that, at least with regard to the natural sciences, historical inquiry represents nothing more than a rough analog to a context of discovery. Styles of reasoning and processes of categorization of natural phenomena play the role for him analogous to a context of justification. On this view, there would then be nothing requiring anything that might be termed a "historical explanation," or even anything (in Hacking's terminology) characterizable as a "style" of historical reasoning, at least in the sense found in the natural sciences. Regarding the human sciences (however one draws that line), Hacking takes a different view. That is, with respect to categories for human kinds, a history of how these emerge and stabilize does constitute a key part of their explanation, unlike laboratory phenomena. Hacking's (1985, 124) scattered remarks on Foucault hint strongly of this view: "I think that we shall lose ourselves in confusion and obscurity for some time yet, in the so-called social and human sciences, because in those domains the distinction between word and thing is constantly blurred. . . . Here Foucault's 'archaeology' may yet prove useful . . . at least to grasp the interrelations of 'power' and 'knowledge' that literally constitute us as human beings."

    2. Work by Alasdair MacIntyre constitutes the sole exception of which I am

aware. I discuss his view below. In a review of the fiftieth-anniversary edition that nicely emphasizes Kuhn's naturalism, Bird (2012) offers in some respects a nice description of Kuhn's philosophical targets and how *SSR* addresses them. However, Bird contents himself with observing that Kuhn's approach to the topics was "multifaceted, involving history, psychology, philosophy, and sociology," a combination that he acknowledges was "unusual" given the then prevailing norms for evaluating arguments in the empirical sciences. As Bird summarizes matters in this regard, "Kuhn's arguments, especially as regards philosophical consequence, are often more implied than stated explicitly" (865). What Bird nowhere acknowledges, despite his recognition of key portions of Kuhn's argument as historical, concerns about how Kuhn succeeded in challenging and overthrowing other extant narratives of the history of science. For it is not as if *SSR* brought new facts to light; its novelty lies in its narrative structure regarding historical episodes already known and much studied. Bird's article might lead an uninformed reader to imagine that no one prior to Kuhn had written a history of science.

3. I have in mind much work by Hacking (e.g., 1995b). But books by Lorraine Daston and Peter Galison also provide important examples.

4. Again, there is a dramatic contrast in the reception by theoretically minded historians between the ignoring of Kuhn and the appropriation of Foucault et al. See Zammito (1993) and Toews (1987). Apart from philosophy, those who do receive extensive discussion for their historicizing turns, e.g., Hayden White and Foucault, offer some (in White's case) or none (so far as I know with Foucault) acknowledgment of any influence by or credit to Kuhn. Foucault's most influential works manifest little or no interest in natural science per se and never seem intent on bringing the sort of questions for which he is famous into the area of scientific change (though, of course, Hacking does precisely this on Foucault's inspiration). This leads, in effect, to about three decades of discussion where those interested in historiography simply assume that nothing that goes on in analytical philosophy could possibly be relevant to their interests. And it is not until the publication of Hacking's key works that any analytic philosopher takes seriously Foucauldian questions regarding the relationship between the historically available stock of ways of self-understanding and the implications of these for other knowledge-related activities. Hacking himself, to add the final turn of the screw, neither self-identifies as a philosopher of history nor, more ironically still, ever exercises the sort of methodological reflection on the methods of history that he lavishes on physics and statistics. To the best of my knowledge, the most judicious and comprehensive account of how the intellectual milieu develops in this regard remains Novick (1988). See also Vann (1998).

5. I shall follow D'Oro in using Hempel's essay as exemplifying the logical positivist position. However, inasmuch as I read the essay somewhat differently than does she, readers might find it helpful to reference as well, e.g., Nagel (1961). Whatever some differences of detail, these works harmonize on the key point on which I insist, viz., the methodological unity of the sciences, and how the methodological unity entails the requirement of the use of covering laws. Neither Hempel nor Nagel ever claims that reasons cannot be causes.

6. A more Kuhn-centric answer to the disappearance question owes to

Pinto de Oliveira (2012, 115), who goes so far as to suggest that Kuhn offers a "new historiography of science." On this account, philosophy of history as it was disappears because replaced by a new historiography crafted by Kuhn. This odd account rests on a reading of Kuhn's texts that might readily be contested. I mention it only to note that although it claims to analyze Kuhn as a historiographer, it does nothing of the sort. For it addresses none of the questions one might have regarding what makes for an adequate historical explanation no matter which general view of the history of science one reads into Kuhn.

7. Although its title suggests a strong relevance to the subject under discussion, I ignore here Kindi's (2005) discussion. For one, she offers no textual evidence for the view she finds in Kuhn. In addition, as I go on to develop, Kuhn's own remarks on historiography simply cannot be reconciled with Kindi's "transcendental" reading and her attribution to Kuhn of certain corresponding "first principles." Mladenovic (2007, 278–82) offers a detailed and compelling debunking of Kindi.

8. See especially Quine (1969) and Friedman (1993, 2002).

9. Hoyningen-Huene (2012, 282) glosses "narrative relevance" as the process of selecting "for material which must be taken into account if the resulting text is to be a proper narrative. Such material includes those facts by which a historical report gains the narrative continuity that it needs . . . or facts which make plausible what would otherwise be implausible." But he has nothing of theoretical moment to say about what makes for a "proper" or "plausible" narrative.

10. Lest it be thought that the considerations just rehearsed represent some passing phase of Kuhn's thought that he later disowns, note that in a biting review essay he published in 1980, he approvingly cites his 1968 essay as expressive of his view on the relation between the history and the philosophy of science. See Kuhn (1980, 183n1).

11. Mink's 1966 work only hint at views that he will later develop, most notably in his 1978 piece, "Narrative Form as a Cognitive Instrument." All reprinted in Mink (1987).

12. A related appreciation of the primacy narrative, though cast in a more critical tone for reasons not examined here, can be found in MacIntyre (1980).

13. Virtually alone among philosophers, MacIntyre has consistently raised issues of *SSR* as a type of philosophy of history and has pursued questions of the historiography needed to account for *SSR* as rationally persuasive. See especially MacIntyre (1980, 1985). I have elsewhere rehearsed my disagreements with MacIntyre and my reasons for favoring Mink's views to his.

Chapter 6

1. An extensive literature exists in the sociology of science that claims to answer questions regarding the constitution of Kuhnian normal science. These sociological claims often invoke a "voodoo epistemology" (Roth 1987) inasmuch as they conjure up unsubstantiated causal claims. They thus prove no more explanatory than the overly rationalistic philosophical accounts they seek to displace.

NOTES TO PAGES 100–115

2. The choice of Gillispie as a reviewer proves interesting inasmuch as Kuhn (1962/2012, 108n11) cites him by name as authoring a history of science shaped to fit the "Procrustean bed" of progressive development from which Kuhn looks to free this subject.

3. Some sense of how this specific dispute about what type of book *SSR* is has long shadowed it can be gleaned by reading, e.g., Burian (1977) and Laudan (1979). For how this debate carries into the twenty-first century, see Richardson (2002), Domski and Dickson (2010).

4. When a historian reads Kuhn, what receives emphasis concerns Kuhn's focus on scientific communities. See Hollinger (1973, esp. 371–75).

5. In a telling footnote, Danto (1962, 168n24) remarks, "It is only necessary to pick a history book at random to find examples of this manner of speaking."

6. Kuhn voices a relentlessly negative and indeed scornful view of those who "reread" history so as to make scientists rational by later lights. See, e.g., Kuhn (1966, 1980).

7. Am I begging the question here in favor of Kuhn by seeming to grant without challenge his account of incommensurability? But incommensurability is not the point at issue in Kuhn's debate with Hempel. For that debate does not concern the correctness or aptness of Kuhn's "first-order" history, so to speak, but rather the legitimacy or implications of his methodology, viz. the use of a history of science to undermine or subvert a priori conceptions of what science is. Nothing I say here contributes to (or is meant to contribute to) that first-order debate. I thank Michael Hicks and Thomas Uebel for emphasizing to me the importance of clarifying this aspect of my argument.

8. Some of the most interesting and important work post-Kuhn focuses precisely on this issue of community re-formation. For an important instance of this, see Galison (1987).

Chapter 7

Portions of this chapter were published in earlier versions in "Naturalism without Tears," in *Handbook of the Philosophy of Science, Volume 15: Philosophy of Anthropology and Sociology,* edited by Stephen Turner and M. Risjord (New York: Elsevier, 2006), 683–708; "The Disappearance of the Empirical," *Journal of the Philosophy of History* 1 (2007): 271–92; and "Epistemology of Science after Quine," in *Routledge Companion to the Philosophy of Science,* edited by Martin Curd and S. Psillos (New York: Routledge, 2008), 3–14.

1. Maffie (1990, 287ff.), in this regard, refers to a division between limited and unlimited naturalists; Kitcher (1992, 74ff., but esp. 75) indicates this divide by distinguishing between traditional and radical naturalists. In each case, the former category contains those who believe that one can both be a naturalist and retain a prior conception of what is necessary for epistemic responsibility, i.e., a nonnaturalistic specification of the norms of proper epistemic functioning. Both Maffie and Kitcher put Alvin Goldman in the former category for their respective pairs, and Quine in the latter. Rosenberg (1996) agrees in general with this diag-

nosis, but goes on to suggest, correctly in my view, that Quine is the bête noire of other erstwhile naturalists because he (Quine) decouples naturalism from realism, progressivity, and other philosophical theses.

2. For Quine (1981, 70–71), methodological monism follows from his rejection of the analytic-synthetic distinction and his consequent acceptance of holism. The "monism" signals that he recognizes no principled distinction in kind (e.g., empirical vs. nonempirical; revisable vs. nonrevisable) among sentences in a language. The monism is methodological inasmuch as the means of evaluating statements is scientific.

3. What counts as a "recognized science" proves to be historically contested and contingent. But that creates no special problem for naturalism as conceived and elaborated in this chapter. Since the various sciences critique and monitor their own normative commitments, one result has to be that the disciplines of which the term "science" may be properly predicated upon will alter as theoretical and related justificatory commitments do. As I argue below, one must view the suggestion that the sciences can only be descriptive and not prescriptive as disingenuous insofar as it presumes on some prior sorting of disciplines as sciences or not, and yet without justifying how such a sorting should proceed.

4. I will not trouble here to try to delineate exactly how to distinguish what separates naturalism and pragmatism. Ellen Suckiel pointed out to me that, with respect to science, pragmatists tend to be naturalists, and vice versa. However, the two might also diverge. Her apposite example involved religious belief. A pragmatist could well find a justification for religious belief; a naturalist would be less likely to do so, barring some at present unknown scientific advantage to, e.g., appeals to intelligent design. Quine (1995) suggests that a naturalist, but not necessarily a pragmatist, could take an interest in questions regarding the unity of science. A pragmatist would not have any clear reason to trouble about this question, but a naturalist could find reason to pursue questions of unity (methodological or ontological) as questions within science. This suggests that one distinguishing feature would be that naturalists use scientific standards (however broadly the term "science" might be understood) as their most general framework for determining the relevance of and the means for answering all questions, while pragmatists do not endorse scientific standards as holding final relevance.

5. I follow in this the sentiment expressed by Sellars (1963, 3): "It is therefore, the 'eye on the whole' which distinguishes the philosophical enterprise. Otherwise, there is little to distinguish the philosopher from the persistently reflective specialist; the philosopher of history from the persistently reflective historian. To the extent that a specialist is more concerned to reflect on how his work as a specialist joins up with other intellectual pursuits, than in asking and answering questions within his specialty, he is said, properly, to be philosophically-minded."

6. Kitcher (1992) identifies antinaturalism with the animus of Frege and those who followed him toward any appeal to psychological or contingent scientific factors. Frege focuses on mathematics and structures presumed to be universal and shared and could envision no role for the empirical in this account. However, as challenges mounted to attempts to stipulate a principled divide between what requires appeals to experience for verification and beliefs that can be held true

come what may, Fregean reasons for precluding the relevance of naturalism appeared less compelling. Friedman's case for a return to antinaturalism reverts to Fregean themes, but at yet higher levels of mathematical abstraction; naturalism cannot be what philosophy should become, because pure mathematics not only "floats free" of the tribunal of experience but actually serves as a constitutive condition for constituting any such tribunal. See, for example, Friedman (1997, esp. 14). However, it does seem to be a consequence of Friedman's position that all philosophy comes to are highly abstract principles, and the only ones that appear to fill that bill belong to extremely abstruse areas of mathematics.

7. In his presidential address to the American Philosophical Association over half a century ago, Nagel (1954–55) articulates a general framework for conceiving of naturalism with which the present chapter chimes. He remarks that he uses the term "partly because of its historical associations, and partly because it is a reminder that the doctrines for which it is a name are neither new nor untried" (7). He goes on to add, as I also emphasize, "If naturalism is true, irreducible variety and logical contingency are fundamental traits of the world we actually inhabit" (10).

8. Solomon thinks this is the case for Quine as well, and here I disagree.

9. Alexander Paseau (2005, 377n1), although content to use the term "naturalism" in his title, quickly alerts his readers that "in general, the term 'naturalism' is overworked in contemporary philosophy. Vague orientation aside, most philosophical naturalisms have little in common with one another." See also van Fraassen (1995).

10. It can easily be overlooked or forgotten that this sweeping characterization of what to count as the relevant unit of empirical significance was one Quine shared with orthodox positivists such as Carnap and Hempel: "In other words, the cognitive meaning of a statement in an empiricist language is reflected in the totality of its logical relationships to all other statements in that language and not to the observation sentences alone. In this sense, the statements of empirical science have a surplus meaning over and above what can be expressed in terms of relevant observation sentences" (Hempel 1950, 59).

11. I would emphasize here that I am *not* claiming that appeals to evidence can never falsify a theory or be probative. I am more concerned with those cases, as discussed throughout this book, where additional evidence does not help settle the issue.

12. Now Toews (1987, 902) does not, and this should startle us, identify the folks just named as philosophers: "Although thinkers like Gadamer, Derrida, Foucault, and Habermas are not scholars in specific disciplines, they might be described in terms of a peculiar combination of intellectual historian and cultural critic."

13. Kuhn, of course, was not the first to make this criticism. Neurath had already criticized Popper on this point, Thomas Uebel noted to me.

14. I owe the emphasis and much of the phrasing of the last two sentences to points made to me by Mark Bevir.

15. I offer one such detailed analysis in Roth (2004). Kuukkanen (2015) urges a similar conclusion.

Conclusion

1. I particularly thank John Vandenbrink for pressing this point on me.

2. See Kuukkanen (2015, 2018) for a dissenting view.

3. This represents a hardening of the position that Kuukkanen (2015) takes in his book and for which I have expressed sympathies and reservations (Roth 2016a).

4. From my perspective, a more nuanced account of how issues such as truth and objectivity operate in my work can be found in the essays by Grigoriev and Zeleňák in Brzechczyn (2018).

5. See Lorenz (1998) for a related analysis of this debate. More generally, the overall philosophical position defended in this book has many points of congruence with what Lorenz terms "internal realism." I do not know whether or not Lorenz would endorse the more general line of argument developed in chapter 3, especially inasmuch as "internal realism" is a philosophical position associated with Hilary Putnam, while this book takes a more Quinean line.

6. A particularly instructive and fascinating example here can be found in van Pelt (2002). Van Pelt was involved in the libel trial initiated by David Irving against Deborah Lipstadt. In brief, Irving denied that Auschwitz had functioned as an extermination camp. Van Pelt's book records in agonizing detail the effort required to overcome what can best be described as Irving's hyperpositivism. Van Pelt's heroic investigation compellingly illustrates the fallacy in the thought that the "facts speak for themselves." It also illustrates what I discuss below as the strategy of "inference to the best explanation."

7. For a thoughtful and comprehensive evaluation of the notion of narrative explanation from a related but slightly different perspective than offered here, see Uebel (2017).

8. I touched on this topic briefly in the discussion of Goldstein's work in chapter 3, part II.

9. Although I do not develop the points here, the contrastive aspect of explanation discussed by Lipton (1993) and by Garfinkel (1981) points to additional ways that what Garfinkel terms the "algebra of explanation" might be developed for essentially narrative explanations. Garfinkel considers a rather broader range of examples than does Lipton, and his remarks about explanatory relativity (e.g., 48) as well as what he terms the "pragmatics of explanation" (172–77) provide further arguments regarding why interest-relativity cannot be factored out of explanations.

Works Cited

Ankersmit, Frank R. 2001. *Historical Representation*. Stanford, Calif.: Stanford University Press.
Apel, Karl-Otto. 1984. *Understanding and Explanation*. Translated by Georgia Warnke. Cambridge, Mass.: MIT Press.
Ayer, Alfred J. 1952. *Language, Truth and Logic*. New York: Dover.
Beatty, John. 2016. "What Are Narratives Good For?" *Studies in History and Philosophy of Biological and Biomedical Sciences* 58: 33–40.
Beatty, John, and Isabel Carrera. 2011. "When What Had to Happen Was Not Bound to Happen: History, Chance, Narrative, Evolution." *Journal of the Philosophy of History* 5: 471–95.
Bird, Alexander. 2012. "*The Structure of Scientific Revolutions* and Its Significance: An Essay Review of the Fiftieth Anniversary Edition." *British Journal for the Philosophy of Science* 63: 859–83.
Blount, Zachary D. 2016. "A Case Study in Evolutionary Contingency." *Studies in History and Philosophy of Biological and Biomedical Sciences* 58: 82–92.
Bosworth, Richard J. B. 1993. *Explaining Auschwitz and Hiroshima: History Writing and the Second World War 1945–1990*. New York: Routledge.
Braudel, Fernand. 1976. *The Mediterranean and the Mediterranean World in the Age of Phillip II*. 2 vols. New York: Harper & Row.
Browning, Christopher. 1998. *Ordinary Men: Reserve Police Battalion 101 and the Final Solution in Poland*. New York: HarperPerennial.
Browning, Christopher. 2004. "Writing and Teaching Holocaust History: A Personal Perspective." In *Teaching about the Holocaust*, edited by Samuel Totten, P. Bartrop, and S. L. Jacobs, 31–49. Westport, Conn.: Praeger.
Browning, Christopher. 2007a. "Founding Holocaust Studies." Unpublished talk.
Browning, Christopher. 2007b. "Raul Hilberg." In *Encyclopaedia Judaica*. 2nd ed. Edited by Fred Skolnik and M. Berenbaum, 9: 100–102. New York: Macmillan Reference USA.
Browning, Christopher. 2007c. "Raul Hilberg." *Yad Vashem Studies* 35: 7–20.
Browning, Christopher. 2008. "Spanning a Career: Three Editions of Raul Hilberg's *Destruction of the European Jews*." In *Lesson and Legacies VIII: From Generation to Generation*, edited by Doris L. Bergen, 191–202. Evanston, Ill.: Northwestern University Press.
Brzechczyn, Krzysztof, ed. 2018. *Towards a Revival of Analytical Philosophy of History: Around Paul A. Roth's Vision of Historical Sciences*. Boston: Brill-Rodolpi.

WORKS CITED

Buchdahl, Gerd. 1965. "A Revolution in Historiography of Science." *History of Science* 4: 55– 69.

Bunzl, Martin. 1996. "How to Change the Unchanging Past." *Clio* 25: 181–93.

Burian, Richard. 1977. "More Than a Marriage of Convenience: On the Inextricability of History and Philosophy of Science." *Philosophy of Science* 44: 1–42.

Bush, Jonathan A. 2010. "Raul Hilberg (1926–2007) in Memoriam." *Jewish Quarterly Review* 100: 661–88.

Carroll, Noël. 2001. *Beyond Aesthetics*. Cambridge, U.K.: Cambridge University Press.

Carroll, Noël. 2007. "Narrative Closure." *Philosophical Studies* 135: 1–15.

Cohen, Jonathan. 1952. "A Survey of Work in the Philosophy of History, 1946–50." *Philosophical Quarterly* 2: 172–86.

Cox, Damien. 2003. "Goodman and Putnam on the Making of Worlds." *Erkenntnis* 58: 33–46.

Creath, Richard. 2010. "The Construction of Reason: Kant, Carnap, Kuhn, and Beyond." In *Discourse on a New Method: Reinvigorating the Marriage of History and Philosophy of Science*, edited by Mary Domski and M. Dickson, 493–509. Chicago: Open Court Press.

Currie, Adrian M. 2014. "Narratives, Mechanism, and Progress in Historical Science." *Synthese* 191: 1163–83.

Danto, Arthur C. 1962. "Narrative Sentences." *History and Theory* 2: 146–79.

Danto, Arthur. C. 1965. *Analytical Philosophy of History*. Cambridge, U.K.: Cambridge University Press.

Danto, Arthur C. 1985. *Narration and Knowledge*. New York: Columbia University Press.

Danto, Arthur C. 1995. "The Decline and Fall of the Analytical Philosophy of History." In *A New Philosophy of History*, edited by Frank Ankersmit and H. Kellner, 70–85. Chicago: University of Chicago Press.

Daston, Lorraine. 2016. "History of Science without Structure." In *Kuhn's Structure of Scientific Revolutions at Fifty: Reflections on a Science Classic*, edited by Robert J. Richards and L. Daston, 115–32. Chicago: University of Chicago Press.

Davidson, Donald. 1973–74. "On the Very Idea of a Conceptual Scheme." *Proceedings and Addresses of the American Philosophical Association* 47: 5–20.

Davidson, Donald. 1980. *Essays on Actions and Events*. New York: Oxford University Press.

Dewulf, Fons. 2017a. "The Emergence of Scientific Explanation in the Work of Carl Hempel." Unpublished manuscript, Microsoft Word file.

Dewulf, Fons. 2017b. "The Place of Historiography in the Network of Logical Empiricism." Unpublished manuscript, Microsoft Word file.

Dewulf, Fons. 2017c. "Revisiting Hempel's 1942 Contribution to Philosophy of History." Unpublished manuscript.

Dewulf, Fons. 2018. "A Genealogy of Scientific Explanation." PhD diss., University of Ghent.

Domski, Mary, and Michael Dickson, eds. 2010. *Discourse on a New Method: Reinvigorating the Marriage of History and Philosophy of Science*. Chicago: Open Court Press.

WORKS CITED

D'Oro, Giuseppina. 2008. "The Ontological Backlash: Why Did Mainstream Analytic Philosophy Lose Interest in the Philosophy of History?" *Philosophia* 36: 403–15.
Dray, William. 1967. "Philosophy of History." In *The Encyclopedia of Philosophy*, edited by Paul Edwards, 6: 247–54. New York: Macmillan.
Dray, William. 1989. *On History and Philosophers of History.* New York: E. J. Brill.
Dummett, Michael. 1978. *Truth and Other Enigmas.* Cambridge, Mass.: Harvard University Press.
Dummett, Michael. 2004. *Truth and the Past.* New York: Columbia University Press.
Durkheim, Emile: 1951. *Suicide: A Study in Sociology.* New York: The Free Press.
Edel, Abraham. 1946. "Is Naturalism Arbitrary?" *Journal of Philosophy* 43: 141–52.
Fay, Brian. 1984. "Review of *Naturalism as a Philosophy of Social Science.*" *Philosophy of the Social Sciences* 14: 542.
Friedländer, Saul, ed. 1992. *Probing the Limits of Representation.* Cambridge, Mass.: Harvard University Press.
Friedman, Michael. 1993. "Remarks on the History of Science and the History of Philosophy." In *World Changes: Thomas Kuhn and the Nature of Science*, edited by Paul Horwich, 37–54. Cambridge, Mass.: MIT Press.
Friedman, Michael. 1997. "Philosophical Naturalism." *Proceedings and Addresses of the American Philosophical Association* 71: 7–21.
Friedman, Michael. 2000. *A Parting of the Ways.* Chicago: Open Court Press.
Friedman, Michael. 2001. *The Dynamics of Reason.* Stanford, Calif.: CSLI.
Friedman, Michael. 2002. "Kant, Kuhn, and the Rationality of Science." *Philosophy of Science* 69: 171–90.
Friedman, Michael. 2010. "Synthetic History Reconsidered." In *Discourse on a New Method Reinvigorating the Marriage of History and Philosophy of Science*, edited by Mary Domski and M. Dickson, 571–813. Chicago: Open Court Press.
Galison, Peter. 1987. *How Experiments End.* Chicago: University of Chicago Press.
Galison, Peter. 1997. *Image and Logic.* Chicago: University of Chicago Press.
Galison, Peter. 2010. "Trading with the Enemy." In *Trading Zones and Interactional Expertise*, edited by Michael E. Gorman, 25–52. Cambridge, Mass.: MIT Press.
Galison, Peter, and D. Stump, eds. 1996. *The Disunity of Science.* Stanford, Calif.: Stanford University Press.
Gallie, Walter B. 1968. *Philosophy and the Historical Understanding.* New York: Schocken.
Garfinkel, Alan. 1981. *Forms of Explanation.* New Haven, Conn.: Yale University Press.
Gillispie, Charles C. 1962. "The Nature of Science." *Science* 138: 1251–53.
Glymour, Clark. 1980. *Theory and Evidence.* Princeton, N.J.: Princeton University Press.
Goldstein, Leon. J. 1976. *Historical Knowing.* Austin: University of Texas Press.
Goldstein, Leon. J. 1977. "History and the Primacy of Knowing." *History and Theory* 16: 29–52.
Goldstein, Leon. J. 1996. *The What and the Why of History.* New York: Brill.
Goodman, Nelson. 1978. *Ways of Worldmaking.* Indianapolis, Ind.: Hackett.

Goodman, Nelson. 1979. *Fact, Fiction, and Forecast*. 3rd ed. Indianapolis, Ind.: Hackett.
Gordon, Peter E. 2010. *Continental Divide: Heidegger, Cassirer, Davos*. Cambridge, Mass.: Harvard University Press.
Habermas, Jürgen. 1988. *On the Logic of the Social Sciences*. Translated by Shierry W. Nicholsen and J. A. Stark. Cambridge, Mass.: MIT Press.
Habermas, Jürgen. 1997. "On the Public Use of History." In *The New Conservatism: Cultural Criticism and the Historians' Debate*, 229–40. Cambridge, Mass.: MIT Press.
Hacking, Ian. 1982. "Wittgenstein the Psychologist." *New York Review of Books*, April 1.
Hacking, Ian. 1983. *Representing and Intervening*. Cambridge, U.K.: Cambridge University Press.
Hacking, Ian. 1985. "Five Parables. " In *Philosophy in History: Essays on the Historiography of Philosophy*, edited by Richard Rorty, J. B. Schneewind, and Q. Skinner, 103–24. Cambridge, U.K.: Cambridge University Press.
Hacking, Ian. 1986a. "The Archaeology of Foucault." In *Foucault: A Critical Reader*, edited by David C. Hoy, 27–40. New York: Blackwell.
Hacking, Ian. 1986b. "Making Up People." In *Reconstructing Individualism*, edited by Thomas C. Heller, M. Sosna, and D. E. Wellbery, 222–36. Stanford, Calif.: Stanford University Press.
Hacking, Ian. 1990. "Natural Kinds." In *Perspectives on Quine*, edited by Robert Barrett and R. Gibson, 129–41. Cambridge, Mass.: Blackwell.
Hacking, Ian. 1992a. "The Self-Vindication of the Laboratory Sciences." In *Science as Practice and Culture*, edited by Andrew Pickering, 29–64. Chicago: University of Chicago Press.
Hacking, Ian. 1992b. "Statistical Language, Statistical Truth, and Statistical Reason: the Self-Authentication of a Style of Scientific Reasoning." In *The Social Dimensions of Science*, edited by Ernan McMullin, 130–57. Notre Dame, Ind.: University of Notre Dame Press.
Hacking, Ian. 1992c. "World-Making by Kind-Making: Child Abuse for Example." In *How Classification Works*, edited by Mary Douglas and D. Hull, 180–238. Edinburgh: Edinburgh University Press.
Hacking, Ian. 1993. "Working in a New World: The Taxonomic Solution." In *World Changes: Thomas Kuhn and the Nature of Science*, edited by Paul Horwich, 275–310. Cambridge, Mass.: MIT Press.
Hacking, Ian. 1995a. "The Looping Effects of Human Kinds." In *Causal Cognition*, edited by Dan Sperber, D. Premack, and A. J. Premack, 351–83. Oxford: Clarendon Press.
Hacking, Ian. 1995b. *Rewriting the Soul*. Princeton, N.J.: Princeton University Press.
Hacking, Ian. 1995c. "Two Kinds of 'New Historicism' for Philosophers." In *History and . . . Histories within the Human Sciences*, edited by Ralph Cohen and M. S. Roth, 296–318. Charlottesville: University of Virginia Press.
Hacking, Ian. 1996. "The Disunities of Science." In *The Disunity of Science*, edited by Peter Galison and D. Stump, 37–74. Stanford, Calif.: Stanford University Press.

WORKS CITED

Hacking, Ian. 1999. *The Social Construction of What?* Cambridge, Mass.: Harvard University Press.
Hacking, Ian. 2012. "Introductory Essay." In Thomas S. Kuhn, *The Structure of Scientific Revolutions*, vii–xlvi. 4th ed. Chicago: University of Chicago Press.
Haddock, Adrian. 2002. "Rewriting the Past: Retrospective Description and Its Consequences." *Philosophy of the Social Sciences* 32: 3–24.
Hawthorn, Geoffrey. 1991. *Plausible Worlds: Possibility and Understanding in History and the Social Sciences.* Cambridge, U.K.: Cambridge University Press.
Hempel, Carl G. 1942. "The Function of General Laws in History." *Journal of Philosophy* 39: 35–48.
Hempel, Carl G. 1950. "Problems and Changes in the Empiricist Criterion of Meaning." *Revue Internationale de Philosophie* 4: 41–63.
Hilberg, Raul. 1985. *The Destruction of the European Jews.* Revised and definitive ed. 3 vols. New York: Holmes & Meier.
Hollinger, David A. 1973. "T. S. Kuhn's Theory of Science and Its Implications for History." *American Historical Review* 78: 370–93.
Hoyningen-Huene, Paul. 1992. "The Interrelations between the Philosophy, History and Sociology of Science in Thomas Kuhn's Theory of Scientific Development." *British Journal for the Philosophy of Science* 43: 487–501.
Hoyningen-Huene, Paul. 1993. *Reconstructing Scientific Revolutions.* Chicago: University of Chicago Press.
Hoyningen-Huene, Paul. 2012. "Philosophical Elements in Thomas Kuhn's Historiography of Science." *Theoria* 75: 281–92.
Kindi, Vasso. 2005. "The Relation of History of Science to Philosophy of Science in *The Structure of Scientific Revolutions* and Kuhn's Later Philosophical Work." *Perspectives on Science* 13: 495–530.
Kitcher, Philip. 1992. "The Naturalists Return." *Philosophical Review* 101: 53–114.
Kolb, David. 2008. "Darwin Rocks Hegel: Does Nature Have a History?" *Bulletin of the Hegel Society of Great Britain* 57–58: 97–116.
Kuhn, Thomas S. (1962) 2012. *The Structure of Scientific Revolutions.* 4th ed. Chicago: University of Chicago Press.
Kuhn, Thomas S. 1966. "Reviews." *British Journal for the Philosophy of Science* 17: 256–58.
Kuhn, Thomas S. 1970. "Notes on Lakatos." *PSA: Proceedings of the Biennial Meeting of the Philosophy of Science Association* 1970: 137–46.
Kuhn, Thomas S. 1977. *The Essential Tension.* Chicago: University of Chicago Press.
Kuhn, Thomas S. 1980. "The Halt and the Blind: Philosophy and History of Science." *British Journal for the Philosophy of Science* 31: 181–92.
Kuhn, Thomas S. 2000. "Rationality and Theory Choice." In *The Road Since Structure*, edited by James Conant and J. Haugeland, 208–15. Chicago: University of Chicago Press.
Kuukkanen, Jouni-Matti.2012. The Missing Narrativist Turn in the Historiography of Science." *History and Theory* 51: 340-363.
Kuukkanen, Jouni-Matti. 2015. *Postnarrativist Philosophy of Historiography.* New York: Palgrave Macmillan.

Kuukkanen, Jouni-Matti. 2018. "The Future of Philosophy of Historiography: Reviving or Reinventing?" In *Towards a Revival of Analytical Philosophy of History: Around Paul A. Roth's Vision of Historical Sciences*, edited by Krzysztof Brzechczyn, 73–94. Boston: Brill-Rodolpi.

Lakatos, Imre. 1970. "Falsification and the Methodology of Scientific Research Programmes." In *Criticism and the Growth of Knowledge*, edited by Imre Lakatos and A. Musgrave, 91–196. New York: Cambridge University Press.

Larvor, Brendan. 2003. "Why Did Kuhn's *Structure of Scientific Revolutions* Cause a Fuss?" *Studies in History and Philosophy of Science* 34: 369–90.

Laudan, Larry. 1979. "Historical Methodologies: An Overview and Manifesto." In *Current Research in the Philosophy of Science*, edited by Peter D. Asquith and H. E. Kyburg Jr., 40–54. East Lansing, Mich.: Philosophy of Science Association.

Lipton, Peter. 1993. *Inference to the Best Explanation*. New York: Routledge.

Little, Daniel. 2010. *New Contributions to the Philosophy of History*. New York: Springer.

Lorenz, Chris E. G. 1998. "Historical Knowledge and Historical Reality: A Plea for 'Internal Realism.'" In *History and Theory: Contemporary Readings*, edited by Brian Fay, P. Pomper, and R. T. Vann, 342–76. Oxford: Blackwell.

MacDonald, Graham, and C. MacDonald. 2009. "Explanation in Historiography." In *A Companion to the Philosophy of History and Historiography*, edited by Aviezer Tucker, 131–41. Malden, Mass.: Blackwell.

MacIntyre, Alasdair. 1980. "Epistemological Crises, Dramatic Narrative, and the Philosophy of Science." In *Paradigms and Revolutions*, edited by Gary Gutting, 54–74. Notre Dame, Ind.: University of Notre Dame Press.

MacIntyre, Alasdair. 1985. "The Relationship of Philosophy to Its Past." In *Philosophy in History*, edited by Richard Rorty, J. B. Schneewind, and Q. Skinner, 31–48. Cambridge, U.K.: Cambridge University Press.

Maffie, James. 1990. "Recent Work on Naturalized Epistemology." *American Philosophical Quarterly* 27: 281–93.

Maier, Charles S. 1997. *The Unmasterable Past: History, Holocaust, and German National Identity (With a New Preface)*. Cambridge, Mass.: Harvard University Press.

Mandelbaum, M. 1977. *The Anatomy of Historical Knowledge*. Baltimore, Md.: Johns Hopkins University Press.

Martin, Raymond. 1989. *The Past within Us*. Princeton, N.J.: Princeton University Press.

Martin, Wallace. 1986. *Recent Theories of Narrative*. Ithaca, N.Y.: Cornell University Press.

Mead, George H. 2002. *The Philosophy of the Present*. Amherst, N.Y.: Prometheus Books.

Megill, Allan. 1989. "Recounting the Past: 'Description,' Explanation, and Narrative in Historiography." *American Historical Review* 94: 627–53.

Miller, Joseph H. 1990. "Narrative." In *Critical Terms for Literary Study*, edited by Frank Lentricchia and T. McLaughlin, 66–79. Chicago: University of Chicago Press.

WORKS CITED

Mink, Louis O. 1987. *Historical Understanding*. Edited by Brian Fay, E. O. Golob, and R. T. Vann. Ithaca, N.Y.: Cornell University Press.

Mladenovic, Bojana. 2007. "'Muckraking in History': The Role of the History of Science in Kuhn's Philosophy." *Perspectives on Science* 15: 261–94.

Morris, Humphrey. 1993. "Narrative Representation, Narrative Enactment, and the Psychoanalytic Construction of History." *International Journal of Psycho-Analysis* 74: 33–54.

Murphey, Murray G. 1973. *Our Knowledge of the Historical Past*. Indianapolis, Ind.: Bobbs-Merrill.

Murphy, Arthur E. 1945. "Book Review: *Naturalism and the Human Spirit*." *The Journal of Philosophy* 42: 400-417.

Murphy, Dominic. 2001. "Hacking's Reconciliation: Putting the Biological and Sociological Together in the Explanation of Mental Illness." *Philosophy of the Social Sciences* 31: 139–62.

Nagel, Ernest. 1954–55. "Naturalism Reconsidered." *Proceedings and Addresses of the American Philosophical Association* 28: 5–17.

Nagel, Ernest. 1961. *The Structure of Science*. New York: Harcourt, Brace, & World.

Norman, Andrew. 1998. "Telling It Like It Was: Historical Narratives on Their Own Terms." In *History and Theory: Contemporary Readings*, edited by Brian Fay, P. Pomper, and R. T. Vann, 153–71. Oxford: Blackwell.

Novick, Peter. 1988. *That Noble Dream: The "Objectivity Question" and the American Historical Profession*. Cambridge, U.K.: Cambridge University Press.

Nowell-Smith, Patrick H. 1977. "The Constructionist Theory of History." *History and Theory* 4: 1–28.

O'Sullivan, Luke. 2006. "Leon Goldstein and the Epistemology of Historical Knowing." *History and Theory* 45: 204–28.

Patton, Lydia. 2015. "Methodology of the Sciences." In *Oxford Handbook of German Philosophy in the Nineteenth Century*, edited by Malcolm Forster and K. Gjesdal, 594–606. New York: Oxford University Press.

Paseau, Alexander. 2005. "Naturalism in Mathematics and the Authority of Philosophy." *British Journal for the Philosophy of Science* 56: 377–96.

Pickering, Andrew. 1984. *Constructing Quarks*. Chicago: University of Chicago Press.

Pinto de Oliveira, Janete C. 2012. "Kuhn and the Genesis of the 'New Historiography of Science.'" *Studies in History and Philosophy of Science* 43: 115–21.

Popper, Karl. 1957. *Poverty of Historicism*. London: Ark.

Prudovsky, Gad. 1997. "Can We Ascribe to Past Thinkers Concepts They Had No Linguistic Means to Express?" *History and Theory* 36: 15–31.

Quine, Willard V. O. 1951. "Two Dogmas of Empiricism." *Philosophical Review* 60: 20–43.

Quine, Willard V. O. 1969. "Epistemology Naturalized." In *Ontological Relativity and Other Essays*, 69–90. New York: Columbia University Press.

Quine, Willard V. O. 1981. *Theories and Things*. Cambridge, Mass.: Harvard University Press.

Quine, Willard V. O. 1995. "Naturalism, or Living within One's Means." *Dialectica* 49: 251–61.

WORKS CITED

Randall, John H., Jr. 1944. "The Nature of Naturalism." In *Naturalism and the Human Spirit*, edited by Yervant K. Krikorian, 354–82. New York: Columbia University Press.

Ricketts, Thomas. 2004. "Frege, Carnap, and Quine: Continuities and Discontinuities." In *Carnap Brought Home*, edited by Steve Awodey and C. Klein, 181–202. La Salle, Ill.: Open Court Press.

Richardson, Alan. 2002. "Narrating the History of Reason Itself: Friedman, Kuhn, and a Constitutive *A Priori* for the Twenty-First Century." *Perspectives on Science* 10: 253–74.

Rorty, Richard. 1980. "Pragmatism, Relativism, and Irrationalism." *Proceedings and Addresses of the American Philosophical Association* 53: 719–38.

Rosenberg, Alexander. 1996. "A Field Guide to Recent Species of Naturalism." *British Journal for the Philosophy of Science* 47: 1–29.

Roth, Paul A. 1987. *Meaning and Method in the Social Sciences*. Ithaca, N.Y.: Cornell University Press.

Roth, Paul A. 1988. "Narrative Explanation: The Case of History." *History & Theory* 27: 1–13.

Roth, Paul A. 1991a. "Interpretation as Explanation." In *The Interpretive Turn: Philosophy, Science, and Culture*, edited by James Bohman, D. Hiley, and R. Shusterman, 179–96. Ithaca, N.Y.: Cornell University Press.

Roth, Paul A. 1991b. "Truth in Interpretation: The Case of Psychoanalysis." *Philosophy of the Social Sciences* 21: 175–95.

Roth, Paul A. 1992. "Hayden White and the Aesthetics of Historiography." *History of the Human Sciences* 5: 17–35.

Roth, Paul A. 1998. "The Cure of Stories: Self-Deception, Danger Situations, and the Clinical Role of Narratives: Roy Schafer's Psychoanalytic Theory." In *Psychoanalytic Versions of the Human Condition*, edited by Paul Marcus and A. Rosenberg, 306–31. New York: State University of New York Press.

Roth, Paul A. 1999a. "The Epistemology of 'Epistemology Naturalized.'" *Dialectica* 53: 87–109.

Roth, Paul A. 1999b. "Naturalizing Goldman." *Southern Journal of Philosophy* 37: 89–111.

Roth, Paul A. 2000. "The Object of Understanding." In *Empathy and Agency*, edited by Karsten Stueber and B. Kögler, 243–69. Boulder, Colo.: Westview Press.

Roth, Paul A. 2002. "Ways of Pastmaking." *History of the Human Sciences* 15: 125–43.

Roth, Paul A. 2003. "Mistakes." *Synthese* 136: 389–408.

Roth, Paul A. 2004. "Hearts of Darkness." *History of the Human Sciences* 17: 211–51.

Roth, Paul A. 2006. "Naturalism without Tears." In *Handbook of the Philosophy of Science, Vol. 15: Philosophy of Anthropology and Sociology*, edited by Stephen Turner and M. Risjord, 683–708. New York: Elsevier.

Roth, Paul A. 2008a. "Epistemology of Science after Quine." In *Routledge Companion to the Philosophy of Science*, edited by Martin Curd and S. Psillos, 3–14. New York: Routledge.

Roth, Paul A. 2008b. "Varieties and Vagaries of Historical Explanation." *Journal of the Philosophy of History* 2: 14–226.

Roth, Paul A. 2012. "The Pasts." *History and Theory* 51: 313–39.

Roth, Paul A. 2013a. "Silence of the Norms: The Missing Historiography of *The Structure of Scientific Revolutions.*" *Studies in History and Philosophy of Science* 44: 545–52.

Roth, Paul A. 2013b. "Whistling History: Ankersmit's Neo-Tractarian Theory of Historical Representation." *Rethinking History* 17: 548–69.

Roth, Paul A. 2016a. "Back to the Future: Postnarrativist Historiography and Analytic Philosophy of History." *History and Theory* 55: 270–81.

Roth, Paul A. 2016b. "What Would It Be to Be a Norm?" In *Normativity and Naturalism in the Philosophy of the Social Sciences*, edited by Mark Risjord, 43–59. New York: Routledge.

Roth, Paul A. 2017a. "Essentially Narrative Explanations." *Studies in History and Philosophy of Science* 62: 42–50.

Roth, Paul A. 2017b. "Philosophy of History." In *The Routledge Companion to the Philosophy of Social Science*, edited by Alexander Rosenberg and L. McIntyre, 397–407. New York: Routledge.

Roth, Paul A. 2018. "Reviving Philosophy of History." In *Towards a Revival of Analytical Philosophy of History: Around Paul A. Roth's Vision of Historical Sciences*, edited by Krzysztof Brzechczyn, 9–27. Boston: Brill-Rodolpi.

Schafer, Roy. 1978. *Language and Insight.* New Haven, Conn.: Yale University Press.

Schafer, Roy. 1983. *The Analytic Attitude.* New York: Basic Books.

Schaffer, Simon, and Steven Shapin 1985. *Leviathan and the Air-Pump.* Princeton, N.J.: Princeton University Press.

Schwartz, Robert. 1986. "I'm Going to Make You a Star." *Studies in Essentialism: Midwest Studies in Philosophy* 11: 427–39.

Scott, Joan W. 1996. "The Evidence of Experience." In *The Historic Turn in the Human Sciences*, edited by Terrence J. McDonald, 379–406. Ann Arbor: University of Michigan Press.

Sellars, Wilfrid. 1963. *Science, Perception, and Reality.* London: Routledge & Kegan Paul.

Sepkoski, David. 2016. "'Replaying Life's Tape': Simulations, Metaphors, and Historicity in Stephen Jay Gould's View of Life." *Studies in History and Philosophy of Biological and Biomedical Sciences* 58: 73–81.

Snyder, Timothy. 2010. *Bloodlands: Europe between Hitler and Stalin.* New York: Basic Books.

Solomon, Miriam. 1995. "Legend Naturalism and Scientific Progress." *Studies in History and Philosophy of Science* 26: 205–18.

Spence, Donald. 1982. *Narrative Truth and Historical Truth: Meaning and Interpretation in Psychoanalysis.* New York: Norton.

Spence, Donald. 1991. "Saying Good-bye to Historical Truth." *Philosophy of the Social Sciences* 21: 245–53.

Spiegel, Gabrielle M. 1990. "History, Historicism, and the Social Logic of the Text in the Middle Ages." *Speculum* 65: 59–86.

Spiegel, Gabrielle M. 2013. "Rhetorical Theory/Theoretical Rhetoric: Some Ambiguities in the Reception of Hayden White's Work." In *Philosophy of History after Hayden White*, edited by Robert Doran, 171–82. New York: Bloomsbury.

Stone, Dan. 2013. "Excommunicating the Past? Narrativism and Rational Constructivism in the Historiography of the Holocaust." *Rethinking History* 21: 549–66.

Stueber, Karsten. 2015. "The Cognitive Function of Narratives." *Journal of the Philosophy of History* 9: 393–409.

Toews, John. 1987. "Intellectual History after the Linguistic Turn: The Autonomy of Meaning and the Irreducibility of Experience." *American Historical Review* 92: 879–907.

Toulmin, Stephen. 1971. "Rediscovering History." *Encounter* 36: 53–64.

Towers, Frank. 2011. "Partisans, New History, and Modernization: The Historiography of the Civil War's Causes." *Journal of the Civil War Era* 1: 237–64.

Trevor-Roper, Hugh R. 1962. "Nazi Bureaucrats and Jewish Leaders." *Commentary* 33: 351–58.

Turner, Stephen. 1994. *The Social Theory of Practices*. Chicago: University of Chicago Press.

Turner, Stephen. 2010. *Explaining the Normative*. Malden, Mass.: Polity Press.

Turner, Stephen. 2018. "What Do Narratives Explain? Roth, Mink and Weber." In *Towards a Revival of Analytical Philosophy of History: Around Paul A. Roth's Vision of Historical Sciences*, edited by Krzysztof Brzechczyn, 130–147. Boston: Brill-Rodolpi.

Uebel, Thomas. 2017. "Philosophy of History and History of Philosophy of Science." *HOPOS: The Journal of the International Society for the History of Philosophy of Science* 7: 1–30.

van Fraassen, Bas. 1995. "Against Naturalized Epistemology." In *On Quine*, edited by Paolo Leonardi and M. Santambrogio, 68–88. New York: Cambridge University Press.

van Fraassen, Bas. 1996. "Science, Materialism, and False Consciousness." In *Warrant in Contemporary Epistemology*," edited by Jonathan Kvanvig, 149–82. Latham, Md.: Rowman & Littlefield.

Vann, Richard T. 1987. "Louis Mink's Linguistic Turn." *History and Theory* 26: 1–14.

Vann, Richard T. 1995. "Turning Linguistic: History and Theory and *History and Theory*, 1960–1975." In *A New Philosophy of History*, edited by Frank Ankersmit and H. Kellner, 40–69. Chicago: University of Chicago Press.

Vann, Richard T. 1998. "The Reception of Hayden White." *History and Theory* 37: 143–61.

van Pelt, Robert J. 2002. *The Case for Auschwitz: Evidence from the Irving Trial*. Bloomington: Indiana University Press.

Velleman, David. 2003. "Narrative Explanations." *Philosophical Review* 112: 1–25.

Walsh, William H. 1977. "Truth and Fact in History Reconsidered." *History and Theory* 16: 53–71.

Weberman, David. 1997. "The Nonfixity of the Historical Past." *Review of Metaphysics* 50: 749–68.

White, Hayden. 1966. "The Burden of History." *History and Theory* 5: 111–34.

White, Hayden. 1973. *Metahistory: The Historical Imagination in Nineteenth-Century Europe*. Baltimore, Md.: Johns Hopkins University Press.

WORKS CITED

White, Hayden. 1999. "Auerbach's Literary History: Figural Causation and Modernist Historicism." In *Figural Realism: Studies in the Mimesis Effect*, 87–100. Baltimore, Md.: Johns Hopkins University Press.
White, Hayden. 2010. "The Politics of Contemporary Philosophy of History." In *The Fiction of Narrative: Essays on History, Literature, and Theory 1957–2007*, edited by Robert Doran, 136–52. Baltimore, Md.: Johns Hopkins University Press.
Williams, Michael. 2001. *The Problems of Knowledge.* New York: Oxford University Press.
Wise, Gene. 1980. *American Historical Explanations.* 2nd ed., revised. Minneapolis: University of Minnesota Press.
Wise, Norton. 2011. "Science as Historical Narrative." *Erkenntnis* 75: 349–76.
Wise, Norton. 2016. "A Smoker's Paradigm." In *Kuhn's* Structure of Scientific Revolutions *at Fifty: Reflections on a Science Classic*, edited by Robert J. Richards and L. Daston, 31–41. Chicago: University of Chicago Press.
Wright, Crispin. 1993. *Realism, Meaning, and Truth.* 2nd ed. Cambridge, Mass.: Blackwell.
Zammito, John H. 1993. "Are We Being Theoretical Yet? The New Historicism, the New Philosophy of History, and 'Practicing Historians.'" *Journal of Modern History* 65: 783–814.
Zammito, John H. 2000. "Reading 'Experience': The Debate in Intellectual History among Scott, Toews, and LaCapra." In *Reclaiming Identity: Realist Theory and the Predicament of Postmodernism*, edited by Paula M. L. Moya and M. R. Hames-García, 279–311. Berkeley: University of California Press.
Zammito, John H. 2004. *A Nice Derangement of Epistemes.* Chicago: University of Chicago Press.

Index

analysis of meaning, 128, 137
Anscombe, G. E. M., 41, 42, 152–53nn9–10
Arendt, Hannah, 16
Auerbach, Erich, 146

Beatty, John, and Isabel Carrera, 76–80
Bird, Alexander, 99, 166n2
Braudel, Fernand, 70–72, 78, 140, 162n9
Browning, Christopher, 17, 73, 74, 163nn10–11
Buchdahl, Gerd, 99–100, 111
Bunzl, Martin, 157n25

Carnap, Rudolf, 20, 21, 140, 147, 170n10; a Carnapian Chronicler, 32–33
Carroll, Noël, 5, 150n7
causal explanations, 4, 5, 6, 11, 12, 16, 67, 73, 87, 98, 116, 146, 151n12
cognitive values, 90–91
Collingwood, R. G., 51, 150n4
comprehension and explanation, relationship between, 13, 116
constructivism, xiii, 55, 57, 140
contingency, 5, 55, 56, 114, 147; historical, 76–78, 105, 121
correspondence theory of historical truth, 25, 26
Cox, Damian, 59–60
Creath, Richard, 19
Currie, Adrian, 80, 163n14, 164n17

Danto, Arthur C., xiii, 4–5, 7–11, 20, 35, 48, 51, 62–63, 84–85, 91, 146, 147, 156n19, 159n21, 157nn23–24, 160n42; on Ideal Chronicle, 8, 9, 10, 14–15, 27–28, 33, 160n40; on Kuhn, 18, 84–85; on narrative structures, 62, 159n31. *See also* narrative sentences

Daston, Lorraine, 102
Davidson, Donald, 9, 29, 30, 33, 63, 87, 161n47
Derrida, Jacques, 170n12
description and justification distinction, 71–72, 101
descriptive and normative distinction, 107–8, 155n18
Dewey, John, 139
Dewulf, Fons, xiii
Dilthey, Wilhelm, 86–87
"disappearance of the empirical," 114, 127–38
D'Oro, Giuseppina, 86–88
Dray, William, 50, 158n28
Dummett, Michael, 47, 48, 53, 54–55, 57, 156n22, 157n27, 160n36, 160n39
Durkheim, Émile, 42

Edel, Abraham, 119
empiricism, 121–29, 137, 141, 170n10
epistemology, 47–48, 128; epistemological realism, 156n20; Kuhn on, 103, 107; in naturalism and science, 115, 120, 122, 124–26
events, status of, 29–31, 33, 35, 37, 50–51, 61–64, 74–75, 107, 143, 145–46, 157n25, 164n16
evolutionary biology, 76–80, 104
experience, 36–37, 45, 48–49, 61, 63–64, 115, 117, 119–20, 123–33; Scott on, 133–37
explanation. *See* causal explanations; comprehension and explanation; historical explanation; narrative explanation; scientific vs. historical explanation

Foucault, Michel, 37, 40, 42, 46, 150n11, 158n30, 166n4, 170n12; Hacking

INDEX

and, 152n5, 153n10, 153n14, 155n17, 165n1, 166n4
Frege, Gottlob, 21, 37, 169n6
Friedman, Michael, 19–20, 21, 104–5, 109, 140, 170n6

Gadamer, Hans-Georg, 116, 129, 170n12
Galilei, Galileo, 60–61
Galison, Peter, 102, 103, 125
Gallie, W. B., 78
Garfinkel, Alan, 154n15, 171n9
Garfinkel, Harold, 135
Gillispie, Charles C., 100, 168n2
Glymour, Clark, xi–xii, xiii
Goffman, Erving, 40
Goldman, Alvin, 120, 168n1
Goldstein, Leon, xii, 49–55, 57, 157nn26–27, 158n30, 159–60nn32–36
Goodman, Nelson, xiv, 36–37, 40, 42, 43, 45, 47, 49, 57, 59–60, 161n43
Gordon, Peter, 20
Gould, Stephen J., 76–77

Habermas, Jürgen, 116, 129, 142, 170n12
Hacking, Ian, xiv, 35–47, 49, 57–59, 63–64, 152–53nn5–11, 153–55nn13–17; "dynamic nominalism" in, 37, 39–40, 152n5; indeterminacies in the past, 35, 37, 44, 47, 59, 153n13; intentionality in, 37, 40–44; on Kuhn, 100, 109, 160n41, 165n1; "memoro-politics" in, 153n14, 155n16; on social sciences, 154n15; on taxonomic classifications, 45, 154nn14–15. *See also under* Foucault, Michel
Haddock, Adrian, 153n13
Hanson, Norwood Russell, 95
Hegel, Georg Wilhelm Friedrich, 4, 105
Hempel, Carl G., xiii, 18, 66, 83–84, 87, 90, 147; on empiricism, 170n10; on goal of science, 91, 108; on historical explanation, 4–5, 11–12, 23, 85–86, 95; Kuhn on, 108, 110, 168n7
Hilberg, Raul, 16–17, 72–75, 78, 140, 141–43, 163n11
historical constitution thesis, 49, 50–51, 54, 57, 63, 159n30
historical explanation: academic silence on, xiii, xiv–xv, 3, 83–86, 95–96;

Danto on, 147; evaluative dichotomy in, xi–xiii, xvi, 127, 139; Hempel on, 4–5, 11–12, 23, 85–86, 95; as narrative explanation, 20–21; nomothetic vs. idiographic modes of, 3–4, 5, 23, 86, 113. *See also* narrative explanation; scientific explanation vs. historical explanation
historical realism vs. irrealism, xiv, xv, 24, 35–36, 47–55, 57, 59, 64, 138, 156nn19–20, 157nn27–29; Goldstein on, 49–50, 52–55
history, analytical philosophy of, 4–6; Danto and, 8, 84–85, 158n30; Hempel and, 4, 86
history and fiction, parallels between, 65, 69, 128, 146–47
Hitler, Adolf, 142–43
holism, 48, 49, 83–84, 93, 101, 109
Hollinger, David, 130
Hollis, Martin, 22
Holocaust, explanations of, 16–17, 53, 69, 72–75, 140, 141–43, 145, 163nn11–12, 171n6
Hoyningen-Huene, Paul, 90–91, 167n9
Huizinga, Johan, 8
Hume, David, 36, 141, 155n18

Ideal Chronicle(r), 29–34, 79; Danto on, 8, 9, 10, 14–15, 27–28; Mink on, 28–29, 62
"inference to best explanation" (IBE), 144–45, 171n6
irrealism. *See* historical realism vs. irrealism
Irving, David, 171n6

Kant, Immanuel, 33, 130, 133, 135, 136–37
Kermode, Frank, 149n2
Kindi, Vasso, 167n7
Kitcher, Philip, 120, 168n1, 169n6
Koyré, Alexandre, 60–61
Kripke, Saul, 60
Kuhn, Thomas, xiv–xv, xvi, 9–10, 15, 18–19, 58, 82–96, 97–112, 130, 131, 138, 140, 152n5, 162n4, 166n2; Danto on, 18, 84–85; historiographic method of, 82, 85, 86, 88, 90–93, 98–106, 110–12, 167nn6–7; narrative sentences and, 18, 104–6, 111;

INDEX

reversal of epistemic authority in, 18, 86; structure of *The Structure of Scientific Revolutions*, 82, 98, 166n2
Kuukkanen, Jouni-Matti, 67, 141, 144, 145, 171n3

Larvor, Brendan, 99
Lavoisier, Antoine, 104, 111
linguistic turn in historiography, 127–30, 137–38
Lipton, Peter, 144, 145, 171n9
Little, Daniel, 5–7, 9, 72
Lorenz, Chris E. G., 171n5

MacIntyre, Alasdair, 40, 94–95, 116, 165n2, 167n13
Maffie, James, 168n1
Maier, Charles S., 142
Mandelbaum, Maurice, 24–26, 28
Martin, Raymond, 163
Martin, Wallace, 68–69, 79
Mead, George Herbert, 52
Megill, Allan, 70–72
metaphysical realism, xiv, 59
methodological exclusivism, 22
methodological monism, 115, 169n2
methodological naturalism. *See* naturalism
Milgram experiment, 17
Mill, John Stuart, 154n14
Mink, Louis, xii, xiii, 5, 8, 9–10, 11–12, 13–15, 20, 35, 50, 62–63, 93–94, 145, 146–47, 150n3, 150n11; on "conceptual asymmetry," 10; on Danto, 62; on Gallie, 78; on history/fiction demarcation, 146–47; on Ideal Chronicle, 28–29; Kuhn and, 93; on narrative form as "cognitive instrument," xv, 147; on "Universal History," xiv, 15, 26, 29; on "untold story" presupposition about the past, 26–27, 50
Mladenovic, Bojana, 88–89
Morris, Humphrey, 66
Murphey, Murray G., 158n30
Murphy, Arthur E., 119

Nagel, Ernest, 170n7
narrative explanation: Beatty and Carrera on, 78–79; Danto on, 4–5, 7–11, 150n4; defining features of, xiv, 9, 10, 11, 14–16, 18, 22–23, 35, 64, 66–68, 75–76; definitions and uses of term, 4–5, 22; "essentially narrative explanations," xiv, 36, 64, 65–66, 68, 71–81, 98, 100, 127, 145, 162n5; Kuhn on, 91–92; legitimacy of, xiv, 9, 18, 139–40, 143, 147–48; metaphysical objections to, xiv, 24–28, 33–34, 35, 47–48, 64; methodological objections to (logical formlessness and evaluative intractability), xiv, 22–24, 64, 65, 70, 75, 140, 145; scholarship on, 4–18; of science, 98–99, 162n4; unavoidability of, xv, 98
narrative form, xi–xiii, 33, 49, 50, 64, 65–66, 68–70, 72, 100; cognitive role of, xv, 147; defining features of, 6, 66; legitimacy of, xiv; moral implications of, xv, 7, 142
narrative sentences, xiv, 13, 27–28, 30, 41, 47, 55–57, 67–69, 71, 74, 75, 80–81, 143; Danto's notion of, 8–11, 145, 146, 153n13, 160n38; in Kuhn, 18, 104–6, 111
narrative theory, xii, 7, 11, 132, 162n3; White on, 149n1
narrative turn in historiography, 67
naturalism, xiv, xv, xvi, 97, 48, 97–98, 141; antinaturalism, 169n6; defined, 116–17, 121, 170n7; Kuhn and, 166n2; methodological, 65, 113–27, 138; pragmatism and, 169n4; supernaturalism vs., 117, 119; types of naturalists, 168n1
natural science and history, xiv, 3, 12, 15, 76, 116; *Erklären* vs. *Verstehen* dispute in, 86–87. *See also* scientific vs. historical explanation
Neurath, Otto, 144, 170n13
New Historicism, 132
Nietzsche, Friedrich, 28
Nolte, Ernst, 143
nominalism, 38, 49, 155n15; Dummett on, 156n22; "dynamic," 37, 39–40, 152n5, 153n11; Goodman on, 156n22; Kuhn's "revolutionary," 152n5, 165n1
nonaggregativity, xiv, 14–15, 16, 18, 22, 26, 64, 66–68, 75, 80, 101
nondetachability, xiv, 14–15, 16, 18, 22, 64, 66–68, 71, 75, 101; Mink on, 93

nonstandardization, xiv, 9, 10, 11, 14–16, 18, 22, 61–62, 64, 66–68, 75, 80, 101, 165n18
Novick, Peter, 20, 128
Nowell-Smith, P. H., 157

Paseau, Alexander, 170n9
Patton, Lydia, 3
Peirce, Charles Sanders, 55
philosophy, aims of, xi, 83
philosophy of mind, 87
Pickering, Andrew, 125
Pinto de Oliveira, Janete C., 166n6
Popper, Karl, 18, 149n1, 170n13
positivism, xii, 3, 84–85, 116, 128, 133, 137, 138, 147; logical positivism, xi–xii, 86–87, 90, 140, 166n5; postpositivism, 118, 132, 133, 147
Prudovsky, Gad, 60–61, 161nn44–45

Quine, Willard Van Orman, 21, 37, 83–84, 109, 137, 144; empiricism and, 83, 122, 124, 170n10; methodological monism and, 115, 169n2; naturalism and, 113, 115, 118–19, 120, 122, 168n1, 169n4; on positivism, 138; on reductionism, 133; on science, 126

Randall, John Herman, Jr., 118–19
Ranke, Leopold von, 24
Rashomon (film), 30–31
Rationalitätstreit, 22
Reagan, Ronald, 27–28, 68, 162n6
relativism, 16, 109, 149n2
Richardson, Alan, 18, 105
Ricketts, Thomas, 151n14
Rorty, Richard, 33, 141, 149n2, 156n23
Rosenberg, Alexander, 168n1
Russell, Bertrand, 21, 52, 139, 140

Santayana, George, 128
Schafer, Roy, 155n16, 161n42
Schaffer, Simon, and Steven Shapin, 125
science: as community of practitioners, 103–7, 109–10; "normal," 97–98, 101, 103–11; norms of, 88, 90, 108, 114–15, 117, 120, 122; relation between history and philosophy of, xv 18–19, 83, 132–33; revolutions in, 18, 89, 95, 101, 103–7, 110–11
scientific vs. historical explanation, 5, 9–10, 78, 81, 82–96, 98, 113, 159n32
Scott, Joan W., 128
Sellars, Wilfrid, xi, 21, 130, 169n5
Sharrock, Wes, and Rupert Read, 88
Snyder, Timothy, 142–43, 146
social sciences, 10, 17, 39, 76, 116; Hacking on, 154n15
Solomon, Miriam, 120
Spence, Donald, 155n16
Spiegel, Gabrielle, 131, 135
Stueber, Karsten, 12–13, 150n9, 151n12
Suckiel, Ellen, 169n4

Toews, John, 129–29, 131, 135, 137, 170n12
Toulmin, Stephen, 95–96
Trevor-Roper, Hugh, 73–74
"truth-value gaps," 47, 48, 57

Uebel, Thomas, xiii
Universal History concept, xiv, 15, 26, 29, 67

van Fraassen, Bas, 121
Vann, Richard, 149–50nn2–3
van Pelt, Robert J., 171n6
Velleman, David, 5, 11, 13

Weber, Max, 6, 39; on ideal types, 89–90
Weberman, David, 157n25
White, Hayden, xii, xv, 7, 50, 67, 68, 69, 75, 142, 145, 146, 149n1, 150n5, 158n30
White, Morton, 11–12, 13
Williams, Michael, 156n20
Wise, Norton, 95
Wittgenstein, Ludwig, vii, ix, 21, 37, 58, 87, 109, 152–53nn9–11
Wright, Crispin, 47, 56, 155n18

Zammito, John, 95, 99, 132–33, 135, 137
Zimbardo, Philip, 17